ENDURE

Tools, Tactics & Habits For

SPIRITUAL STAMINA

by

BEN GREENFIELD

TABLE OF CONTENTS

5   INTRODUCTION

PART I: COMMON TEMPTATIONS

22   LUST & PRIDE

28   CONTROL

44   SEX, PORN & POLYAMORY

83   THE TREE

PART II: MASTERY OF PASSIONS & DESIRES

96   HONEY

103   MARSHMALLOWS

114   TEMPERATE

PART III: PURPOSE & PRODUCTIVITY

129 SOUL

136 CREATE

155 CHOP WOOD, CARRY WATER

165 SEATBELTS & SENTRIES

174 FLOW

189 ANALOG

204 BOOKENDS

212 PRAYER

PART IV: LOVING OTHERS & LOVING GOD

234 SHOES

246 BABIES

PART V: END OF LIFE

259   DEATH

269   HELL

276   FOREVER

PART VI: LIVING FULLY

289   SIMPLICITY

299   LAUGH

308   CONCLUSION

314   ADDITIONAL RESOURCES

INTRODUCTION

There was a time in my life when, rightly so, you'd likely have labeled me as a mildly masochistic, somewhat insane, seriously hardcore endurance athlete. You know, one of those guys who is likely to be wearing a swimming Speedo or cycling shorts under my jeans and running shoes tucked away under the seat of my car, just in case the opportunity arose to swim, bike, run or engage in any other form of forward repetitive motion at random points throughout the day.

In the past several years, I have certainly backed off quite a bit from buffeting my body with bouts of extreme sufferance, but for nearly two decades, I spent much of my existence traveling the globe and challenging myself with some of the most difficult and grueling events on the face of the planet, from the famed 72-hour Agoge Race (previously called the "Spartan Death Race") at 38 degrees below zero in the backwoods of Vermont to over a dozen of the hardest Ironman triathlons on the face of the planet to days upon days spent suffering through Navy SEAL training for civilians on the beaches of the Pacific Ocean off the coast of San Diego, and much, much more.

It actually all began in high school.

During seventh grade basketball practice, I discovered that while I wasn't necessarily the highest jumper or fastest sprinter on the team, I could wax the floor with my teammates or competitors when it came to lasting an entire game without a substitution, or simply running countless numbers of laps and ladders on the court. It seemed my athletic talents seemed to mimic my academic talents: I wasn't necessarily the smartest student, but I was definitely the most tenacious, studying for hours without a break until I had achieved a state of mastery over any given element of academia, from sketching long division and multiplication tables for long nights in my bedroom, to playing the same violin concerto over and over and over again, to reading science chapters until I was blue in the face—and quite doggedly and tirelessly never giving up on anything.

When, at 14 years old, I fell in love with tennis, I began to run the hills behind my family's country home in North Idaho, often trudging uphill for miles at a time, day after day, a smile half-plastered across my face as I embraced what is oft-referred to in the field of endurance sports as "the suck" while simultaneously experiencing the rush of dopamine, endocannabinoids and other feel-good neurochemicals that shifted me deeper and deeper into the so-called "runner's high." During my high school tennis matches, I was the guy who could play an all-day tournament in the blazing sun on a tennis court surface that could fry an egg, go for a run or hit the gym after the tournament, then wake up the next morning and come back with a big smile on my face, ready for more.

Halfway through my short-lived collegiate tennis career, I signed up for my first actual road running race: a ten-mile slog straight up the side of a mountain, with the starting line at the bottom of the mountain and the finish line at the top. Although I had no clue what I was doing, and had never raced cross-country, 5K, 10K, half-marathon, marathon or anything of the like in my life, I managed to slowly but systematically plod up that giant slope one step at a time with the same grit and determination that had fueled my daily runs up the hills behind my house, passing other runners one-by-one until I reached the finish line nearly a mile ahead of all my competitors but one—a 50-year-old local, undefeated phenom who held the course record for the race.

I was beginning to take mental notes. I had begun to identify what type of activities my body seemed to be really good at performing and my brain seemed hard-wired to crave. And of course, I had a strong hunch that, despite being tall, broad-shouldered and more muscular than a traditional cross-country runner or skinny endurance athlete, I was kind of *good* at this whole endurance thing.

In college, I fell in love with bodybuilding, which is arguably—based upon the oodles and oodles of sets and reps involved, and the amounts of tissue-burning lactic acid one practically bleeds out their eyeballs while engaged in that sport—the "endurance" sport of weightlifting. For this, I'd typically wake at 4 am to train for a couple hours at the gym before my first classes of the day, then return to the gym later that evening for intense cardio and interval training, often stopping at certain points during the academic day to teach spin classes at the gym or swim laps at the University of Idaho pool.

Then I had a bright idea: I was already swimming, cycling and running, and somewhat burnt out on bodybuilding, so why not apply my skill set to something new, particularly the brutal swim-bike-run sport of *"triathlon"*—the very definition itself of multi-sport endurance? So one evening, I attended the University of Idaho triathlon club meeting and—that very night—registered for my first triathlon, scheduled to occur three months later. After ninety days of swimming, biking, running and studying up every nitty-gritty endurance element from cycling aerodynamics to hydration and nutrition protocols, I recall standing at the pool edge on the morning of the race, hearing the starting gun sound, then slipping into a state of pure, red-hot burning intensity for the next hour of the triathlon. While I had no clue what I was doing, didn't know how to "pace" myself, and felt a deep sense of wanna-be triathlete imposter syndrome, I wound up beating the entire field and setting the course record for the competition.

After that race, I was officially hooked.

Over the next decade, I competed in 147 additional triathlons in America, South America, Europe, Asia, and beyond, including Short Course World Championships, Half-Ironman World Championships, Ironman World Championships and a grand total of 5,569 miles of brutal, hot, endurance competition. Along the way, I sprinkled in additional cross-training via marathons, open water swimming competitions, cycling races, and even water polo.

Just like my experiences in high school basketball and tennis, I was known in triathlon as the guy who simply wouldn't stop. I wasn't the fastest. I wasn't the most naturally talented or biomechanically efficient. I wasn't the most experienced.

But I just.

Didn't.

Stop.

I'd nearly always start the race in the middle of the swim pack, gradually move my way up through the bike portion of the triathlon, and continue plodding on with steadfast determination, clicking off race markers mile-by-mile and picking off competitors one-by-one throughout the run.

Later, as a trained exercise physiologist, I actually discovered the scientific reasoning behind *why* my body seemed hardwired for endurance. See, in exercise physiology, there is a concept known as the "lactate threshold." Quite simply put, this threshold is the point of exercise intensity at which the body begins to accumulate burning lactic acid faster than that lactic acid can be "buffered" by the muscles. Once this threshold is exceeded, exercise becomes increasingly difficult, and failure or fatigue sets in quickly.

But in some individuals, the percentage of maximum pace or maximum effort at which the lactate threshold occurs is uncannily high. In other words, let's say that you and I are going to have a footrace over the course of a mile. And let's say that you've got a much higher top-end speed than I do, and can definitely run faster than me, especially for the first quarter or half or so of that mile.

I, on the other hand, may not have the same foot speed as you, but while you gradually slow down as lactic acid accumulates in your muscles over the course of that mile, I'm able to maintain a much higher average speed because I can manage all my lactic acid much better than you can yours. So, every little bit of that mile I creep up on you and eventually pass you before the finish line, simply because my tolerance for lactic acid is higher than yours. Perhaps the best example of a famous athlete who didn't have the fastest speed but possessed a ridiculously high lactate threshold is celebrated cyclist Lance Armstrong, who was also known for his grit, tenacity and ability to "go" at a decent pace for very long periods of time.

Turns out, this whole lactate threshold thing is actually testable, and, after having undergone multiple bouts of blood lactate testing for swimming, cycling and running—a protocol in which one exercises at a gradually more difficult pace while stopping every few minutes to test blood levels of lactic acid via a finger prick—I discovered that I was actually born with an uncannily high ability to be able to buffer the burn, so to speak.

Well, then, if endurance is my jam, I figured I might as well run my winners, literally and figuratively. So over twenty years—from the age of 19 until I was 39 years old—I kept plodding along. I jumped into adventure races, which include map and way-finding, cave spelunking, kayaking, mountain climbing, swimming, cliff jumping, rucking, trekking and beyond, all in one race. I competed in multi-mile open water and ocean swim races. For years, rarely a month went by that I didn't complete a century (100-mile) organized bike ride or cycling competition. I became a member of the Spartan professional obstacle course racing team, and spent four years engaged in that sport, which involved everything from hauling sandbags, to climbing ropes, to crawling under barbed wires, to jumping over fires, to swinging from bars and other obstacles. I learned to shoot a bow, and began to enter hunting competitions that required running, shooting, hiking, more obstacle course racing, and even hauling over a hundred pounds in a backpack over miles and miles of steep, rough terrain—while running!

Yep, if a sport involved any shred of stamina, steadfastness or sufferance, I'd happily sign up to be at the starting line.

And of course, along the way, I applied that same stubborn tenacity to academia, to business and to life in general, often working five to six jobs at a time while sleeping four hours a night, starting and building new companies in the health and fitness industry, investing, advising, coaching, consulting and juggling as many balls as I possibly could, because, frankly, I like to work long and work hard. Bring on the lactic acid, baby.

So why am I telling you all this?

Because, as you may have predicted, the concept of *enduring* is a topic very near and dear to my heart.

WHAT IS SPIRITUAL STAMINA?

So yes, I know endurance. It's a language I've spoken for quite some time.

But it's one thing to have the physical or mental endurance and stamina required to sit on a hard bicycle seat to pedal and sweat for six hours, or grit one's teeth through bitter cold ocean waves for thousands upon thousands of swim strokes, or wake up at 4 am and strap on a pair of running shoes to pound the pavement for mile upon mile...

...and quite another thing to possess spiritual stamina.

Yes, spiritual stamina.

See, in the same way you can train your brain, heart, muscles and lungs to resist fatigue, train your cardiovascular system to build new blood vessels for oxygen and fuel delivery, and train the central governor in your brain to possess the staying power to keep pushing through no matter how physically fatigued you are or how much your body is screaming at you to throw in the towel and succumb to exhaustion, you can also train your *spirit* to resist temptation, to master carnal passions and desires, to combat lust and pride and to hold fast with perseverance, persistence and patience when all the allures of the world seem to be working in cahoots to derail your spiritual health and your ability to make full impact for God with the purpose you've been given for life.

In his book *Disciplines Of A Godly Man*, author Kent Hughes writes:

> *"...the statement from Paul to Timothy regarding spiritual discipline in 1 Timothy 4:7—'train yourself to be godly'—takes on not only transcending importance, but personal urgency. There are other passages which teach discipline, but this is the great classic text of Scripture. The word 'train' comes from the word gumnos, which means 'naked' and is the word from which we derive our English word gymnasium. In traditional Greek athletic contests, the participants competed without clothing, so as not to be encumbered. Therefore, the word 'train' originally carried the literal meaning, 'to exercise naked.'*
>
> *By New Testament times it referred to exercise and training in general. But even then it was, and is, a word with the smell of the gym in it—the sweat of a good workout. 'Gymnasticize (exercise, work out, train) yourself for the purpose of godliness' conveys the feel of what Paul is saying. In a word, he is calling for some spiritual sweat! Just as the athletes discarded everything and competed gumnos—free from everything that could possibly burden them—so we must get rid of every encumbrance, every association, habit, and tendency which impedes godliness. If we are to excel, we must strip ourselves to a lean, spiritual nakedness."*

Unfortunately, as I write in my book *Fit Soul*, while most of us inherently know that caring for our soul with the same, lean spiritual, naked intensity and habitual routine with which a gymnast might train their body, we somehow shove it to the side because, let's face it—life gets busy, and it just seems far more practical and immediately useful to go hit the gym rather than sit cross-legged on the floor meditating and praying, spending an extra five minutes in bed in the morning gratitude journaling, or prioritizing relationships during a long and joyful family dinner. The concept of putting on our spiritual armor and equipping ourselves to withstand all the temptations and flaming arrows that the world inevitably flings at us each day; training our spirit to, by the grace of God, withstand the pride of life, the pride of the eyes and the lust of the flesh; and viewing our spiritual life as a training ground for battle is, sadly, often an afterthought.

Just imagine if you wanted to gain the superior fitness of an Olympian, or the chiseled body of a movie star, or the lightning-fast brain of a rocket scientist. Would your workout consist of cranking out a tiny handful of push ups before bed each night, eating one healthy meal a week, and reading picture books of airplanes to train your brain? I would surely hope not. Yet it can be so simple to stray into a habit of our spiritual stamina and endurance training to consist of saying a simple prayer before bedtime, digesting a few verses or a couple minutes of the Bible before rushing off to work in the morning, or meditating that one time for that *one* precious social media photo.

Fact is, as I also write in *Fit Soul,* I personally spent about 20 years of my life, up until I was in my mid-30s, barely tending to my spirit—until I realized that my own unhappiness and constant striving for the next big physical, mental, business, and personal achievement and obstacle to overcome was simply leaving my spirit even more shriveled, shrunken, unfit, and neglected and leaving me unfulfilled, unhappy and unable to fully love others and to make a maximum, purpose-filled impact with my life for God's glory. Perhaps most concerningly, my lack of devotion to spiritual fitness and all the chinks in my spiritual armor was leaving me wide open to falling, failing and being swept up by, as Galatians 5:19-21, says *"...sexual immorality, impurity and debauchery; idolatry and witchcraft; hatred, discord, jealousy, fits of rage, selfish ambition, dissensions, factions and envy; drunkenness, orgies, and the like."*

Ultimately, in a state of God-given conviction, I realized that in order for me to be both truly impactful and purposeful for God, to not be a washed-up, weak spiritual warrior, and to be a true father, leader and legacy-builder for my family, I needed to apply just as much forethought, seriousness and training to my spiritual stamina and endurance as I had been applying to my physical and mental training. I needed to follow the instructions of Ephesians 6:10–18, which says:

> *"Finally, be strong in the Lord and in his mighty power. Put on the full armor of God, so that you can take your stand against the devil's schemes.*
>
> *For our struggle is not against flesh and blood, but against the rulers, against the authorities, against the powers of this dark world*

and against the spiritual forces of evil in the heavenly realms.

Therefore, put on the full armor of God, so that when the day of evil comes, you may be able to stand your ground, and after you have done everything, to stand.

Stand firm then, with the belt of truth buckled around your waist, with the breastplate of righteousness in place, and with your feet fitted with the readiness that comes from the gospel of peace. In addition to all this, take up the shield of faith, with which you can extinguish all the flaming arrows of the evil one. Take the helmet of salvation and the sword of the Spirit, which is the word of God.

And pray in the Spirit on all occasions with all kinds of prayers and requests. With this in mind, be alert and always keep on praying for all the Lord's people."

So that's exactly what I did, and while, in the first chapter of my book *Fit Soul*, I describe to you the entirety of my journal from poverty-stricken spiritual detraining to wealth-infused spiritual fitness, I can give you a brief glimpse now of how I became fitted with the full armor of God: belt, breastplate, boots, shield, sword, helmet and prayer.

Ultimately, I began to train my spirit the same way I train my body and mind. See, I pride myself on maintaining a streak of physically rigorous workouts nearly 365 days a year, taking a cold shower or cold soak daily, doing three or four brutally hot sauna sessions a week, walking at least 15,000 steps per day, foam rolling at least ten minutes per morning, getting a massage at least twice per month, taking a carefully selected handful of supplements both morning and evening, stopping every 30 minutes of work to move or stretch for two minutes, reading at least three books per week, writing at least 200 words per day, practicing guitar for a minimum of ten minutes per day, etc., etc., etc.

Why not apply that same determination, temperance and mastery of passions and desires to my spiritual fitness? And what would happen if I did? After all, if I can stare at a blank wall running on a treadmill for three hours, surely I could read a chapter of my Bible each morning, couldn't I? Could I take the concept of stamina—commonly defined as the bodily or mental capacity to sustain a prolonged stressful effort or activity—and apply that concept to my spirit?

So I began to attend church on a regular basis, not as an afterthought or occasional visit, but with a reverent and worshipful attitude...

I turned to God daily, praying for clarity, wisdom, insight and a life drawn closer to union with Him...

I continued to pray without ceasing, throughout the day, and not just before meals or at church...

I studied the spiritual disciplines that I taught you in *Fit Soul* and that you'll also discover within the pages of this book, and began to incorporate gratitude, service, silence, meditation and Scripture memorization into my daily routine...

I returned to my childhood love for music, and steeped myself in praise and worship songs...

I set aside my selfish tendencies and gave more time, tender care and teaching to my wife and twin sons...

I read at least one chapter a day from my Bible, and followed a Bible reading plan the same way I'd devotedly follow a workout plan...

I memorized at least one verse from the Bible each week...

I gathered my family for gratitude, meditation and prayer each morning, and re-gathered them for self-examination, purpose, prayer and thanksgiving each evening...

I began to volunteer more in my local community and at my church...

I recorded one new worship song on my guitar each month...

You get the idea, I began to plan, systematize, structure and apply just as much seriousness to my spiritual training as I would to my physical training had I, say, signed up for an Ironman triathlon, but of course with the realization that the spiritual "race" is a race with a far more important, meaningful finish line—a race that results in everlasting glory and eternal happiness found in God, and not just a perishable blue ribbon or a shiny gold medal.

The fruits began to pour forth into my life, particularly when it came to me feeling far more equipped to be able to resist temptation.

For example, as you'll read in Chapter 3, one temptation I've struggled with for much of my life has been sexual infidelity, lust and porn. But as I grew closer to God and closer to my wife through my focus on building spiritual stamina, I suddenly found myself able to walk past beautiful, attractive women on the street, in grocery stores, at the gym, or at clubs or restaurants without nary a thought of lusting after or objectifying that woman or cheating on my wife.

When insulted, treated rudely, or disparaged by others, I found myself able to respond in a spirit of love and forgiveness, rather than becoming angry, lashing out or experiencing a gut response of bitterness, rage or resentment, finding myself more able to make relationships transformational instead of purely transactional (read more about that in Chapter 4 of *Fit Soul*).

When stressed or in an unpleasant or annoying situation, I felt myself more free and able to, in the words of holocaust survivor Victor Frankl choose an attitude of gratefulness, acceptance and contentment no matter the circumstances (you can read more about satisfaction and completeness in Chapters 8 and 9).

At the end of a hard and demanding day of work, I was able to turn to God, prayer, meditation and worship instead of weed, wine, cocktails, kava or plant medicines for mental relief or relaxation (you'll read more about my perspective on responsible use of such compounds in Chapter 5).

I became better, as you'll read about in Chapter 6, with patience and delayed gratification.

I found myself more purposeful with work and connected to applying my personal purpose statement to loving God and loving others as I "chopped wood and carried water" each day, a concept I'll explore in Chapter 10.

I became less begrudged and hesitant and more motivated and inspired to carve out unselfish time for charity, volunteering and giving, which I tell you more about in Chapter 21.

I released my unhealthy, white-knuckled grasp on control and began to see the OCD-like tendencies I describe in Chapter 2 melt away.

I became more connected to my family as they joined me on the same journey of morning and evening prayer, meditation, gratitude, service and self-examination you'll discover in Chapter 15.

I stepped into others' shoes more and developed heightened amounts of both sympathy and empathy, as I tell you about in Chapters 16 and 17.

As you learn in Chapters 18 and 19, I discovered more about what really happens when we humans die, how exactly that shapes our lives, and the importance of full union with God and perspective on life and deathbeds in general.

I danced more, sang more, laughed more, dreamed more and created more—in the same way I teach you how to do in Chapter 9 and, as a result, experienced a greater sense of awe and beauty in God's creation.

Ultimately, an overall sense of peace, love and joy began to saturate my entire day, and night.

It turns out that—in the same way one gradually sees their body morph as they begin to hit the gym each day, or their brain morph as they begin to read, learn new things, memorize facts or play musical instruments on a consistent basis—a deep and meaningful spiritual transformation occurs when the spirit is trained with the same forethought, planning, specificity and systematization as the body and mind. In other words, spiritual stamina is *trainable*.

You too can possess this same steadfast endurance, this same power to withstand hardship and stress, and this same inward fortitude necessary to persist in the face of temptation, failure and hard times. But you must set your jaw and prepare for, within the pages of this book, a journey of...

...patience...

...planning...

...acceptance...

...forbearance...

...persistence...

...detachment...

...tenacity...

...doggedness...

...resoluteness...

...guts and grit.

Just as with any massive, transformative goal in life, you must now view yourself standing on the training field, a wooden bucket full of steel maces, kettlebells, and heavy rocks before you; sandpits, hot pavement and steep hills surrounding you; plush couches, free food, icy cold lemonade and a cocktail bar distracting you; and make a decision as to what path you will choose.

In the whole scheme of your life—your eternal life—this kind of focus on spiritual training is so, so incredibly important. How important? Just look at 1 Timothy 4:8-9 in the Bible, in which Paul says:

> *"For bodily exercise profits a little, but godliness is profitable for all things, having promise of the life that now is and of that which is to come. This is a faithful saying and worthy of all acceptance."*

Read that passage carefully. Now, bodily exercise and physical training isn't exactly scoffed at as a complete waste of time, as of course that type of training can equip us to be more impactful with the short life we've been given here on earth in our current bodies—allowing us to better love God, love others and savor God's creation. But compared to spiritual endurance and spiritual training, it absolutely pales in comparison, because training the spirit is an act of building godliness and becoming more and more sanctified each day with the ultimate outcome being *eternal* glory and a finish line party that lasts *forever*. Of course, it's easy to think short-term—up to the 70 or 80 or 90 or 100 years we might live on this planet—and to train for simply managing our bodies during that timespan. But it's quite another thing, and quite an exciting thing, to consider that you have the ability to be able to train your soul to be prepared for eternity, and to equip yourself to bless others with that same forever life. What a great and rewarding priority in your life that should and must be!

HOW TO ENDURE

I've already given you plenty of resources above and also mentioned many others elsewhere (such as in my podcasts, articles and books featured or reviewed on my website) to begin upon your path to spiritual endurance, such as my previous book *Fit Soul*, the *Spiritual*

Disciplines Journal **(SpiritualDisciplinesJournal.com), and the** *Spiritual Disciplines Handbook* **by Adele Calhoun that I mention quite often.**

But nothing has been more dear to me and nothing will be a closer and more helpful companion to you—even more than the book you're reading right now—on this journey to self-mastery, endurance and spiritual stamina than a Bible. Consider just a few of the verses sprinkled throughout Scripture that you can use as inspiration, motivation and direction for your spiritual training.

1 Corinthians 10:13: "No temptation has overtaken you except such as is common to man; but God is faithful, who will not allow you to be tempted beyond what you are able, but with the temptation will also make the way of escape, that you may be able to bear it."

Mark 13:13: "But he who endures to the end shall be saved."

James 1:12: "Blessed is the man who endures temptation; for when he has been approved, he will receive the crown of life which the Lord has promised to those who love Him."

James 1:2-4: "My brethren, count it all joy when you fall into various trials, knowing that the testing of your faith produces patience. But let patience have its perfect work, that you may be perfect and complete, lacking nothing."

Colossians 1:11: "Strengthened with all might, according to His glorious power, for all patience and long-suffering with joy."

Romans 12:12: "Rejoicing in hope, patient in tribulation, continuing steadfastly in prayer."

Hebrews 12:1-3: "Therefore we also, since we are surrounded by so great a cloud of witnesses, let us lay aside every weight, and the sin which so easily ensnares us, and let us run with endurance the race that is set before us, looking unto Jesus, the author and finisher of our faith, who for the joy that was set before Him endured the cross, despising the shame, and has sat down at the right hand of the throne of God. For consider Him who endured such hostility from sinners against Himself, lest you become weary and discouraged in your souls."

And finally, perhaps two of my favorites:

Philippians 4:13: *"I can do all things through Christ who strengthens me."*

Isaiah 40:31: *"But those who wait on the Lord shall renew their strength; they shall mount up with wings like eagles, they shall run and not be weary, they shall walk and not faint."*

Yes, your Bible is your training manual for spiritual endurance. And you can consider this book as a complete guide to getting jump-started into that journey. Now it's time to take one deep breath, to release your fears about whether or not you will have enough time to train, set aside any sense of spiritual "imposter syndrome," to place full trust in God that He will clothe and feed you even if you're working less, working out less or even sleeping less to make your spiritual endurance training a priority and to take that first step forward.

Summary

Do you struggle with temptation, and often find yourself succumbing to it?

Do you get confused or overwhelmed by the variety of ways one can pray, meditate, read the Bible or "be spiritual?"

Do you lay awake at night feeling as though although you checked a lot of productivity boxes, at the end of the day, you are still restless and unfulfilled?

Do you want to live a fully impactful life that inspires others to greatness and defies the sad status quo of what the world accepts as adequate spiritual health?

Do you want to ingest more beauty, dance more, sing more, dream more, create more, and experience with a fuller sense of peace, love and joy all of God's creation?

I don't know about you, but I crave this kind of meaning.

However, it doesn't just *happen*. You must, as I write in Chapter 11, trust God, and then strap on your sword. We are in this together, you and I, fighting a battle for our very soul. And we must come prepared.

This book Endure, written and inspired by my own personal temptations, struggles and failures, and informed by what I've studied and learned along the way, will serve as part of that very preparation for you.

Quite simply, *Endure* is structured into six parts.

First, in Part 1, you'll discover common temptations, obstacles, pitfalls and struggles you'll face along the way, and learn exactly how to deal with them.

Part 2 will address mastery of passions and desires, and how to strike a balance between savoring God's creation and stoic self-discipline.

Part 3 delves into purpose and productivity, revealing how to work deep, create beauty, and simultaneously experience rest and refreshment.

In Part 4, you'll learn how to love others and love God more fully, while creatively weaving the Golden Rule into your life.

Part 5 addresses what happens at the end of your life, and how to find meaning in both life and death.

Finally, in Part 6, from simplicity to laughter, you'll learn more about how to be most glorified in God by being most satisfied in Him.

By the conclusion of *Endure*, you will have discovered and learned how to implement the same tools, tactics and habits for spiritual stamina that were inspired by great philosophers, thinkers and theologians of ancient and modern ages, including Augustine, Plato, the Apostles Paul, Peter and John, the kings David and Solomon, C.S. Lewis, Naval Ravikant, Anthony DeMello, Derek Sivers, Doug Wilson, Randy Alcorn, John Piper, many, many others, and of course, Jesus Christ himself.

Each chapter will also end with a quick call-to-action: a chance for you to jot down just a few thoughts about questions I ask you in each Chapter Summary. So it is time for that very exercise right now.

How about you? How is your own spiritual stamina? Do you tackle and train it with the same ferocity as you do your body and mind? Do you crave the confidence and protection afforded by living your life equipped in the full armor of God?

If the answer to the third question above is "not really" and your answer to the fourth question above is "absolutely," then, now is the time to start. I invite you to join me on this journey through the pages of Endure, and, in the spaces below, to answer the following question:

Why do I desire more spiritual stamina and endurance?

For resources, references, links and additional reading and listening material for this chapter, visit GetEndure.com/Introduction.

BEN GREENFIELD

PART I

COMMON TEMPTATIONS

Obstacles, pitfalls and struggles you'll face, and how to deal with them.

CHAPTER I

LUST & PRIDE

I'm constantly inspired by the deep wisdom of Jesus, and have been recently captivated by his extraordinary transformation following a forty-day stint of fasting, reportedly in a rugged mountain wilderness location near the Jordan River. It was after this experience that Jesus returned to Galilee as an entirely new man (for just a hint of the power of this type of fasting protocol, I recommend you read the book *Atomic Power With God*) and commenced performing a host of impressive miracles.

But Jesus' time in the wilderness went far beyond the simple act of solitude and fasting. Matthew 4:3-10 describes the extreme temptations from Satan that Jesus faced during this time:

"And the tempter came and said to him, 'If you are the Son of God, command these stones to become loaves of bread.'

But he answered, 'It is written, 'Man shall not live by bread alone, but by every word that comes from the mouth of God.'

Then the devil took him to the holy city and set him on the pinnacle of the temple and said to him, 'If you are the Son of God, throw yourself down, for it is written, 'He will command his angels concerning you, and on their hands they will bear you up, lest you strike your foot against a stone.'"

Jesus said to him, 'Again it is written, 'You shall not put the Lord your God to the test.'"

Again, the devil took him to a very high mountain and showed him all the kingdoms of the world and their glory. And he said to him, 'All these I will give you, if you will fall down and worship me.' Then

Jesus said to him, 'Be gone, Satan! For it is written, 'You shall worship the Lord your God and Him only shall you serve.'"

While it may seem as though these temptations may have been unique to the son of God, they are actually an identical reflection of the three distinct temptations every one of us mere humans face on a near-daily basis.

THE LUST OF THE FLESH

The first temptation that Jesus faced was the "lust of the flesh"—in this case, the desire for food (*"If you are the Son of God, command these stones to become loaves of bread."*)

From the dawn of time, humankind has had to deal with this lust of the flesh, most notably beginning with the Garden of Eden, in which Adam and Eve were tempted by the fruits from the tree of the knowledge of good and evil. This lust of the flesh is a temptation to derive physical pleasure from an attachment or an otherworldly object that isn't necessarily "bad" in and of itself (after all, God created all things for good), but if used in a dishonorable way or accompanied by addiction can certainly be problematic.

These lusts can range from food and supplements to medications and drugs to exercise and sex to social media and television. For me, personally, examples of lusts of the flesh that I must deal with on a daily basis include food, plant medicines such as marijuana, attractive women, and escapism through physical activity and exercise. You can learn about how those types of temptations nearly derailed my entire journey of spiritual fitness in the Who Am I? chapter of my book *Fit Soul*.

Notably, with this first temptation, and the two that follow after it, I learn from the story of Jesus above exactly what to do when presented with a fleshly attachment, addiction, or temptation. In this case, I can say to Satan when presented with these temptations exactly what Jesus said: *"I shall not live by bread alone, but by every word that comes from the mouth of God."*

And where does one find "every word that comes from the mouth of God?" You guessed it: *the Bible.* If a Bible is near you (or installed on your phone/computer) at all times, you can simply escape to God's word when faced with a temptation of the lust of the flesh, even by doing something as simple as turning to Psalms or Proverbs and simply beginning to read the words of King David, who frequently called out to God during periods of struggle and stress.

THE LUST OF THE EYES

The lust of the eyes is a second temptation Jesus faced, in this case the offer for unfettered access to kingdoms, cities, wealth, all the world's riches and beyond (*the devil took him to a very high mountain and showed him all the kingdoms of the world and their glory. And he said to him, "All these I will give you, if you will fall down and worship me."*)

Beginning again in the Garden of Eden, in which the fruit of the tree of the knowledge of good and evil was "pleasant to the eyes" of Adam and Eve, each of us also face a temptation of the lust of the eyes on a daily basis. This can include coveting our neighbor's spouse, children, family, or belongings; consumption of pornography; desiring others' material possessions or wealth and status; being envious of the body or lifestyle someone is displaying on Instagram or Facebook; or wishing we could have the souped-up car, motorcycle, or bicycle pulled up next to us at the stoplight.

I'll admit that I'm constantly pulled towards a bit of "grass is always greener" syndrome—wishing I had someone else's house, life, belongings, body, wisdom, or unique skills, and often tempted towards discontentedly casting my own eyes upon the visual appeal and anticipation of ownership of these things as I'm washed over with feelings of desire and anticipated pleasure from something somebody else has that I don't.

Yet in the same way that dwelling upon God's word can save us from the lust of the flesh, the simplicity of Scripture offers us an "out" when we are tempted with the lust of the eyes. What did Jesus tell Satan when Satan tempted him with the lust of the eyes?

> *"You shall worship the Lord your God and Him only shall you serve."*

That's right: All you need is to be able to worship God and a relationship of deep union with God to resist the temptation of the lust of the eyes. You can read in my book *Fit Soul* about to how develop your union with God, so that you can turn to Him in worship, trust, and dependence when you are confronted with anything from porn on your smartphone to your neighbor's spiffy new lawnmower. It's that simple.

The Pride Of Life

The final temptation we all-too-often face is the pride of life (*Then the devil took him to the holy city and set him on the pinnacle of the temple and said to him, "If you are the Son of God, throw yourself down, for it is written, 'He will command his angels concerning you,' and 'On their hands they will bear you up, lest you strike your foot against a stone.'"*)

No surprises here: This was also one of the first temptations humankind faced when Adam and Eve desired to be wise by partaking of the forbidden fruit. The pride of life is a temptation for greatness, power, fame, glory, knowledge, and the superior lifestyle that we all feel the constant urge to attain at all costs—not for God's glory, but for our own glory. This can include a desire to get credit or glory for any great thing we accomplish (rather than being content if nobody notices but God), a desire for others to hold us in high esteem so we can "make a name for ourselves," a desire to feel more valued or more important than others around us, or to be put into positions of power over others in a way that puffs up our own ego for the sake of bragging rights.

I like to think of this temptation as "politician syndrome," as I see it displayed amongst many power-hungry politicians, but also amongst executives and hard-charging, high-achievers who aren't pursuing glory for the sake of magnifying God, but rather for the sake of magnifying themselves.

And how did Jesus deal with this temptation?

He simply said to Satan: *"You shall not put the Lord your God to the test."* In other words, when you are tempted towards greatness for greatness' sake, turn to God and acknowledge that He is Almighty and you are merely a creation that He designed to bring glory to Him. Who are you to test God as to whether He is God or *you* are god? So remind yourself the next time you are tempted towards the pride of life that there is only one God, it's not you, and your greatest calling is to glorify God, and not yourself.

Summary

Like Jesus, we all face the lust of the flesh, the lust of the eyes, and the pride of life. But in a very simple and easy-to-understand way, Matthew 4:3-10 tells us exactly how to resist these temptations: Read the Bible, worship God, and acknowledge His greatness.

Furthermore, 1 Corinthians 10:13 tell us that:

> *"There hath no temptation taken you but such as is common to man: but God is faithful, who will not suffer you to be tempted above that ye are able; but will with the temptation also make a way to escape, that ye may be able to bear it."*

That's right: God promises us that no matter how hard a temptation is, He will always provide an escape route. With God's word constantly saturating our minds and hearts, we can resist, for we know that the word of God is quick, and powerful, and sharper than any double-edged sword. My prayer for you on this day is that God would deliver you from temptation, and that this short read will give you the three mighty tools you need to do just that.

How about you? What temptations do you face? When encountering those temptations, what have you found to be helpful for keeping you on the straight and narrow path? If you don't really know how to deal with those temptations, then don't worry, because that's what this book will teach you, but for now, simply take a pause for a time of breathing, self-examination and silence, then list some of your major temptations below:

For resources, references, links and additional reading and listening material for this chapter, visit GetEndure.com/Chapter1.

CHAPTER II
CONTROL

I'm going to come right out and admit it...

...I think I have OCD.

No, no, no, I haven't actually been "officially diagnosed" with Obsessive-Compulsive Disorder (OCD). It's nothing that dramatic.

But I'm pretty darn sure I certainly have grown significantly in the past several years certain OCD-like tendencies, which I've found seems to be quite common amongst my peers as we age and develop distinct habits, rituals, and routines that—while lending stability, control, and productiveness to one's life—can reach a certain point to where those same habits become almost too rote and non-negotiable, often to the detriment of social life, family life, personal progression, exploration, creativity, and learning; experiencing new things in a free, fun, flowing manner; and simply *being* instead of *doing*.

For example, when I step back and analyze my own daily routine, I've noticed the development of several OCD-like tendencies, including:

- *Feeling "less-than-myself" unless I fully complete a morning self-care and spiritual routine that includes strategies such as meditation, journaling, face-washing, oil-pulling, tongue-scraping, nutritional supplements, foam-rolling, stretching, breathwork, etc. Should I miss any component of this established routine (which seems to have grown more and more elaborate over the years) I simply feel a bit "off" the rest of the day, with a nagging worry at the back of my mind that I didn't "stick to my morning routine" or didn't do everything I could have done to optimize my body and brain for the day. Are these types of morning or evening rituals bad? Absolutely not. I actually don't know any successful, productive people who do not have some kind of a relatively structured and occasionally elaborate morning routine, but when that routine dictates zero allowance for more free-flowing activities such as random fun family breakfast outings or occasionally sleeping in to snuggle in bed with my wife, or that routine interferes with work obligations by causing me to show up late for a call or be inadequately prepared for a meeting or writing session because I was "checking all my boxes," it becomes obsessive, problematic, and selfish.*

- *Extreme rigidity with workouts and exercising to the extent that if I do not finish the exact workout that I have planned for the day, for the exact amount of time I have scheduled for that workout, with the exact exercises I have programmed, I become annoyed and anxious. If a social event my wife has planned or an outing with the kids suddenly, at the last minute, interferes with that workout, it significantly rubs me the wrong way, even if it's something as simple as cutting a stretching session five minutes short or going on a family hike instead of doing my planned kettlebell or weight training workout. I'll also often become anxious if I look at my wearable tracker results and see that I haven't reached my allotted 15,000-step count for the day, and even go on random walks that tear me away from social events just so I can "catch up" on my step count. I'll sometimes find myself checking my continuous blood glucose monitor, sleep tracker, or activity tracker nearly as often as some people check their social media accounts (meaning, more than once per hour, which I don't think is a healthy and productive use of time). Again, these are the same types of physical disciplines that have kept me extremely fit and healthy, but increasingly seem to threaten my very sanity should they ever be altered by something outside my control or some "annoying" obligation that is actually more important than adhering to my planned workout. Of course, this should all be viewed in light of the fact that these habits developed when I was a pro athlete, but now that I'm not a pro athlete anymore seem to have stuck around in near full amounts.*

- *Intense control of food and meal composition and timing, including: painstaking analysis of packaged food labels to ensure not even the slightest semblance of anything I perceive as unhealthy to be present in even the most minuscule amounts; refusal to eat a meal until the exact amount of time has arrived I have planned on eating it (e.g. ensuring an intermittent fast lasts at least 12 hours, and refusing to eat even if I'm hungry because it's only been, say 11.5 hours, or refusing to go to a lunch meeting at 12:30 because I hadn't planned on eating lunch until 1 pm); putting off family meals or dinners until the exact time that they fit into my own personal schedule; resistance to allowing others to cook for me unless I know the exact list of ingredients they* are putting into my meal, hence some amount of low-level anxiety at any restaurants; and a near-obsession with tracking parameters such as blood glucose and ketones to ensure I'm constantly staying within my targeted range.

- *Sacrificing anything to ensure my circadian rhythm and sleep/wake times are optimized, including: not going outside to star-gaze with my kids if it's too close to the beginning of my bedtime rituals; refusing to splurge on a late-night dinner date with my wife if it doesn't allow me to adhere to my normal evening sleep time; avoiding social events that may put me in a scenario in which I'm "out past my bedtime;" refusing to sleep in a bed unless it has exactly three pillows (one for under my head, one for on top of my head and one for between my legs); and becoming anxious and borderline insomniac if I I'm ever unable to go to bed without my sleeping mask, foam earplugs, lavender essential oil, blue light blockers, etc., etc., etc.*

- *Most notably, an ever-increasing lack of fun, free-flowing play, which has instead been replaced by strict scheduling, order, checklists, habits, rituals, disciplines, and a distinct and significant lack of spontaneity that also often serves as work or habit-based escapism that distances me from the needs of my loved ones.*

These are just a few examples I've identified from my own life, but I hope you get the idea.

So...

...have you ever struggled with the same issues?

If so, do you, like me, wonder how these kinds of extreme control issues gradually develop?

Which ingrained habits, tendencies, or inherent genetic predispositions does all this stem from?

And most importantly, is there a solution?

After all, I know for a fact that I'm not the only health enthusiast that deals with OCD-like tendencies. I have many, many friends and acquaintances who are biohackers, nutritionists, personal trainers, exercise enthusiasts, and the like who all seem to face similar uphill battles of control. And of course, that's just the tiny subset of people in "my world," and doesn't include the executive who is a monster at the office if everyone is not arranged perfectly, the mother who can't sleep at night due to extreme control over her household, or the grown man or woman with few friends in life because they insist upon controlling every social scenario they create or find themselves in.

So I think it's high time that—particularly in this chapter—I put all the cards on the table and talk openly about my own issues, the underlying causes, and the solutions I've personally found so that I can hopefully help you out just a bit with any OCD or control issues you may have.

What Is OCD & What Causes It?

We all have our own little quirks, habits, and behaviors that we know we might be better off without, or at least may be better off being more flexible with. Sure, many of us could use *more* self-control and order in our lives. But when habits and thoughts spin out of control, becoming so intense and intrusive that they seem to take over against our will or what we know would be a more sane and normal approach to routine, they can turn into all-consuming rituals that are irrationally and often selfishly performed to rid us of an overwhelming sense of fear, dread, and anxiety. This signifies that we may be on a slow slide towards excessive control tendencies or mild OCD.

The National Institute of Mental Health (NIMH) defines OCD as *"...a common, chronic, and long-lasting disorder in which a person has uncontrollable, reoccurring thoughts (obsessions) and/or behaviors (compulsions) that he or she feels the urge to repeat over and over."*

People with OCD can have symptoms of obsessions, compulsions, or both, and these symptoms can interfere with all aspects of life, such as work, school, and personal relationships.

Obsessions are defined by the NIMH as *"...repeated thoughts, urges, or mental images that cause anxiety,"* including:

- Fear of germs or contamination

- Unwanted, forbidden or taboo thoughts involving sex, religion, or harm
- Aggressive thoughts towards others or self
- Having things symmetrical or in a perfect order

Compulsions are defined as repetitive behaviors that a person with OCD feels the urge to do in response to an obsessive thought, including:

- Excessive cleaning and/or handwashing
- Ordering and arranging things in a particular, precise way
- Repeatedly checking on things, such as repeatedly checking to see if the door is locked or that the oven is off
- Compulsive counting, counting things for no reason, or not being able to finish activities until you've counted to a certain number

Other common characteristics of OCD-like tendencies include uncontrolled eating or drinking, nail-biting, compulsive shopping and gambling, substance abuse, impulsive sexual behaviors, and excessive ruminating about relationships, self-image, and self-esteem.

Now there is one important caveat here: People often tend to confuse OCD with a far less disabling issue named obsessive-compulsive personality disorder (OCPD), and it's actually a bit more accurate to describe my own OCD-like tendencies—and the tendencies of many people who suspect they may have OCD—as OCPD, and not true OCD.

So what sets these two apart?

Basically, when obsessions and compulsions are significant enough to cause significant functional impairments, it's usually OCD. In contrast, in OCPD, obsessions and compulsions are more like slight personality quirks or idiosyncrasies. For example, a person with OCPD may hang on to some object because they believe they may need it someday, but a person with OCD may, in a sort of hoarding compulsion, fill every square foot of their house with worthless trash they know they'll never need.

People with OCPD tend to have trouble "seeing the forest for the trees" and are typically list-makers who get so hung up on minute details that they don't see the big picture. In a classic case of the "best" being the "enemy of the good," their quest for perfection often interferes with their getting things done. People with OCPD tend to mess up things that are good enough in their quest to make everything perfect in every detail. They are relatively set in their ways and habits, inflexible, and unwilling to compromise. In the view of someone with OCPD, if a job is to be done right, it must be done exactly their way. Because of this, they tend to be checklist-driven micromanagers who are unwilling to delegate. (Interestingly, this personality type is twice as common in males than females.)

However—although I imagine this may be much to the chagrin of a dyed-in-the-wool psychiatrist or personality disorder specialist—for purposes of simplicity and clarity, for the remainder of this chapter, I'm simply going to use the term OCD as a catch-all phrase to describe both OCD and OCPD. Hopefully, that's OK with you.

So with that quick clarification, let's move on: What causes OCD in the first place?

Researchers have offered a variety of explanations. For example, there is a link between OCD and unbalanced levels of serotonin, a neurotransmitter that relays messages between neurons. There are also significant genetic factors at play. For example, if you listen to my intriguing podcast with Dr. Mansoor Mohammed of TheDNACompany—which I'll link to on the resources page for this chapter—you'll hear Dr. Mohammed explain how my own serotonin pathways (and interestingly, those of my twin boys)—specifically those related to the COMT and 5-HTTLPR genotypes—result in decreased expression of serotonin transporters and dysregulated serotonin secretion and reuptake, resulting in a strong tendency towards reward and pleasure-seeking behavior, a propensity to addictive, binge-like, or manic behaviors, propensity to endlessly ruminate on worries and tasks, and proneness to—you guessed it—OCD-like tendencies.

This neurotransmitter and genetic hardwiring, while allowing one to be a highly productive and organized individual, can also cause a bit of a glitch in a section of the brain called the caudate nucleus, basically causing the frontal lobe of the brain to become somewhat overactive. This allows the brain to become flooded and often overwhelmed with many thoughts, impulses, anxieties, and worries that enter their mind. (Incidentally, one of the most meaningful tips Dr. Mohammed gave to me during that podcast was to ensure that I write down any to-dos, tasks, or notes that enter my brain as soon as possible after I think of them because otherwise, my brain will grab onto those thoughts like a bulldog and cause me to become hyper-focused and anxious that I may forget or lose track of them.)

But while genetics and nature can certainly play a role in OCD, there are also environmental factors and nurturing factors that can also contribute. For example, in the past two decades, as a former bodybuilder, then a serious Ironman triathlete, then a professional Spartan competitor—all while acting as a family man, CEO, and founder of a variety of businesses in the health, nutrition, and fitness sector—I've had to set up robust planning and organizing mechanisms in my own environment that have required me to become a creature of habit who relies upon a strict, nearly obsessive, schedule to simply keep track of and accomplish everything I need to do in any given week. Throw hefty bouts of speaking, biohacking, and immersive journalism into the mix, and I've also got tons of toys to try, books and research papers to read, books to write, and habits to pile on already existing habits, resulting in many, many things to "do" each day that tend to, especially after years and years, stack on each other to create an incredibly complex existence that necessitates even more OCD and control.

As you can imagine, this can become a bit of a vicious cycle.

In addition, childhood experiences can play a role in the development of or tendencies towards OCD. Many people with control issues or OCD grew up in households headed by either a very rigid father or a dominating mother, which can result in low self-esteem and the subsequent development of controlling compulsions. These types of folks, early in life, were often given the impression by their parents that they need to be perfect, and hence, develop a tendency to try to control their social environment. They build up their own safe, little perfect world that they can easily control, and, as a result, family, friends, and social obligations are often pushed outside this world due to the relatively spontaneous nature of these relationships.

In my own case, I was both raised in a very rigid and controlling home and was also often given the impression that much of my personal value was determined by how perfect I was or how perfect I appeared to be to the outside world, which you can learn a lot more about in my book Fit Soul.

Ultimately, I'm not really a "label" guy. I'll admit that I often have a bit of a visceral reaction when I hear people blame their personal issues on past trauma, or the way their mother and father raised them, or biochemical imbalances and the like. I often feel as though these labels or reasons for personal faults can take too much precedence and can be used as a crutch to shame others or blame experiences for what is truly a personality or character fault that someone simply needs to turn over to God, repent of, and then do the hard work to fix. Yet, at the same time, I think we all have inherent tendencies towards certain sins and faults, and in my own case, the genetic, environmental, and deeply-rooted "blessing" of being a creature of habits, rituals, routines, order, and systems has gradually become a "curse" of being a creature void of creative, spontaneous flow.

The question is, what does one do about these tendencies? I'll now share with you what I have been finding helpful as I have identified control issues in my own life and set about to fix them.

Three Ways To Release Control Issues & OCD Tendencies

Before I explain the three strategies I have personally found most helpful to release control and OCD tendencies, I must first emphasize that I am not encouraging or endorsing a chaotic, unscheduled, free-wheeling existence with no scheduling, control, organization, or routines. Allow me to repeat and re-emphasize what I wrote earlier in this chapter:

> *"Things become problematic when habits and thoughts spin out of control, becoming so intense and intrusive that they seem to take over against our will or what we know would be a more sane and normal approach to routine, because they can turn into all-consuming rituals that are irrationally or often selfishly performed to rid us of an overwhelming sense of fear, dread, and anxiety."*

So do not be ashamed or embarrassed if you are a somewhat controlling and orderly Type-A individual (like me). The world needs those types of people, especially due to the great deal of stability they can lend to society, just as much as the world needs creative, free-flowing artists (like my wife) for healthy doses of joy, inspiration, and spontaneity. But do indeed guard against control and identify when it, or OCD-like tendencies that accompany it, threaten to produce excessive anxiety, selfish habits, social isolation, or lack of creative, free play.

Next, I'd had quite a few people ask me whether plant medicines or so-called "psychedelics" may help break the type of OCD or control "loops," upon which the ego can become hardwired and reliant, so I'd be remiss not to briefly address that question. Long story short is that I certainly think there can be some efficacy to these type of compounds for dissolving the ego and releasing significant amounts of control, but if you find yourself relying upon such substances to "reboot" your system over and over again, it is, in my opinion, indicative of the need to fix the issue with a more permanent solution, such as those I'll present below. I highly suspect that the thoughtful integration process that should ideally occur after any plant medicine or psychedelics treatment, along with a deeper knowing of and belief in God, is responsible for any results from such an experience that will actually "stick."

That being said, **the first major realization that has helped me is to recognize and acknowledge that the Creator of this universe is a God of both order and spontaneity.**

1 Corinthians 14:33 tells us: *"For God is not a God of disorder but of peace."*

For example, God's created universe is orderly. It was created in a sequenced six-day span, with sun, moon, and stars to regulate time, seasons, and the circadian rhythms of earth's inhabitants, and heavenly bodies that operate with clock-like precision and predictability.

Your body is another example of God's orderliness. Biological mechanisms such as the complex cardiovascular system that snakes miles throughout the body, a supercomputer brain that fires thousands of neurotransmitters per second to regulate breath, heart rate, pain, temperature, respiration, thought, and more, symmetrical patterns such as Pi and the Golden Ratio that are symbolized in elements of nature such as fingertips and leaves and millions of other chemical and physical reactions occur nearly every second of the day. If one of these factors falls out of order, creation slowly begins to crumble.

God also created and scheduled orderly and sequential time variations as a way for earth to mark changes, including the rising and setting of the sun, the perfectly timed rotation of the earth upon its axis, the waxing and waning of the moon, and many others. Hebrews 1:3 and Colossians 1:17 tell us that everything in the universe was created by God to be good and perfect, and for millennia, it has remained in working order based on these built-in laws of time. Throughout the Old Testament, God continues to lay down order with specific laws, customs, and rituals such as Passover, sacrifices and anointings, days of atonement, symbolic clothing and lists of rules such as the Ten Commandments. God's Church has continued to reflect this order with practices such as celebrations of religious holidays, dedicated prayer times, a liturgical calendar, and weekly taking of the sacraments.

Yet while God is a God of order—and while Paul tells the Corinthians, *"Let all things be done decently and in order"* (1 Corinthians 14:40)—God is also a fierce, wild, and spontaneous God, and Paul also tells the Corinthians *"where the Spirit of the Lord is, there is liberty"* (2 Corinthians 3:17). In Chapter 19 of *Fit Soul*, I cite an intriguing essay that describes a fitting description of God's fierceness, wildness, dangerousness, and spontaneity:

> *"...God is dangerous, wild, and unpredictable. He is dynamite and a kidnapper. That's the God of Abraham...the God of Abraham does not pen Hallmark cards. He is not a corporate risk manager. He is not a cruise director aiming to make our trip as pleasant and comfortable as possible. He is here to overturn tables and create people who can run alongside Him. 'If you have run with the footmen, and they have wearied you, then how can you contend with horses?' (Jeremiah 12:5). He wants people like horses, people whose necks are 'clothed with thunder,' 'mock at fear,' and do not stop at the sound of the trumpet. It's not about power; it's about character and tension and Trinity."*

Throughout history, the same God who freely paints splatters of yellow, orange, and red across a sunset and sunrise, fashions and forms the funkiness of the hippopotamus, platypus, and giraffe, and coordinates miracles that can often defy the laws of the order of nature (such as talking donkeys, burning bushes, and floating axes) has also inspired great works of poetry, art, fiction, architecture, and many other creative forms of human expression. God is a Creator who takes joy in our own human creations, and creation, of course, often requires a certain deal of creativity and release of tidy, predictable control.

The trick is to use wisdom, discernment, prayer, and understanding to know how to weave into your own life *both* order and spontaneity. Think about it this way: Water is free, flowing, playful, and unpredictable, yet a series of intricately ordered and well-arranged hydrogen and oxygen molecules are what actually comprise the mass of waters that boundlessly lap across our planet. A dark and wild forest is broad-sweeping, unconstrained, and borderless, yet upon closer inspection can be comprised of row upon row of ordered trees consisting of atoms, electrons, and protons that operate according to specific laws of chemistry and physics. Earth itself, if a person attempted to walk its circumference, would appear to be a creative, variable, and oft-erratic conglomerate of random deserts, lakes, rivers, oceans, mountains, and valleys, yet if that same person were suddenly swept into space to peer at earth from above, it would appear to be a tidy and symmetrical orb rotating at a perfectly predictable rate.

So, aim to arrange your own life similarly: Create calendars, systems, habits, rituals, routines, and organizations, but use these structures as the foundation for a life that is creative, flowing, and playful. Work hard *and* play hard. Research scientific papers, run on a treadmill, and speak systematically, *but also* read fiction, dance, and sing. Go out to the garage to do your end-of-the-day planned 30-minute bike ride, but simply smile, dismount, and don't let smoke come out your ears if your spouse pops their head out the garage door at the 26-minute mark to announce that dinner is ready.

And don't chew too much off at once. I recommend you begin with a Sunday. Take that single Sabbath day of the week and schedule (perhaps aside from visiting church at the proper time or setting a time to have a dinner party or something like that), *absolutely nothing*.

Try it. Just once. See how it feels. Personally, I'd categorize it as glorious.

Second, trust in God and turn your anxious thoughts over to Him. I talk plenty about trust in Chapter 4 of *Fit Soul*, but allow me to expound upon what I wrote there just a bit more.

Philippians 4:4-9 tells us to:

> "Rejoice in the Lord always: and again I say, Rejoice. Let your moderation be known unto all men. The Lord is at hand. Be careful for nothing; but in every thing by prayer and supplication with thanksgiving let your requests be made known unto God. And the peace of God, which passeth all understanding, shall keep your hearts and minds through Christ Jesus. Finally, brethren, whatsoever things are true, whatsoever things are honest, whatsoever things are just, whatsoever things are pure, whatsoever things are lovely, whatsoever things are of good report; if there be any virtue, and if there be any praise, think on these things. Those things, which ye have both learned, and received, and heard, and seen in me, do: and the God of peace shall be with you."

Verses 4 and 5 build upon what I noted earlier regarding a healthy mix of both joy and spontaneity along with control and order. Those verses tell us to rejoice in the Lord always, but also to let our "moderation" be known to all men because the Lord is at hand. If you have trusted in God and allowed His Holy Spirit to fill you with the peace that comes through salvation in Christ, you enable yourself to both live a life with self-control and playfully rejoice all the time.

In Verse 6, we are told to "be careful for nothing." This translates literally to "be anxious for nothing." We are then instructed to submit our requests to God with a grateful heart and then to allow God to guide our hearts and minds. Verse 7 tells us that the result of that gratefulness will be both peace and protection, which are, of course, the opposite of anxiety.

Verse 8 then tells us to dwell upon things that are true, honest, just, pure, lovely, and of good report. I can think of no better way to do this than to steep ourselves daily in the Bible—through hearing, reading, memorizing, singing, praying, and meditation (all of which I teach in great detail how to do in Chapter 11 of *Fit Soul*). As you crack open the Bible daily, you may also find the website that I'll link to on the resources page for this chapter, which includes specific Bible verses about anxiety and OCD quite encouraging and helpful. Finally, Verse 9 tells us that when we do all these things, God will give us (and here is that word once again) peace.

In summary, have self-control and engage in moderation, then rejoice in all things, be constantly grateful, pray to and trust God to give you wisdom and discernment over what is a useful habit and what is not, and read the Bible daily.

Finally, I read a fantastic book entitled *Brain Lock.* In it, Dr. Jeffrey Schwartz lays out four key and scientifically proven steps to manage OCD and OCD-like tendencies, showing before-and-after PET scans of actual changes in the hardwiring of controlling brains when these steps are taken:

- *First, you* **relabel**, which means you train yourself to identify what's real and what isn't and refuse to be misled by intrusive, destructive thoughts and urges. This includes full presence and awareness to be able to recognize when a habit, routine, or ritual has become selfish, harmful or distracting, then labeling it as an obsession and/or compulsion. One especially helpful component of relabeling includes bringing into play the "Impartial Spectator," a concept that Adam Smith used as the central feature of his book *The Theory of Moral Sentiments*. Smith defined the Impartial Spectator as the capacity to stand outside yourself and watch yourself in action, which is essentially the same mental action as the ancient Buddhist concept of mindful awareness or the modern psychological practice of trying to step outside yourself and view yourself as the leading character in a movie or book, then assessing how you would feel about that character if they were displaying the same harmful habits you are currently engaged in.

- *Second, you **reattribute***, meaning that you understand that those thoughts and urges are merely mental noise and false signals being sent from your brain—neurochemicals and neurotransmitters that may be biological blessings in some regards, but are ultimately holding you back from happiness. Obsessions and compulsions can simply be your brain doing "funny things," and you must simply recognize that.

- *Third, you **refocus*** by learning to respond to those false signals in a new and more constructive way, working around the false signals by refocusing your attention on more constructive behavior that can serve as a replacement or modification to your existing harmful habit, for example, by adapting a sixty-minute daily workout to instead be a thirty-minute workout, followed by thirty minutes of creative, free play with your children, reading fiction, or tinkering around on a piano. This step is where Dr. Schwartz has noted the most significant changes in brain chemistry to take place.

- *The final and fourth step is to **revalue***, or to place value on the positive change in habit or new replacement activity for that habit, value on the joy and freedom that pours into your life as a result of release of control, and recognition of the little or no value you actually found in the initial unwanted thought or urge. At this point, Dr. Schwartz describes that the automatic transmission in your brain officially begins to start working properly again.

Biblical counselors John and Janie Street, authors of *The Biblical Counseling Guide for Women*, have actually developed a Christian method based on Dr. Jeffrey Schwartz's four steps described above. Below are two of the foundational verses they utilize for the four steps they adapted from his book:

> *"Do not be conformed to the pattern of this world but be transformed by the renewal of your mind, that by testing you may discern what is the will of God, what is good and acceptable and perfect." (Romans 12:2)*

> *"...put off your old self, which belongs to your former manner of life*

and is corrupt through deceitful desires, and to be renewed in the spirit of your minds, and to put on the new self, created after the likeness of God in true righteousness and holiness." (Ephesians 4:22-24)

Based on these verses, the Streets adapted Schwartz's four steps to the following:

1. *Repent*: Identify and confess all obsessive thoughts that control you as sinful habits because they assume you are able to thrive and live by rigid rules of thoughts and behaviors, based on your own works, rather than by faith and trust in God.

2. *Relabel*: Similar to Schwartz's step, simply relabel the recurring thoughts and behaviors—even those you feel could be helpful but are ultimately manifested fruits of selfishness in your life—as anxious and fearful tendencies. Do not fear loss of control. Fear God only.

3. *Replace*: Substitute those anxious thoughts with trust in a good and loving God who loves and provides for you no matter whether you are perfect or fully in control—in any state of messiness and sinful tendencies. You don't control problems out of your life—only God does.

4. *Refocus*: Focus upon the two greatest commandments: loving God and loving others. Release self-focus and shift the focus instead to your Creator, to your friends, and to your family.

Both books cited above, *Brain Lock* and *The Biblical Counseling Guide for Women* (yes guys, you can read it, too) will be helpful for anyone who has control issues or OCD. Read them if you can for more detailed instructions and clarity related to the steps I've cited above.

SUMMARY

Paul says in Colossians 3:9–10, *"You have put off the old self with its practices and have put on the new self, which is being renewed in knowledge after the image of its creator."*

There is hope. Your old self can become a new self. You can release the shackles of control, fear, and shame and replace them with the flowing robes of faith, trust, peace, love, and joy. Science has even proven that the renewing of one's thoughts can create real, measurable, and observable changes in the brain, based on the same cellular mechanisms behind the biology of belief (read Bruce Lipton's *Biology of Belief* and Chapter 15 of *Fit Soul* for a more complete understanding of those mechanisms).

So, in summary:

1. Recognize and acknowledge that the Creator of this universe is a God of both order and spontaneity, and proceed to weave healthy doses of both order and spontaneity into your own life, especially if you're currently skewed towards the former.

2. Trust God, rejoice in all things, be constantly grateful, pray to and trust God to give you wisdom and discernment over what is a useful habit and what is not, and read the Bible daily.

3. Read *Brain Lock*, or at least follow the four steps from it that I have described above (relabel, refocus, reattribute, and revalue), or use the steps from *The Biblical Counseling Guide for Women* (repent, relabel, replace, and refocus).

I pray that the thoughts I have presented above will help many others with OCD, OCPD, or other control issues. Now, it's your turn. Have you struggled with these same issues? What elements in your own life do you think you try too hard to control? What have you found to be helpful or what do you plan to implement from this chapter to help you with those tendencies?

For resources, references, links and additional reading and listening material for this chapter, visit GetEndure.com/Chapter2.

CHAPTER III
SEX, PORN & POLYAMORY

Woo, boy. I guess it's time to open a can of worms.

I'm going to address a few somewhat controversial but absolutely temptation-related topics I've received quite a few questions about, and so I figured that in this somewhat hefty chapter, I'd "kill three birds with one stone" and tackle them all at once.

The topics at hand are, in no particular order of importance:

1. *Polyamory*
2. *Pornography*
3. *Sex*

Obviously, all three topics are rife with potential for opinionated discussions and often trigger intense responses based on one's sexual history and personal beliefs, so I fully understand that you may not necessarily agree with what I'm about to write. But this is important. After all, sexual health is just as important for your physical, mental, and spiritual fitness as lifting weights, meditating, or praying.

I'll begin by addressing polyamory, then move on to pornography and sex.

What's Polyamory?

Polyamory, the practice of engaging in multiple romantic (and typically sexual) relationships, with the consent of all the people involved, might very well be the biggest sexual revolution since the 1960s. Several of my notable friends in the authoring and health and fitness communities,

such as Chris Ryan, Neil Strauss, Aubrey Marcus, Kyle Kingsbury, and Paul Chek, are just a few influencers who I consider have taken what I consider to be a significant part in popularizing polyamory. Folks like this will often readily claim that polyamory is a path to integrating sexual freedom, honesty, and openness—while still retaining a semblance of commitment.

But others think polyamory, in addition to creating inevitable scenarios of jealousy and relationship angst, poses an existential threat to Western Civilization, societal stability, and family legacy, and I'd tend to agree.

It's important to raise this issue not only because an increasingly significant number of people seem to be pursuing polyamorous, open, or swinging relationships, but also because the nature of societal views on marriage can have long-lasting implications for children, communities, economies, civilizations, and future generations.

Sure, I fully realize that many would argue that sexual relationships are a matter of individual choice, nobody else's business, and *"what happens in my bedroom stays in my bedroom, bro."* But, I'll certainly make it a business of non-apologetically sticking my nose into other people's sex lives—or any other aspects of their lives, for that matter—if I feel that those sexual choices may significantly affect the world I live in and the world my children grow up in.

I also fully realize that I cannot, in a single chapter of a book, thoroughly address this topic. That would require a full book. And yes, yes, yes, I've read my friend Chris Ryan's book, *Sex At Dawn*, which is largely an argument against monogamy and for polyamory. I've also read the quite decent antithesis to Ryan's book, *Sex At Dusk*, by Lynn Saxon, a book that presents the polar opposite view. I've even quite recently read Doug Wilson's hilarious fiction book, *Ride, Sally, Ride*, which is a witty exposé of what can happen when we slide from the devaluation of marriage all the way down to sex dolls being recognized as "humans with rights." (At the time I'm writing this, that particular book is also being turned into what promises to be a very funny movie). You may want to consider reading all three books above to better form your own opinions around this topic.

But—despite not having the bandwidth to write a book on polyamory—I can at least, in this brief section, share with you my own thoughts and concerns regarding polyamory (before moving on to the equally inciting topics of porn and sex).

However, before filling you in on my personal thoughts regarding polyamory, I'll first define what polyamory is a bit more thoroughly than I did above. In a nutshell, polyamorous relationships, also known as "open" relationships, are based upon the concept of "consensual non-monogamy," which is the idea that relationships can theoretically be loving, committed, and serious, without necessarily being sexually exclusive.

Many proponents of polyamory would say it's a bit of a libertarian approach to sex and marriage, meaning that if you can choose to have more than one child, more than one friend, and more than one work colleague, you should also be free, should you so desire, to choose more than one sexual partner. Among married couples, you may also be familiar with a flavor of polyamory called "swinging," or, essentially, sexual partner-swapping. There's also polygamy, which is a bit similar to polyamory, but occurs within the context of a marriage, and is simply the practice or custom of having more than one wife or husband at the same time.

Openness to a so-called "poly" lifestyle appears to be surprisingly common. For example:

- *4 percent* to *5 percent* of all adults are in open or polyamorous relationships;
- *20 percent* have at least tried some kind of open or polyamorous relationship at some point;
- *17 percent* of adults aged 18-44 have had sex with someone else with the consent of their partner (and 9 percent among adults aged 45-54);
- *28 percent* of adults say it is not natural for humans to be in a monogamous relationship
- *29 percent* of adults under 30 consider polyamory to be morally acceptable (compared to 6 percent of adults over 65).

So that's what polyamory is, and that's how surprisingly common it is.

The Problem With Poly

Now...why do I, and others, consider polyamory to be problematic?

First, polyamorous relationships tend to be rife with jealousy, particularly sexual jealousy. This makes sense. From an ancestral standpoint, we humans have deep-rooted desires for relationship features such as paternity certainty (e.g. who's your real daddy?), protecting pair bonds, and reducing sexual disease transmission. This jealousy, as I've witnessed in many of my polyamorous friends, can be stressful, difficult to manage, and can often create intense emotional turmoil in a relationship. Of course, jealousy—along with broken agreements and dishonesty—can also be a feature of monogamous relationships. But, the fact is that if you're in a polyamorous relationship, you know your partner is sleeping around and also often know with whom they are sleeping around, the *potential* for jealousy, stress, and emotional turmoil threatens to be much higher; and this is exactly what I have witnessed in my polyamorous friends. Their relationships with both their spouse and their "open others" seem to be a constantly stressful drama, chock full of emotional meltdowns and bitter arguments *(e.g. "You did what with who, and you've never done that with me?")*.

Furthermore, polyamory seems to require a significant amount of trade-offs in terms of time, energy, money, and mating efforts to juggle multiple partners—partners who are simultaneously also trying to do the same with their multiple partners. Where does Dad sleep when Mom's boyfriend comes over for the night? Where does little Johnny go during this time? If the polyamorous relationship occurs in a scenario in which multiple partners are living within the same household, who decides which bed the man or woman shares for that night, and who watches the kiddos when Mom or Dad are out on date-night with their extra partner? There's even a term, "poly-drama," used as a moniker for these types of sticky, often unforeseen problems that sometimes aren't considered, since they are often overshadowed by the prospect of sexual freedom and getting to enjoy multiple partners.

Speaking of kids, who exactly does a child who lives in a polyamorous house appropriately and accurately call father? Who do they call mother? When it comes to paternity certainty—a man's confidence that his kids are really his—is there a mental shift in the way a man cares for a child not his own vs. a child who he is confident is his direct blood relative? If a man is indeed concerned about this, or a woman wants to guarantee she has a child by one specific man in the relationship, does this increase the expenses of paternity testing, or on a more serious note, the likelihood of a desire for abortion? As you can imagine, when it comes to the children, polyamory can introduce a host of additional confusions that go beyond the stress of juggling multiple partners.

SEX, PORN & POLYAMORY

Disease risk may also be amplified in the case of polyamory. Monogamy reduces the spread of sexually transmitted infections (STIs), and although STIs have become far less common over the last several centuries, any time there are more sexual partners in any scenario, the likelihood of STIs—even in an era of vaccines, medications, PReP, condoms, and "safe sex"—could potentially be higher in a polyamorous relationship (though I'll admit that's not proven), or at least the threat thereof could require far more time, energy, and even more mental stress based around contraceptive practices and disease risk. Heck, I know if I knew my wife's genitals were being rubbed against a few different gentlemen each month or year, I'd certainly have a gnawing worry at the back of my mind about what exactly could have been on one of those dicks that was now on my own.

Next, folks like Jordan Peterson have astutely noted the potential sexual-egalitarian and violence-reduction benefits of monogamy. This may be in part because monogamy decreases the ability of males to monopolize women, while simultaneously helping to equalize mating opportunities and decrease violent competition among males. Peterson puts it this way:

> *"Men get frustrated when they are not competitive in the sexual marketplace (note: the fact that they DO get frustrated does not mean that they SHOULD get frustrated. Pointing out the existence of something is not the same as justifying its existence). Frustrated men tend to become dangerous, particularly if they are young. The dangerousness of frustrated young men (even if that frustration stems from their own incompetence) has to be regulated socially. The manifold social conventions tilting most societies toward monogamy constitute such regulation...socially-enforced monogamous conventions decrease male violence. In addition (and not trivially), they also help provide mothers with comparatively reliable male partners, and increase the probability that stable, father-intact homes will exist for children."*

I mostly agree with Jordan on this point (just read Chapter 7 of *Fit Soul* to read my detailed opinions on father-intact homes), although I believe that social or governmental enforcement of monogamy should not exist. Instead, I think children should be taught about the values of marriage and the stability that monogamy affords, then be free to make their own choice. As a self-professed libertarian, I don't really want the government "ordering" me to be a one-woman man any more than I want them ordering me to be a two or three or four-woman man. But at the same time, I should also be free to express my own opinions on the matter, and teach my children what I consider to be valuable, ethical, and (more on this briefly) Biblical views on marriage.

The societal stability afforded by monogamous societies is also a hefty consideration here. From everything I've researched, the only societies that have ever succeeded in becoming large-scale technological civilizations are societies that have adopted monogamous marriage as the gold standard for long-term pair bonds and family formation. As the paper, *The Puzzle of Monogamous Marriage* succinctly notes:

> *"...it is worth speculating that the spread of normative monogamy, which represents a form of egalitarianism, may have helped create the conditions for the emergence of democracy and political equality at all levels of government. Within the anthropological record, there is a statistical linkage between democratic institutions and normative monogamy. Pushing this point, these authors argue that dissipating the pool of unmarried males weakens despots, as it reduces their ability to find soldiers or henchmen. Reduced crime would also weaken despots' claims to be all that stands between ordinary citizens and chaos. Historically, we know that universal monogamous marriage preceded the emergence of democratic institutions in Europe, and the rise of notions of equality between the sexes. In Ancient Greece, we do not know which came first but we do know that Athens, for example, had both elements of monogamous marriage and of democracy. In the modern world, analyses of cross-national data reveal positive statistical relationships between the strength of normative monogamy with both democratic rights and civil liberties. In this sense, the peculiar institutions of monogamous marriage may help explain why democratic ideals and notions of equality and human rights first emerged in the West."*

In other words, monogamy has historically been central to the emergence of complex societies, and while a small indigenous hunter-gatherer village may be able to survive for long periods of time in a scenario of wife and husband swapping, you'd be hard-pressed to name a single great country that has emerged built upon a foundation of polyamorous or polygamous vs. monogamous relationships. I suspect that an additional reason this may be so is that, from a legacy and legal standpoint, married couples can far more easily do things such as prepare a living trust as an estate planning tool to more quickly transfer assets upon death, keep family matters private, minimize taxes, and develop a scenario in which a stable and long-lasting legacy is built for generations to come.

One reader on my website made an astute comment regarding this idea of monogamy and cultural stability:

> *"We have to trust that God has set up boundaries for morality in our lives because He as our creator knows what is best for us. In his great book, Civilizing Sex, Patrick Riley analyzes every ancient culture and what led to their destruction and he boils the key to civilization down to one word – monogamy. Have you ever thought about why you don't know any Babylonians or Assyrians but you do know at least one Jewish family? There is one simple reason Jewish culture has survived for 3500 years – monogamy. No society has ever survived the breakdown of the family and we would be fools to think ours will."*

Of course, considering I believe the Bible to be the absolute truth and the firmest foundation that exists upon which to build a society—I'd be remiss not to also share with you what the Bible says about marriage and sexual partnerships.

What The Bible Says About Marriage

So...is there any evidence of a Biblically-based, stable marriage that includes multiple partners?

After all, many of the great men of the Bible—such as Abraham, Jacob, David, Solomon, along with a number of Old Testament patriarchs and kings (as was typical of many ancient Middle-eastern chieftains)—all had multiple wives. But while the Bible describes the practice of polygamy and polyamory, it never actually *condones* this practice, and, as a matter of fact, I can't find a single passage in Scripture where such a relationship is ever portrayed in a positive light or results in a happy, satisfied, and stable marriage scenario. Additionally, in every such case, the practice of keeping multiple wives results in pretty big problems, including Solomon's many wives leading him into idolatry and destroying his faith in God;

extreme bitterness between Abraham's wife Sarah and her maid Hagar with whom Abraham was sleeping; Rachel's sinful jealousy of Jacob's wife Leah, which led to Joseph being betrayed and sold by his half-brothers; and the rape of one of King David's daughters (Tamar) by one of his sons (Tamar's half-brother Amnon) and Amnon's subsequent murder by Tamar's brother Absalom.

Sheesh. What a poly-drama mess.

Polygamy had mostly disappeared in Israel by the time of Jesus Christ, and in the New Testament, Paul's instructions in Titus 1 and 1 Timothy 3 clearly specified that deacons and elders must be *"the husband of one wife."* He goes on to say in 1 Corinthians 7 that a man is to have his own wife and a woman is to have her own husband. Jesus also explicitly states in Matthew 19:3-9 that a man should have only one wife: *"Have ye not read, that he which made them at the beginning made them male and female, And said, 'For this cause shall a man leave father and mother, and shall cleave to his wife: and they twain shall be one flesh?'"*

God intended that marriage should work this way from the very beginning. The Bible clearly says in Genesis 2:22-24: *"Then the rib which the Lord God had taken from man He made into a woman, and He brought her to the man. And Adam said, 'This is now bone of my bones and flesh of my flesh; she shall be called Woman, because she was taken out of Man.' Therefore a man shall leave his father and mother and be joined to his wife, and they shall become one flesh."*

Like many orders, rules, and laws in the Bible, I'm certain that God had a reason for inspiring Jesus to speak of and the Biblical apostles to write of the values of a "one-woman man" and a "one-man woman." Our Creator is certainly aware of many of the practical, legal, logistical, and societal downfalls of polyamory and polygamy, and aware of our human tendencies to engage in bitter and stressful bouts of jealousy and arguments in a multi-partner scenario. Furthermore, many Biblical writers refer to the exclusivity and sacredness of sexual love as being a symbol for the exclusivity and sacredness of our relationship with God. In other words, we should worship one God, and we should marry one spouse. We shouldn't worship a variety of idols, nor marry or sleep with a variety of sexual partners. Adopting this monogamous practice of sexual commitment, loyalty, and honesty can create order, stability, honesty, patience, kindness, love, and a host of other societal and spiritual fruits that simply seem far more difficult to attain in a polyamorous or polygamous society or relationship.

Based on this, I believe that monogamy was inherent to God's plan for humanity from the very beginning of Creation. I'm well aware that there are a host of arguments otherwise, but—and I realize this is fully anecdotal—in my experience and interactions with swingers, open relationship advocates, and polyamorous or polygamous friends, I can't personally name any single polyamorous or polygamous couple I know who has not been what I can best describe as either A) frequently miserable, depressed, or worried; B) constantly complaining of relationship stress and jealousy; and/or C) possessed of relatively confused children—all as a result of juggling multiple sexual partners.

Summary

Of course, rampant and unfettered access to multiple digital sexual partners (i.e. porn) along with many people's complete lack of knowledge or experience with true, sacred, spiritual sexual intercourse is no doubt contributing to poly-popularity—and may even make the prospect of multiple sexual partners be all-the-more natural and appealing. So, in the next sections of this chapter, stay tuned as I tackle two other important considerations for sexual health: porn and sex.

In the meantime, allow me to share with you one of my favorite songs that I often sing to my best friend, lover, and wife of 18 years: Jessica Dawn Greenfield...

...the name of the song is "Forever & Ever, Amen" by Randy Travis. You can watch it or listen to it on YouTube. As you listen or watch, pay close attention to the lyrics, also written below:

> *"You may think that I'm talking foolish*
> *You've heard that I'm wild and I'm free*
> *You may wonder how I can promise you now*
> *This love that I feel for you always will be*
> *But you're not just time that I'm killin'*
> *I'm no longer one of those guys*
> *As sure as I live, this love that I give*
> *Is gonna be yours until the day that I die*
> *Oh, baby, I'm gonna love you forever*
> *Forever and ever, amen*

As long as old men sit and talk about the weather
As long as old women sit and talk about old men
If you wonder how long I'll be faithful
I'll be happy to tell you again
I'm gonna love you forever and ever
Forever and ever, amen
They say time take its toll on a body
Makes a young girl's brown hair turn gray
Well, honey, I don't care, I ain't in love with your hair
And if it all fell out, well, I'd love you anyway
They say time can play tricks on a mem'ry
Make people forget things they knew
Well, it's easy to see it's happenin' to me
I've already forgotten every woman but you
Oh, darlin', I'm gonna love you forever
Forever and ever, amen
As long as old men sit and talk about the weather
As long as old women sit and talk about old men
If you wonder how long I'll be faithful
Well, just listen to this song
I'm gonna love you forever and ever
Forever and ever, amen
I'm gonna love you forever and ever
Forever and ever, forever and ever
Forever and ever, amen."

Trust me: I've been a guy who's "wild and free" and I've been a guy who's given love that's gonna be hers (and *only* hers) until the day that we die, and I can tell you the latter is far, far better, happier, more satisfying, more fulfilling and—though saying it may put me at the risk of coming across as too aesthetic and irrational—feels so, so right.

Finally, to wrap up this section of the chapter, I'll recommend to you several excellent additional reading resources on this matter, including:

- On sperm competition and the biological origins of hypergamy: *Promiscuity: An Evolutionary History of Sperm Competition by Tim Birkhead*

- On jealousy, and how it differs from envy: *The Dangerous Passion by David*

M. Buss

- *On male violence and the competition for sex and status:* Why We Fight *by Mike Martin*

- *On the intersection of religion and competition for sex, as well as the abuses of church institutions:* Alpha God *by Hector Garcia*

- *On intersexual dynamics, including the dangers of polyamory:* The Rational Male *by Rollo Tomassi*

- *On how the Protestant church systematically undermined kinship ties, enforced monogamous expectations, and built the cultural foundation of the Industrial Revolution:* The Weirdest People In The World *by Joseph Henrich*

How about you? What are your thoughts on polyamory? Are you a one-woman man or a one-man woman? Why is (or, perhaps, isn't yet) that important to you?

_____
_____
_____
_____
_____
_____
_____
_____
_____
_____
_____
_____
_____
_____
_____
_____
_____
_____
_____
_____
_____

Porn

So, here we are—part two of a matter that I think cannot be ignored if we are to explore all avenues of sexual health...

...*namely, porn.*

But before I delve in, allow me to be brutally honest with you about my own experience with porn. When I was 12, while employed as a janitor, I discovered "dirty" magazines and posters hidden away in the broom closet of my father's jet-boat production facility in Lewiston, Idaho. The pornographic materials were essentially "just" pin-up girls posing in bikinis or "tastefully" nude, but I found it all intriguing nonetheless and tucked a few posters and magazines away to bring home to my bedroom. They weren't my father's, and instead belonged to a few choice male employees of the company, but it was somewhat ironic that at that same time, my father was famous in the local newspaper—the Lewiston Morning Tribune—for his local anti-porn campaign, detailed in a 1990 article by Mohsin Askari entitled "Porn Fighter Goes Back on the Warpath." Askari's article includes the following quip:

> "Within a month, Greenfield said, he hopes to have another boycott campaign underway and he has targeted 18 businesses at Lewiston-Clarkston which operate about 25 stores. He intends to extend the boycott to other towns in the region also. 'We hope that a boycott will be sufficient, but I wouldn't rule out picketing,' he said... Greenfield, who last year set up affiliation with the American Family Association as its Lewiston-Clarkston chapter, said his organization will provide 'concerned citizens' with a list of stores and a boycotting strategy... 'Those magazines, they promote statutory rape. They promote incest. They have encouraged that sex at any age is healthy. They have sought to tear down every traditional Christian value that promotes the typical family,' Greenfield said. 'That kind of philosophy contributed to teenage pregnancy and sexual disease, like AIDS.' He does not want his money to support businesses which sell magazines that support such philosophies."

I vaguely recall this time of my father's life, particularly when he came home one day after work and described how he purchased every last porn mag at the local 7-11 for the purposes of throwing them in the dumpster outside the gas station.

Other articles featuring my father's local anti-porn, pro-family efforts included "How To Fight Lewiston-Clarkston's Town Bully" (*subtitle: "Gary Greenfield of Lewiston has decided which magazines you shouldn't read and which movies you shouldn't see, but he's not going to let you make the final judgment about them. He's not even going to let you see them."*) and "If Porn Boycott Is Out, What About Others" (including the anecdote *"Greenfield was identified as the "town bully" because he is willing to organize a boycott of those establishments which promote the degradation of women."*) I'll link to the full articles on the resources webpage for this chapter should you care to read them in their somewhat ancient entirety.

Anyways, despite my father's valiant efforts to put a stop to such degradation of women, I personally—as many young red-blooded American males did and of course, still do—continued to find porn absolutely intriguing. Being raised in a very strict household in which open talk of sex, porn, and other similar matters was frowned upon, I soon found myself, throughout high school, using the internet (which was painfully slow in those days, but still a readily available source of porn), magazines, and any other materials I could get my hands on to get aroused and to learn about sex. At the time, I was ashamed of and very secretive about my use of porn, but by the time I got to college, porn was widely accepted among myself and most of my male friends as a totally normal and expected component of our sexual existence. I'd grown jaded. Even after getting married, I continued to turn to porn as a frequent source of sexual pleasure and entertainment—particularly when my wife wasn't around, if I was just bored at night without much else to do, or occasionally, and quite sadly, even as something I'd look at before sex with my wife so I could get more turned on. As is quite common (and for reasons you'll discover later in this chapter), over years of porn use, I gradually couldn't even get aroused by photos of scantily clad or nude women, and instead needed high-res videos, hardcore action, threesomes, and beyond to experience any type of meaningful sexual pleasure.

It wasn't until after my twin boys were of toddler age that I really stepped back and analyzed whether I wanted my sons to be raised by a father who was incapable of finding deep, meaningful sexual satisfaction with his wife, let alone being unable to even become sexually aroused without incorporating some kind of fringe pornographic media. I found myself, while surfing the internet for photos and videos of women, unable to think about how I'd really feel if that woman being objectified and paid to pose were my own daughter, or wife, or sister, or mother and whether I really wanted my boys to grow up with the same sexual addiction or harsh objectification of women. It was also during that time that I discovered websites such as Fight the New Drug (FightTheNewDrug.org) or Your Brain on Porn (YourBrainOnPorn.com), which helped me become painfully aware of many of the deleterious brain and neurotransmitter issues associated with porn. This almost instantly placed porn for me into the same mental department into which I'd place addiction issues such as alcohol or drug abuse. Finally, as I grew in deep love for my wife and began to cherish all the benefits and blessings of a committed, monogamous relationship, I simply couldn't look at porn without feeling as though I was betraying her.

Now here's where I "got lucky." I'm one of those guys who—by the grace of God—has always been able to start or quit just about any activity cold turkey. Call it willpower, stubbornness, an all-or-nothing approach, or whatever you'd like, but that's just the way I've always been able to operate. As author and Navy SEAL Jocko Willink dictates in his book Extreme Ownership, *sometimes changing a habit doesn't come down to psychological tricks, talk therapy, or mental magic to make that change—instead, sometimes you simply buckle down, discipline yourself, and just do it.*

So one day, when I was about 30 years old, I simply *stopped* looking at porn. Of course, leading up to that moment, I'd come to a growing realization and conviction that the cons of porn far outweighed the pros of the instant sexual arousal and pleasure, that I was digging myself into a deeper and deeper hole of seeing women as mere sexual objects, and that if I was truly going to be a father, leader, and king for my family, I couldn't waste a single, additional precious minute of my life burning my eyeballs out staring at a pixelated screen of skin or scrolling through photo after photo of hedonistic indulgence. That's not how everybody quits porn, but that's how I did it. No special website filtering and blocking software, no men's accountability groups (although now I use a very good one called "Canopy" for my sons), and no pastoral therapy sessions. I simply told myself, *"No more,"* and then I walked away from porn for good.

And thus now we come full circle, with me, just like a chop off the ol' block, getting on my own porn soapbox to hopefully help a few boys or men (or women) who struggle with the time-wasting, brain-numbing, human-objectifying nature of this all-too-readily accessible bastardization of the sacred sexual experience to swear it off altogether. In the next several pages, I'll share with you what I think the root problem with porn is, how porn problematically affects our brains and our neurotransmitters, the pain porn can cause in our relationships,

and the nature of "just looking" vs. full-blown adultery in general.

Your Brain On Porn

Most of us know what porn is. As United States Supreme Court Justice Potter Stewart famously stated in a 1964 court case on pornography and obscenity: "I know it when I see it."

But, so that we are all entirely clear as to what I'm talking about when I say "porn," let's just go with the Merriam-Webster definition, which I think is appropriate enough:

1: the depiction of erotic behavior (as in pictures or writing) intended to cause sexual excitement

2: material (such as books or a photograph) that depicts erotic behavior and is intended to cause sexual excitement

3: the depiction of acts in a sensational manner so as to arouse a quick intense emotional reaction

So that's what porn is. But I think too few of us, especially us men, know what porn does.

Let's begin with what a brain on porn looks like, which I briefly mentioned in my introduction to this chapter section when I alluded to two very helpful websites (FightTheNewDrug.org and YourBrainOnPorn.com) that feature in-depth articles, videos, audios, and research to help educate you; a child being taught about porn; or a loved one trying to help a spouse, friend, or family member navigate through porn issues to better understand the impact of porn on the central nervous system and neurotransmitters.

Basically, the moment you look at or scroll through a series of erotic photos or videos, the reward system in your brain switches on. This reward system includes the ventral striatum and orbitofrontal cortex areas of your brain—both of which help elicit the good feelings you get when you do something good or experience something pleasurable, whether that be a dark chocolate bar, an orgasm, or a favorite song. As these areas of your brain become repetitively hyper-activated in response to viewing porn, your brain creates deeper and more networked reward circuits in response to porn as it learns, especially over repetitive exposure, that porn is a reliable way to experience the dopamine response associated with intense pleasure.

For example, a 2016 functional magnetic resonance imaging (fMRI) in the journal *NeuroImage* showed elevated activity in the ventral striatum when males viewed something arousing, showing that the brain's reward system was churning out extra dopamine. An analysis of each participant's self-reported porn consumption habits showed that many of the subjects reported symptoms of porn addiction. When comparing the fMRI data and survey results, the researchers noted that the degree of ventral striatum activation significantly correlated with the degree of porn addiction each participant reported. People who reported signs of porn addiction experienced greater degrees of ventral striatum activity when they looked at porn, which means their brains were better equipped to experience a pleasurable response to porn.

The amygdala, a part of the brain involved in stress, emotional behavior, and motivation, is also activated when viewing porn. For example, research on people with compulsive sexual behavior or sexual addictions to experiences such as porn suggests that altered connectivity and increased activity in the amygdala are linked to heightened reward-seeking behavior. Most notably, these studies show a change in a person's "appetitive conditioning," which means their biological activation of reward pathways is greater in response to sexual stimuli. This research also shows that porn is a habit that trains the brain to seek rewards and a feel-good response through porn. This is concerning because these are the same reward pathways that can become gradually desensitized through repeated exposure, meaning that more and more porn or greater variations of porn are necessary to be able to continue to experience arousal in response to viewing porn. This can easily create a slippery slope from being satisfied and aroused with "innocent" bikini websites to needing to view relatively disturbing foursomes, child abuse, bestiality, and beyond in order to become sexually aroused, not to mention that "plain-jane" sex with a single committed partner sparks less and less formation of pleasurable neurotransmitters in the central nervous system. Perhaps this is why many men who use porn frequently experience porn-induced erectile dysfunction.

Besides these addiction and pleasure desensitization responses to porn, there are two other concerning effects of frequent porn use. First, a 2017 study found that many porn users are compulsive, distressed, or both; and a host of additional research shows that frequency of porn consumption correlates with depression, anxiety, stress, and social problems. Second, a 2014 study, and also additional research since, showed that the volume of gray matter in a porn user's forebrain was negatively correlated with the volume of porn they viewed, meaning that porn may produce structural brain differences and a shrinking of gray matter quite similar to what one would experience with, say, excessive marijuana use. By the way, I'll link to all these studies on the resources webpage of the chapter should you want to read more.

Now don't get me wrong, I enjoy a good romp in the bedroom with my wife and the occasional bout of weed-smoking, but there's a big difference between the effects those activities have on the brain compared to a nightly visit to PornHub and a marijuana addiction. I don't know about you, but my brain is pretty important to me, as are the biological responses I receive to any pleasurable element of life that produces dopamine. The fact that porn use may shrink my brain or numb my pleasure responses certainly makes me think twice about porn being a part of my life.

How Porn Changes Our Relationships

But it gets worse. Porn can also significantly change the way you view and treat members of the opposite sex, especially and most concerningly your spouse or significant other.

The best way I can describe this is that porn use can create a very similar relationship scenario to what you'd experience if you were actually cheating on your partner with a real person. It can also, even if you're not in a committed relationship, set you up to be more likely to cheat, be unfaithful, or be less committed to a future relationship.

Sure, I realize that many will say...

> ..."I'm just looking! That's not cheating! It's not as if I actually stuck my dick in her!"...

or...

> ..."This sex doll, vaginal stimulating toy, ball of kleenex with lube, strap-on (insert-erotic-toy-or-image-of-choice-here) isn't actually a real human, so how could it be wrong?"

or...

> "I'm not touching, feeling, or engaged in any kind of spiritual or psychological commitment to this pixelated image on my screen, so it's nothing like cheating!"

But, as I'm prone to do when researching for articles, podcasts and books, and for all my important decisions in life in general, I look at this through the lens of my go-to handbook on morality: the Bible.

Matthew 5:27 and Matthew 5:28 are key verses related to this topic, and part of Jesus's famous Sermon on the Mount. They address one of the ten commandments, namely *"You shall not commit adultery."* In this case, adultery is widely defined as sexual relations between a man and a married or betrothed woman who was not his wife.

In the World English Bible translation, the text from the Sermon on the Mount reads:

> *"You have heard that it was said,*
> *'You shall not commit adultery;'*
> *but I tell you that everyone who gazes at a*
> *woman to lust after her has committed*
> *adultery with her already in his heart."*

In other words, Jesus equates sexual lust or sexual coveting as adultery. Put more succinctly: *"If you're lookin', you're cheatin'."* And just so you know, the word translated as woman here is gyne, which can mean either woman or wife, so the sin lies not in simply lusting after the woman some other guy is married to, but a woman in general.

In this case, "lookin'" is not simply noticing or appreciating the beauty of, say, a pretty woman walking down the street or waltzing across the screen on your computer or the pages of a magazine. That's completely natural. There's absolutely no need to feel guilty about that type of natural sexual desire or appreciation of human beauty. Instead, this type of lust or coveting that Jesus is referring to would instead involve not just noticing and appreciating that woman, but instead scanning her up-to-down, head-to-toe, boobs-to-ass-to-heels intensively; "eye-f*^ckin" her; taking some mental snapshots of her for your spank bank later that night; swiveling your head to get a better look at the short skirt or tight jeans as she passes by; or, in the case of porn, whipping your member out and pleasuring yourself right there on the spot.

So, why would Jesus warn about that type of activity being the equivalent of adultery?

Put simply, in the same way that unforgiveness, bitterness, hate, and anger can destroy the sanctity of relationships and create a slippery slope into actual murder (a concept Jesus also visits in his Sermon On The Mount)*, unfettered sexual lust can create a slippery slope into actual, real, physical cheating.*

Here's the way I think about this "slippery slope" that can be created by "just looking"...

...First, you view an erotic image, porn, or an attractive woman in a lustful manner...

...Next, you begin to think about her, often with increasing frequency, and often while sexually aroused and/or masturbating...

...That image or those images continue to saturate your mind, sometimes serving as a self-pleasuring substitute for actual, real sex with your partner, and sometimes—even more problematically—popping into your head *while* you're having sex with your partner, thus serving to smash apart the spiritual intertwining and sacredness of sex that I'll visit in more detail later in this chapter. (After all, how deep and connected do you feel to your partner and how honestly and lovingly can you gaze into his or her eyes during lovemaking while you're simultaneously imagining the erotic images you were obsessed with the night before, that attractive human you saw walking down the street earlier that afternoon, or some kind of porn that involves multiple partners, animals, children, or minors?)...

...Worse yet, if we're not talking about lusting after porn, but instead after a real, physical human being (let's say, in this case, your tantalizing next-door neighbor), you continue to think about that person sexually (even if subconsciously), especially while you're near him or her, with him or her, or talking to him or her, and even when you're having sex with your partner. Perhaps one day, when your guard is down or your partner is out of town, you find yourself dropping by to help that neighbor move her couch or fix a faucet; and before you know it, you're making out with them on the living room floor. Or maybe that hottie who you've been chatting with via e-mail or you're in some kind of online group (and who you just happen to have been mentally making love to for months) happens to show up as an attendee at an out-of-town conference you're attending, and their hotel room is on the same block as yours. After a few-too-many glasses of wine at the conference dinner, you run into them on the elevator and five minutes later your tongue is in their mouth and you're fumbling in your back pocket for your hotel room keycard.

Folks, I'm not making this stuff up. This is how this sh*t goes down. This is how the "innocent" act of "just looking" gradually, and often quickly, degrades into not only sexual dissatisfaction, dopamine desensitization, and erectile dysfunction, but also sexual activities that go far beyond looking. This is how marriages get torn apart, families become separated, and entire generational legacies that took years to create become destroyed in a single one-night stand.

As a man thinketh, right?

See, Jesus was *smart*. He didn't just say this kind of stuff to keep us from having fun, to make Christianity a continual rite of self-denial, or to make life feel like a real drag. He knew exactly what makes life better, what makes relationships more meaningful, what brings order to society (just read the part on polyamory for more on that), and perhaps most importantly, what kind of attitudes and practices equip us to live out the Golden Rule of loving our neighbor (which includes our partner) in as full and glorious a way as possible. Heck, when you actually incorporate the kind of love that Jesus preached into your life, and you practice and dwell upon that love on a daily basis, your *desire* to lust, covet, cheat, and engage in any other acts of sexual immorality considerably *wanes* because you've grown to love God, love your partner, and love your family so much that the last thing you'd ever want to do is throw a giant, ugly wrench into that entire sublime scenario.

Ultimately, I hope what I'm saying here makes sense: If you commit adultery with your eyes and in your heart, you'll quickly find yourself readily capable of committing real adultery that tears your life apart. What begins in the brain will soon manifest materially. What you dwell upon mentally—whether consciously or subconsciously—weaves its way into your life in surprisingly real and tangible ways (you can read more details about that in Chapter 15 of my book Fit Soul) can be a good thing or (in the case of porn) a very, very bad thing.

How A Brain On Porn Makes Men & Women Weak

Finally—and this first part is for you fellas who desire to be better fathers, leaders, and kings for your household—you should know that porn makes you a weakling, particularly hardcore porn in which you're watching other men get it on with a woman or women.

How so? Recently, pastor, author, and my multi-time podcast guest Doug Wilson wrote an article on his website entitled "Pornography for Cuckolds," in which he thoroughly explains how males who get aroused and sexually satisfied watching other males having sex with females become programmed to be more likely to want to "share" their women with other men and to shirk their role as a protector, provider, and procreator—since those *other* males appear to be doing a fine and dandy job with those tasks.

Here's how Doug explains it:

> "In older forms of soft 'porn' (think pin-up girls), there was a straight-forward problem for Christian men. There was a picture of a beautiful woman, and that woman was not your wife. 'You should not desire her, or covet her, or lust after her.' Thus far the plain Scriptures. And it seems incredible to us today that a Christian man back in the day could have been stumbled by that picture painted on the front of his grandfather's B-17 in World War II, but there you go.
>
> But fast forward. We refer today to 'hard core' pornography, by which means video of people having sex, live action of couples copulating. And because we are approaching this thoughtlessly, we think that it is the same thing as the B-17 problem, only way more of it. We think that risque on the left and hard core on the right are the settings on the same dimmer switch. But no. The nature of the problem has been completely changed, and the magnitude of the change has almost entirely escaped our notice...
>
> ...we are accustomed to refer to alpha males and beta males. I would submit that our current forms of pornography are creating a limp new category, the gamma male. This is the poor enervated sap who is shaped and molded and catechized by watching this stuff. How so?

When a lion is having his dinner on the wildebeest he just took down, and there is a circle of hyenas about twenty yards out, what does that tell you? It tells you that the hyenas want what the lion has, and that they are in no position to challenge him in order to get some. They are what we might call gamma hyenas.

And when a man finds a particular woman beautiful and attractive, and then he satisfies himself by watching as another man takes her, he is deadening all the remaining vestiges of masculinity within him. It is not a hyper-masculine impulse to watch other people get it on. It is the opposite. It is one of the hyenas strutting in front of the other hyenas, doing his best leonine imitation. It is not a cosmopolitan decadence. It is not worldly wise. It is not the experience of a man of the world. It is getting your jollies through losing, which is, as sexual perversions go, down near the bottom...

...civilizations are built by men who have families to feed. Cultures are built by men who can say a phrase like "my wife" without embarrassment. Men who have been trained in real masculinity are jealous and protective of their wives. So a man who is not jealous of his wife is not a real man. And pornography, especially of the sort we are talking about here, cauterizes all those basic God-given masculine impulses.

A man who is devoted to one woman will be jealous. He will be unwilling to share her, and for his part, he will be devoted to her alone. As I said, this kind of man with this kind of sexual focus is the kind of man who builds civilizations. A man who is willing to share sexually is a man who has nothing but contempt for the women he is sharing with another man, or with other men. This is the logic of the man who resorts to prostitutes. And as Scripture tells us, he wastes his substance. He doesn't build cultures; he creates economic craters.

So a man in bondage to such pornography is almost certainly lying to himself. Yes, he says, he has a problem. He is highly-sexed. He has more desires than other men. The testosterone is just sloshing around inside him. He is ahead of all those other men, and there are always unique problems that such manly men have.

In reality, he is just a mangy hyena, with a hidden stash of wildebeests getting eaten by lions on his computer."

So how about you?

Are you a man who is designed to be an alpha male lion but who is instead watching a bunch of fake actor gamma male hyenas do what you're supposed to be out doing in the real world with an actual, physical, real partner—preferably a partner you love, care for, provide for, and to whom you are deeply committed? If so, you may want to think twice about the manner in which you are virtually castrating yourself. If you're a woman who knows such a man, you may also want to share this book with him.

Next, I would encourage you, especially if you are a woman, to listen to or read a sermon by pastor John Piper entitled "The Tragic Cost Of Her Cavernous Thirst" (I'll link to it on the resources webpage for this chapter). In the sermon, Piper describes the story of the "woman at the well," as told in the Bible like this:

> *"But He needed to go through Samaria.*
>
> *So He came to a city of Samaria which is called Sychar, near the plot of ground that Jacob gave to his son Joseph. Now Jacob's well was there. Jesus therefore, being wearied from His journey, sat thus by the well. It was about the sixth hour.*
>
> *A woman of Samaria came to draw water. Jesus said to her, 'Give Me a drink.' For His disciples had gone away into the city to buy food.*
>
> *Then the woman of Samaria said to Him, 'How is it that You, being a Jew, ask a drink from me, a Samaritan woman?' For Jews have no dealings with Samaritans.*
>
> *Jesus answered and said to her, 'If you knew the gift of God, and who it is who says to you, 'Give Me a drink,' you would have asked Him, and He would have given you living water.'*
>
> *The woman said to Him, 'Sir, You have nothing to draw with, and the well is deep. Where then do You get that living water? Are You greater than our father Jacob, who gave us the well, and drank from it himself, as well as his sons and his livestock?'*

Jesus answered and said to her, 'Whoever drinks of this water will thirst again, but whoever drinks of the water that I shall give him will never thirst. But the water that I shall give him will become in him a fountain of water springing up into everlasting life.'

The woman said to Him, 'Sir, give me this water, that I may not thirst, nor come here to draw.'

Jesus said to her, 'Go, call your husband, and come here.'

The woman answered and said, 'I have no husband.'

Jesus said to her, 'You have well said, 'I have no husband,' for you have had five husbands, and the one whom you now have is not your husband; in that you spoke truly.'"

So what does this story have to do with porn, polyamory or sex in general? Consider this woman, particularly the fact that she had gone through sexual relationships with six men, including five marriages. Yet she is still desperately unsatisfied and "thirsty." Piper comments that it seems she can't find in a man what she craves and thus moves from the one to the other, desperately believing men are the "water" she is thirsty for, or they can't find what they are craving in her and one after the other eventually drops her. Or both.

In either case, this woman, despite having ample access to sexual partners, has been left with a deep emptiness. I'd imagine she could go her whole life marrying and "trying" new men, or scrolling through as much porn as her heart desires, without ever having her thirst quenched. One of the evidences that you too may have not drunk the water of life, or that you are quenching its spring, is that you, like this woman, are constantly moving from one sexual experience to the next, seeking to fill the void and infinite abyss in your soul that only Jesus can fill.

As the words of Revelation 22:17 say, *"Let the one who is thirsty come; let the one who desires take the water of life without price."*

Summary

First, my apologies to you female readers who may have felt this to be, aside from that last part, a bit of a one-sided talk to men. *I get it*. But you need to understand that I'm a guy, and so many of the analogies and descriptions that I use are written from that subjective viewpoint.

However, I understand that (although it's definitely less common amongst women) many women also view porn and struggle with many of the same issues, including polyamory, I've discussed earlier. So, everything I wrote here also applies to you. You, too, can become dopamine desensitized, experience lower amounts of sexual arousal without the stimulus of novel erotic imagery, devalue your partner, objectify males, or cheat on and leave your family.

Second, to simplify and summarize everything I've just told you, allow me to share with you how I openly discussed the matter of porn with my twin 12-year-old sons when I opened this conversation with them at that age. Here's what I told them, which is exactly what I've told you, but here it is in a more succinct manner:

- *Porn impacts your brain in such a way that anything pleasurable in life, including sex, becomes less pleasurable...*

- *Porn causes you to treat women like sexual objects, rather than as real, precious human beings made in the image of God...*

- *Porn destroys the deeply sacred and spiritual experience of loving sexual intercourse with a real partner...*

- *You'd never desire for your sister, mother, daughter, or any other female you love and cherish to be eye-candy for other men, so don't pour fuel or funding on the fire of an entire industry designed to take advantage of and sexually objectify women...*

- *Women, or any other sexual partners, weren't made to be "shared around the village." Instead, firm family foundations, stable societies, and long-lasting legacies are built upon committed and meaningful relationships between two individuals who follow the Golden Rule and love each other in the same way they would want to be loved...*

I encourage you to share the same message with your children or with others, particularly with your *sons* if you have any.

Finally, there's plenty more I haven't even touched on but that others have in far more detail, including peer-reviewed research on the deleterious effects of porn on the heart, the deleterious effects of a brain on porn, and the deleterious effects of porn on society in general, and a quite concerning increase in sexual coercion, sexual aggression, and even sexual violence. To dig into all of that, please visit the resources webpage for this chapter and also Fight the New Drug (FightTheNewDrug.org) and Your Brain on Porn (YourBrainOnPorn.com), along with the excellent book *Your Brain on Porn: Internet Pornography and the Emerging Science of Addiction*.

How about you? Do you use porn? Do you consider how it may be affecting you physically, chemically or emotionally? If so, how do you feel before, during and after? What void are you seeking to fill?

SEX

Thus far, I've first shared with you my thoughts on polyamory, open relationships, and multiple sexual partners. Next, I've detailed what I think the root problem with porn is, how porn problematically affects our brains and our neurotransmitters, the pain porn can cause in our relationships, and the nature of "just looking" vs. full-blown adultery in general.

And in addressing both polyamory and porn, I alluded multiple times to the potential for both to cheapen and bastardize the special, sacred, spiritual, and reverent nature of true, loving sexual intercourse between two committed partners.

Next, I'll explain exactly what I mean by "sacred sex," why I think most couples really don't experience sex in all the glorious pleasure that it can actually be, and how you can make your own sex life much, much better.

Why is this so important?

Frankly, sex is a subject you can't ignore.

After all, the world is obsessed with sex.

From the moment we wake up to the moment we go to bed, we are constantly bombarded by a culture that seems obsessed with the message that sex is good, sex is free, sex doesn't have consequences, and you should be free to explore as many different avenues of sex as you desire.

Furthermore, we're often told that sex can be casual, sex can be no big deal, and you can and should have sex with as many people as you want (in fact, in many cases, the more the better). For those who have decided to save themselves for a marriage partner, this can be quite a conundrum, since a common belief is that by the time you get married you should have some semblance of sexual experience, know exactly what you want in bed, be free to "try before you buy," never be tied down sexually, and therefore have already experimented with and honed your sexual chops with a wide variety of partners. This is all accompanied by the mistaken belief that the practice of and desire for sex with multiple partners will somehow magically disappear once you find that "right person" and settle down with them. After all, unless you have sex before you get married, how do you know if you're even getting a good deal?

So, not only are we surrounded by this message and a generation of young people growing up and wondering how to navigate this entire confusing sexual realm, but we're also bombarded by screens and imagery that significantly mold our sexual worldview. Often, especially via porn, modern media destroys our expectations of what sex could and should be and decimates our understanding of what a healthy relationship with sex should be like. Porn in particular erects (heh!) unrealistic expectations that are not rooted in love and intimacy, but rather in a desire to give rather than to take—showcasing an unattainable version of sex that often denies the humanity of the other person in our sexual relationship. Sex, therefore, turns into an exploration of "what's in it for me," rather than a golden rule-based philosophy of how we can serve the other person.

Are you getting the idea that you should care about this topic, not only for yourself, but for generations to come? If so, keep reading.

The Importance Of Sacred, Spiritual Sex

I can't say that I fully experienced sex the way sex was "meant to be" until I was probably in my mid-30s.

Up until that point, I'd roughly define my experience with sex as kind of a mutual masturbation with my partner in which we pretty much vigorously rubbed both of our bodies together while grunting, groaning, and moaning until we reached some kind of a mutual orgasmic peak, then perhaps cuddled for a little while, cleaned up, and moved on.

It's only been for the past decade or so, through engaging with my wife Jessa in everything from Tantric breathwork and other forms of breathwork to plant medicine to eye gazing to to a deep spiritual bonding through mutual meditation and prayer that sex has absolutely transformed into a deeply spiritual and sacred experience that I'm frankly shocked I was missing out on for so much of my life.

So what do I mean when I refer to sex being sacred?

The dictionary defines sacred as *"made or declared holy, dedicated or devoted exclusively to a use, purpose, or person worthy of reverence or respect."* The root of the word is derived from the Latin sacra, which means *"sacred, holy, consecrated,"* and is often used to describe something considered to be highly blessed or revered. The noun, singular version of the word sacred is *sacrum*, which you're no doubt familiar with as the term used to describe a specific bone of your pelvic regions, but sacrum also translates to *"a holy thing or place."*

While we so often—especially in our modern, logical, rational, scientific times—separate the sacred and spiritual from the physical and fleshly (a conundrum I discuss in my podcast episode on environmentalism and the sacred intelligence of plants with Gordon Wilson), these Latin roots imply something altogether different, as do other ancient belief patterns. For example, Tantra—the esoteric traditions of Hinduism and Buddhism that developed in India from the middle of the 1st millennium CE onwards—teaches that the seat of the so-called kundalini (spiritual energy or life force located at the base of the spine) or Shakti (spiritual energy of ability, strength, effort, power, and capability) energies originate in this second sacral chakra of the pelvis regions; and, particularly when aroused through Tantric-like sexual practices, these energies travel up the physical spine to deep spiritual centers housed in the higher energetic crown chakra near the top (crown) of the head—centers that we now know from the study of neuroscience physically manifest in a host of pleasurable and mind-altering neurotransmitters and bonding hormones emitted by anatomical regions of the brain.

When you think about it, this makes sense. After all, the culmination of sexual intercourse is the inception of life. It is the very method via which a unique spirit and soul is brought forth into the world. To acknowledge that life force and sexual energy originate from the same source definitely makes one think differently about their sacrum and pelvis, especially when it comes to the way in which those body parts interact with another human being. In other words, the very fact that sex is capable of bringing forth a new life into the world makes sex incredibly sacred, and something to indeed be blessed, revered, and treated with deep respect and consideration.

In addition, a mutually satisfying sexual exchange that naturally intensifies the strength of a relationship is sacred because of its unique role in bonding two human beings together. Sure, sex can take place without bonding, but when sex occurs between humans with two open hearts who are using Tantric sexual practices such as slowing down, awakening each of the senses, tuning into subtle energies via breath and body awareness, releasing judgment and blame, expressing intense gratitude, and savoring the present moment in an act of intentional mindfulness, there is a rare intimacy of bonding that cannot be created in any other human interaction I can think of. Sex can bring people together and keep people together (in a much more fun and pleasurable way than other bonding activities such as, say, natural disasters, war, or political turmoil).

Speaking of politics, perhaps this strong bonding power of sex is why sex can act as such a powerful political manipulation tactic. Sex can indeed be highly political and is something that has been used repeatedly in history as a way to advance political agendas and motives. Case in point: the recent Chinese spy Fang Fang sex scandal (headline of an article I'll link to on the resources webpage for this chapter is "Don't Govern While Horny!"), which of course has been preceded by countless historical instances of so-called sexpionage (the use of sexual activity, intimacy, romance, or seduction to conduct espionage), with many such examples thoroughly highlighted in the book *Sex, Power, and Politics: Exploring the Femme Fatale's Mastery of the Political throughout History*, and even in Bible stories such as Samson and Delilah or other Biblical femme fatales such as Judith, Esther, and Jael—all women who used their feminine charms and sex appeal to dispatch an enemy of Israel.

One comment left by a reader named Veronica on my website really got me thinking more about how profound the biological and energetic bond is that we experience during sex. Among other observations, she noted: *"...just imagine what our bodies can be subjected to with actual, physical sexual interactions; the energies, toxins, hormones, foreign DNA...fluids that are so readily absorbed... taking onboard our physical body and its energetic fields..."* It really is a powerful thought when you dwell upon it: During sex, you are exchanging with another human being's most intimate of fluids, saliva, urine, skin cells, biome, and other biological matter while simultaneously deeply enveloped in that being's heart and brain's electromagnetic field, all while physically dancing in close coordination with the energies of each of their chakras, from sacrum to crown.

Based on all this it's shocking how standard it is—especially in a modern, Westernized, speed-dating, serial-divorcing, polyamorous society—for sex to be...

...a casual event appropriate for a random fling or one-night stand that is largely disconnected from any emotion of love or commitment, despite it being near impossible to disconnect the physical and the spiritual aspects of sex, no matter

how calloused one has become...

...something that can be shared in a polyamorous style *with a wide variety of lovers, absent of devotion or loyalty to any one particular partner, resulting in what I can best describe as a random series of "weak bonds" vs. a single "strong bond," similar to having 5,000 shallow relationships with Facebook friends but no close and deeply appreciated physical friends...*

...an opportunity to create a 90+ billion dollar porn industry *based around us viewing strangers engage in and largely bastardize via sexual objectification, orgies, beastiality, child abuse, and beyond what should instead be a private, blessed, revered, spiritual, and sacred act...*

...a quite nonchalant "que sera sera" approach amongst many married couples that if "sex happens, it happens," with almost no forethought, calendaring, or planning to create intentional and highly meaningful sexual experiences similar to what I discuss in *the podcast episode "Recapture the Rapture: Biohacking Sex, Tantric Breathwork, Plant Medicines For Orgasmic Enhancement & Much More!" with Jamie Wheal....*

In other words, most of us could do a better job recognizing sex for the sacred experience that it is and taking sex far more seriously—not in a sober and boring sort of way, but rather with the same type of mindfulness, preparation, education, and immersion as we might devote to becoming a concert pianist, a watercolor maestro, or a finely tuned athlete.

As a matter of fact, in the same way that I think children should be taught from an early age to have an intimate understanding of how to use their breath and prana life force to control their emotions and physiology, I also believe a core part of any human's educational curriculum should include some kind of formal training in how to truly become physically, mentally, and spiritually intertwined during the act of lovemaking—including learning and incorporating the type of Tantric practices I'll describe later in this chapter.

WHAT THE BIBLE SAYS ABOUT SEX

Of course, coming from a Christian background, I've repeatedly witnessed my Bible-believing friends shy away from any element of fancy lovemaking or deep, immersive sexual experiences with their spouse, often considering a sacred approach to sex to be associated with some type of extreme sexual infatuation of orgiastic Pagan ritual origins or an obsession with fleshly, carnal, lust-infused pursuits. God forbid any good Catholic or Protestant be caught with a Kama Sutra floating about their bedside. This Victorian-esque pessimistic and pragmatic approach to sex is perhaps best illustrated by the words of Queen Victoria when she purportedly instructed the Christian ladies in her realm to simply "Lie back and think of England."

But the great Creator made all things good (see 1 Timothy 4:4 and Genesis 1:31), including our sacrum, our genitals, and sex. Sure, in the same way we can bastardize alcohol, cannabis, or any other potential vice; gluttonize on wine, milk, and honey; or become addicted and attached to exercise or other pleasurable pursuits, we can certainly make sex sinful (e.g. such as via the incorporation of polyamory and porn as described earlier); but that doesn't mean that recognizing the special sacredness of sex or practicing mindful, connected sex with our spouse is a sin. Christianity is generally considered to be a somewhat sexually repressive religion, and furthermore, since Christians are known for being opposed to gay sex, pre-marital sex, and extramarital sex, it is often assumed by many Christians that erotic sex is "bad" or "shameful" or "unspeakable" in and of itself—but nothing could be further from the truth!

For example, I would challenge any Christian—who considers sex to simply be a quick way to, perhaps, conceive a child or make a partner feel briefly satisfied—to spend some time reading the Song of Solomon, an entire Scriptural poem that can be shockingly, sublimely, and sensually sexy, including elements of extravagant lovemaking, male and female oral sex, breasts compared to fawns, a man's penis as sweet fruit and his genitalia as a bag of myrrh, and a woman's genitalia as a garden of pomegranates that should be eaten, with lips and mouths described as "honey and milk."

From the very beginning, sex was part of the created order. In the Garden of Eden, Adam and Eve were *"naked and were not ashamed"* (Genesis 2:25). In the Book of Proverbs, the wise father instructs his son to *"rejoice in the wife of your youth, a* lovely deer, a graceful doe. Let her breasts fill you at all times with delight; be intoxicated always in her love" (Proverbs 5:18–19). Hebrews 13:4 says *"Let marriage be held in honor among all, and let the marriage bed be undefiled,"* indicating that sex should be not be a cause for shame, but should be honored (back to that sacred sacra!), cherished, and enjoyed as a good gift from God.

Heck, we husbands actually owe sex to our wives! In 1 Corinthians 7:3-4, the Apostle Paul writes that *"The husband should give to his wife her conjugal rights, and likewise the wife to her husband. For the wife does not have authority over her own body, but the husband does. Likewise the husband does not have authority over his own body, but the wife does."* In other words, sex was to be mutual and husbands actually owed sex to their wife, while the wife had the right to claim sex from her husband. This idea that sex within a marriage was to be free, generous, and reciprocal was actually a revolutionary thought in the ancient world. Perhaps more disruptive to our modern perceptions of sex, it also means that— despite many young men and women being taught that they should only have sex when both partners desire it—this passage of the Bible indicates that in the context of a marriage, sex should be gifted to a partner whenever that partner desires it!

In addition to encouraging couples to engage in generous and reciprocal sex within a marriage relationship, the Bible indicates that *frequent* sexual intercourse is a good thing. Paul also says *"Do not deprive one another, except perhaps by agreement for a limited time, that you may devote yourselves to prayer; but then come together again, so that Satan may not tempt you because of your lack of self-control."* (1 Corinthians 7:5). Based on the idea that if we drink deeply from our own cisterns we will be less tempted to draw from our neighbor's well (Proverbs 5:15), as is encouraged in the Old Testament, in the New Testament, frequent sexual intercourse is encouraged as a guard against a wandering eye and a lustful heart. Married couples are encouraged to set aside at most a few days of mutually agreed upon abstinence to instead focus on prayer or other spiritual practices, but then to come together quickly lest they be tempted to sexual immorality.

Next, and contrary to the belief of many Christians I know, sex is *not* just for "making babies." Don't get me wrong: children are a blessing from the Lord and there is certainly an encouragement and blessing in the Bible in multiple locations when it comes to bringing new human life into the world through procreation (*e.g. ...God said to them, "Be fruitful and multiply and fill the earth and subdue it"*). But even before God spoke those words, He first, in Genesis 2:18 says: *"It is not good that the man should be alone; I will make him a helper fit for him,"* then, in

Genesis 2:24, *"Therefore a man shall leave his father and his mother and hold fast to his wife, and they shall become one flesh."* This indicates that sex and partnership between the first male and female were first and foremost about intimate friendship and becoming one flesh (bonding!). As a matter of fact, the Hebrew term used in this passage implies more than physical union. It means "becoming one person." It means union. It means bonding. So sure, sex, when done right, often results in children, but it doesn't need to be done purely or only for the purpose of making children.

All of this being said, I must also emphasize that while the Bible supports and celebrates human sexuality, it also makes it very clear that you can be fully and entirely human without sexual intercourse being a part of your life.

After all, Jesus didn't have sex. Neither did the prophets Jeremiah or Elijah or John the Baptist. The Apostle Paul was even asked by early Christians whether abstinence or celibacy were necessary for true spiritual health. And while Paul noted what I've written above, speaking of the need to be sexually generous and reciprocal in a marriage and the benefits of married couples having sex on a regular basis, he also, in 1 Corinthians 7:7, says that he has the *"gift"* of not having to had to go to the trouble of getting married in the first place. See, in Paul's view, much work is needed to be done before the return of Christ, and since those who are married are obligated to take time for their spouses and tend to their spouses' needs, those who are married cannot be fully committed to being a missionary for Christ (1 Corinthians 7:25-38). Thus, according to Paul, it is better to remain single, but if you cannot stand the heat and sexual temptations while being committed to a life of abstinence, it is better to *"marry than to burn"* (1 Corinthians 7:8-9).

So while sex is indeed fully natural, blessed, and reverent—and highly important in the eyes of God—it does not define our worth as human beings. We are worthy because we were created in the image of God, and whether or not we have sex does not define that worth. A person can live a rich, meaningful, and honorable life without ever having had sex. Ultimately, in the eyes of God, marriage and sex are good, but so also are singleness and celibacy. If you are a man or a woman reading who is not married and does not have sex with a husband or wife (yet or perhaps ever in the future), perhaps that simply means that, like the Apostle Paul, God has set you aside to work wonders for His kingdom, and that's nothing to be ashamed or frustrated about. Sex does not define you as a human.

Three Practical Tips For Sacred, Spiritual Sex

After reading all of this, I'm sure you're wondering exactly what I've meant when I've alluded several times above to Tantric sex, and the heightened meaning, thrill, and excitement of being spiritually intertwined with your lover during sacred lovemaking. So I'd like to finish with three quick practical tips and resources for engaging in this kind of sacred, spiritual sex. These tips only scratch the surface of "the places you can go" with sex, and for even more—including how to combine many of the tactics below with additions such as microdoses of plant medicine or psychedelics, the perfect style of music, other breathwork styles and much more—listen to my podcast with Jamie Wheal entitled "Recapture the Rapture: Biohacking Sex, Tantric Breathwork, Plant Medicines For Orgasmic Enhancement & Much More!"

My first tip for you is to be mindful and aware of your breath, especially during sex. Quality breathing, even during sex, can improve cognition and circulation, focus, attention, and provide you with a boost of lovemaking energy. Appropriate breathing techniques can also help you relax, concentrate, and last longer in the bedroom.

The lower the nervous system stress you have during sex, generally the more connected, exciting, and fulfilling sex will be. Deep breathing is crucial to remaining calm because it is linked to your parasympathetic nervous system, the reflex responsible for the "rest and digest" response. Shallow breathing, on the other hand, is more closely associated with the sympathetic nervous system, the reflex responsible for the "flight or fight" response. Irrespective of the "type" of sex you are having, sex in a relaxed, parasympathetic state is much more appealing than getting it on under acute stress (as anyone knows who has tried to "duck away for a quickie" during a day of work and found themselves unable to get as deeply aroused, as, say, in the evening after a glass of wine).

During sex, try to breathe in deeply and imagine the breath flowing into your genitalia. This will enhance pleasure and allow a sexual rhythm to unfold between you and your partner. As pleasure increases and you are both reaching climax or intensity, slow your movement down and continue to breathe even deeper. This focus on breath may seem as if it is taking you away from focusing on your partner, but what is actually happening is you are deepening your connection to your partner through breathing rhythmically, aligning your breath, and slowing it down—inhaling as your partner inhales, and exhaling as your partner exhales.

Finally, regarding breath, ensure you are breathing through your nose. This brings in more oxygen than breathing through your mouth and can provide you with a "natural high" from the accumulated nitric oxide. It also engages your core and pelvic floor in such a way that can enhance your sexual experience. If you want to dive deeper into the power of nasal breathing, check out Patrick McKeown's book, *The Oxygen Advantage: Simple, Scientifically Proven Breathing Techniques to Help You Become Healthier, Slimmer, Faster, and Fitter*, and my podcast with Patrick. Another very helpful resources for becoming a true "breathwork ninja" for sex, work, workouts, and beyond, is the breath course I recently took myself and my twin boys through and also the Breathwork and Meditation Series taught by my friends Christine Hassler and Stefanos Sifandos, a couple who also came to my house and taught my wife and I a Tantric breathwork course, which we discussed in the podcast "Breathwork vs. Psychedelics, Tantric Sex, Relational Alchemy, Questions That Lead To Love & Much More With Stefanos Sifandos & Christine Hassler," all of which I'll link to on the resources webpage for this chapter.

Second, embrace grunts, groans, and sound. When it comes to this kind of audible lovemaking, you may feel self-conscious—but please don't. It is natural to make all sorts of sounds, particularly in association with intense pleasure. Inhibiting this natural function can retract intimacy. When you are not vulnerable and open, even with your sounds, your partner can feel that and move with trepidation. Opening your voice when feeling pleasure is useful in connecting and deepening intimacy, arousal, and sexual exploration. Push your edge here a little and make satisfied sounds even though you may feel uncomfortable doing so.

Third, explore Tantra. Tantric sex revolves around sexual practices that focus on creating a deep, intimate connection with yourself and your partner. During tantric sex, the aim is to be present in the moment to achieve a sensual and fulfilling sexual experience.

To be in more of a Tantric space, you can practice the following:

- Make sex non-linear. It needn't be about direction and orgasm. Explore the body, the mind, stop, connect, talk, feel, be silent, breathe, go back to intercourse, then finally come back to feeling. Eat during sex, or be sensual through sounding and breathing (see above) or movement. Explore each other through all of your senses.

- Make eye contact and gaze into each other's eyes deeply. Take your time absorbing your partner and really feel their expression.

- Slow things down and don't rush. Place your inner focus on your pelvis, then bring it to your heart, your mind, hands, thighs, and then to your partner's body. Be fully present to the environment and the room.

- Synchronize your breath. At the same time, you and your partner can breathe in deeply through your noses, hold for 5 seconds, then exhale through the mouth. Feel each other's abdomen expanding on the inhale by pressing against one another, and then hold and feel the release by paying close attention to it. For males, if you are getting close to orgasm you can try *Kapalbhati breathing*. As you are about to ejaculate, forcefully exhale all the air out through your mouth, then engage in an automatic deeper (yet passive) inhale through your mouth. Kapalbhati breathing helps prolong/lengthen ejaculation in males. This level of self-control also transfers to other areas of life, reinforcing discipline and confidence. The book *The Multi-orgasmic Male* by Mantak Chia is quite good for learning this technique.

- *Yab-yum* is a position where you can practice matching breath and also eye-gazing. One partner sits with their legs crossed, and the other partner sits on their partner's lap, wrapping their legs around their waist (usually the female sits on the lap). You can rub your genitals against each other, engage in penetrative sex, or just sit there in the moment (clothed or unclothed).

Tantric sex is essentially about being in tune with and fully mindful of both your body and the body of your partner. It involves slowing down the moment of peak sexual arousal and instead coming back into the presence of your breath, your body, and your partner's breath and body. Tantric sex involves full-body orgasmic experiences, multi-orgasmic experiences, and non-ejaculatory practices to prolong sexual intimacy—based on the premise that if two people can remain in this space long enough, they can experience a profound spiritual connection. For more on Tantric sex, check out the book *Tantra—Sex, Secrecy, Politics and Power in the Study of Religion* (available as a free PDF that I'll link to on the resources webpage for this chapter).

Summary

Ultimately, sex can be a highly spiritual, sacred, and incredibly special experience. But unfortunately, many people never experience sex in this way due to lack of sexual knowledge and instruction, dilution of spiritual connectedness in sexual relationships by engaging with multiple partners, cheapening and bastardization of the entire sexual experience via immersion in porn, and a belief among some that sex should be plain, unimaginative and functional.

But as you've discovered in this chapter, God made sex and declared it good—not just for the creation of children, but for satisfaction, bonding, and long-lasting, fulfilling, and meaningful relationships.

And, as you've already learned, you can defy the cheapened and bastardized version of sex so prevalent in modern culture and modern media by discovering sacred, spiritual sex with a committed partner whom you love as you yourself would want to be loved.

Finally, to better understand the sacred and spiritual nature of sex, I highly recommend the following resources, all of which I'll link to on the resources webpage for this chapter:

- Book: *The Enlightened Sex Manual: Sexual Skills for the Superior Lover* by David Deida.

- Book: *Finding God Through Sex: Awakening the One of Spirit Through the Two of Flesh* by David Deida.

- Article: 11 Steps to Sacred Sex.

- Podcast: Recapture the Rapture: Biohacking Sex, Tantric Breathwork, Plant Medicines For Orgasmic Enhancement & Much More! With Jamie Wheal.

- The entire sex chapter of my book *Boundless*.

- This article I wrote on effectively pairing breathwork with sex to also enhance the sacredness of sex.

How about you? Do you engage in sacred, spiritual sex? If so, do you have particular Tantric practices or other tactics you use to enhance the

sexual intercourse experience, or are there other ways in which you currently do or plan to in the future make sex more meaningful and sacred? Take a few moments now to think about how you currently think of sex, then leave your thoughts below.

For resources, references, links and additional reading and listening material for this chapter, visit GetEndure.com/Chapter3.

CHAPTER IV

THE TREE

I've always wondered about the story of the tree of the knowledge of good and evil, and, more specifically, the nature of the tree itself.

Just in case you're not familiar with this tree, a quick explanation may enlighten you as to why I'm quite curious about it.

The first time I encountered this tree was when I was a young boy, reading the book of Genesis in the Bible, specifically Chapters 2 and 3. The story goes like this, pretty much verbatim:

> *"This is the account of the heavens and the earth when they were created, in the day that the Lord God made them. Now no shrub of the field had yet appeared on the earth, nor had any plant of the field sprouted; for the Lord God had not yet sent rain upon the earth, and there was no man to cultivate the ground. But springs welled up from the earth and watered the whole surface of the ground.*
>
> *Then the LORD God formed man from the dust of the ground and breathed the breath of life into his nostrils, and the man became a living being. And the Lord God planted a garden in Eden, in the east, where He placed the man He had formed. Out of the ground the Lord God gave growth to every tree that is pleasing to the eye and good for food. And in the middle of the garden were the tree of life and the tree of the knowledge of good and evil.*
>
> *...Then the Lord God took the man and placed him in the Garden of Eden to cultivate and keep it. And the Lord God commanded him, "You may eat freely from every tree of the garden, but you must not eat from the tree of the knowledge of good and evil; for in the day that you eat of it, you will surely die."*

Later, after God created a woman to be a suitable helper for the man Adam, the story continues:

> "Now the serpent was more crafty than any beast of the field that the Lord God had made. And he said to the woman, 'Did God really say, "You must not eat from any tree in the garden?"' The woman answered the serpent, 'We may eat the fruit of the trees of the garden, but about the fruit of the tree in the middle of the garden, God has said, 'You must not eat of it or touch it, or you will die.'"
>
> 'You will not surely die,' the serpent told her. 'For God knows that in the day you eat of it, your eyes will be opened and you will be like God, knowing good and evil.'
>
> When the woman saw that the tree was good for food and pleasing to the eyes, and that it was desirable for obtaining wisdom, she took the fruit and ate it. She also gave some to her husband who was with her, and he ate it. And the eyes of both of them were opened, and they knew that they were naked; so they sewed together fig leaves and made coverings for themselves.
>
> Then the man and his wife heard the voice of the Lord God walking in the garden in the breeze of the day, and they hid themselves from the presence of the Lord God among the trees of the garden. But the Lord God called out to the man, 'Where are you?'
>
> 'I heard Your voice in the garden,' he replied, 'and I was afraid because I was naked; so I hid myself.'
>
> 'Who told you that you were naked?' asked the Lord God. 'Have you eaten from the tree of which I commanded you not to eat?'
>
> And the man answered, 'The woman whom You gave me, she gave me fruit from the tree, and I ate it.'
>
> Then the Lord God said to the woman, 'What is this you have done?'
>
> 'The serpent deceived me,' she replied, 'and I ate.'
>
> So the Lord God said to the serpent:
>
>> 'Because you have done this,

> cursed are you above all livestock
> and every beast of the field!
> On your belly will you go,
> and dust you will eat,
> all the days of your life.
> And I will put enmity between you and the woman,
> and between your seed and her seed.
> He will crush your head,
> and you will strike his heel.'

To the woman He said:

> 'I will sharply increase your pain in childbirth;
> in pain you will bring forth children.
> Your desire will be for your husband,
> and he will rule over you.'

And to Adam He said:

> 'Because you have listened to the voice of your wife
> and have eaten from the tree
> of which I commanded you not to eat
> cursed is the ground because of you;
> through toil you will eat of it
> all the days of your life.
> Both thorns and thistles it will yield for you,
> and you will eat the plants of the field.
> By the sweat of your brow
> you will eat your bread,
> until you return to the ground—
> because out of it were you taken.
> For dust you are,
> and to dust you shall return.'

And Adam named his wife Eve, because she would be the mother of all the living. And the Lord God made garments of skin for Adam and his wife, and He clothed them. Then the Lord God said, 'Behold, the man has become like one of Us, knowing good and evil. And now, lest he reach out his hand and take also from the tree of life, and eat, and live forever...'

Therefore the Lord God banished him from the Garden of Eden to work the ground from which he had been taken. So He drove out the man and stationed cherubim on the east side of the Garden of Eden, along with a whirling sword of flame to guard the way to the tree of life."

Now what's interesting is that there are plenty of ideas floating around out there, especially in theological circles, about the mystery of what exactly this tree *was* and *why* God put it there in the first place. Why is this important? Frankly, what you're about to read will, I think, serve you quite well when it comes to resisting temptations and desires, along with more of the temperancy I write about in Chapter 7.

What Was The Tree Of The Knowledge Of Good And Evil?

As you may have noticed, the tree of the knowledge of good and evil is actually one of two specific trees in the story of the Garden of Eden in Genesis 2-3 above, along with the tree of life.

In Jewish tradition, this tree, and the eating of its fruit, represents the beginning of the mixture of good and evil together. According to this tradition, before that breaking of God's law, the two were separate, and evil had only a nebulous potential existence, and it was not in human nature to desire it. Eating the forbidden fruit changed this, and thus was born what is called in Hebrew the yetzer hara, or the "evil inclination."

From a Christian perspective, church father and theologian Augustine of Hippo taught that the tree should be understood both symbolically and as a real tree, and that the fruits of that tree were not inherently evil, because everything that God created "was good" (more on that in Genesis 1:12—and also in Chapter 5). Rather, it was the disobedience of Adam and Eve that caused disorder in God's creation, and that all humankind inherited sin from Adam and Eve's original sin.

The tree appears in Islam religion, too. The Quran never refers to the tree as the "tree of the knowledge of good and evil" but rather as "the tree" or as the "tree of immortality." Muslims believe that when God created Adam and Eve, He told them that they could enjoy everything in the garden except this tree, but forbade them to eat from the tree so that they would not become angels or immortal (the Quran also mentions the sin as being a "slip," and that consequently, Adam and Eve repented to God and were forgiven).

As far as the identity of the actual "forbidden fruit" on the tree, of course, in most Western cultures and art, the fruit is often depicted as an apple (quite possibly because of a misunderstanding of two unrelated words mălum, a native Latin noun which means "evil," and mālum, another Latin noun, borrowed from Greek μῆλον, which means "apple"). Interestingly the larynx (the large prominence that joins the thyroid cartilage in the human throat) is noticeably more prominent in males and is often called an Adam's apple, derived from a notion that it was caused by the forbidden fruit getting stuck in Adam's throat as he swallowed it.

But other proposed possibilities include grape, pomegranate, fig, carob, etrog or citron, banana, pear, and even magic mushrooms. For example, the non-canonical Book of Enoch describes the tree as *"like a species of the Tamarind tree, bearing fruit which resembles grapes extremely fine; and its fragrance extended to a considerable distance. I exclaimed, How beautiful is this tree, and how delightful is its appearance!"* (1 Enoch 31:4). In Islamic tradition, the fruit is usually either identified with wheat or with grapevine.

And yes, I even mentioned "magic mushrooms." For example, one fresco in the 13th-century Plaincourault Abbey in France depicts Adam and Eve in the Garden of Eden, flanking a tree that has the appearance of a gigantic Amanita muscaria, a commonly known psychoactive mushroom (it's the spotted red-and-white one that looks like the Mario Mushroom). Plant medicine enthusiast and ethnobotanist Terence McKenna (brother of my former podcast guest Dennis McKenna) proposed that the forbidden fruit is a reference to psychotropic plants and fungi, specifically psilocybin mushrooms, which he theorizes played a central role in the evolution of the human brain (it's actually not uncommon to encounter theories about so-called "psychedelic medicines" in the Bible—several of which I'll link to on the resources webpage for this chapter—although there are none of them that I think are relevant to our salvation or particularly important in the scheme of things).

But my own personal conundrum with the tree of the knowledge of good and evil isn't so much curiosity about what kind of tree it was or what kind of forbidden fruit it produced, and more a matter of

wondering *why* God planted it there in the first place. After all, wouldn't everything have been just *perfect* without it?

SO WHY DID GOD CREATE THE TREE OF THE KNOWLEDGE OF GOOD AND EVIL?

There are many theories about why God may have originally created the tree of the knowledge of good and evil.

*But I think the most compelling notion is that the tree really wasn't there to "test" or "tempt" Adam and Eve to see if they would obey or disobey. Rather it was there to provide an opportunity to either delight only in God and the true life He gives, **or** to take an alternative path to satisfaction. By refusing to eat of the fruit, Adam and Eve would have affirmed the totality of their satisfaction as being fully rooted in God. In other words, God is enough. In Him, Adam, Eve, you and I can discover the fullness of life.*

But if we do not live life through the lens that God is most glorified in us when we are most satisfied in Him, and instead seek satisfaction in other "forbidden trees"— in lust, in pride and delights of the eyes and the flesh that I discuss in Chapter 1— we can show where our true desires lie, even if those temptations are not eternally satisfying. The Dutch philosopher Spinoza claimed that "desire is the very essence of a man." This means that if you watch what a person desires, it can reveal their true character. And boy-oh-boy, from money to power to prestige to popularity to food to drugs and beyond, there are plenty of abusable and desire-satiating shiny pennies and forbidden fruits scattered throughout every day of each of our lives, aren't there (even including our precious, "noble and laudable" temptations like exercise, food, and self-care)? However, as I talk about extensively in my book *Fit Soul*, no matter how impressive our attainments and no matter how good we eventually feel about ourselves and our accomplishments, these will never be enough.

It's not that desire is bad.

God made us to desire.

He made us to produce, to sense, and to feel pleasurable neurochemicals like dopamine and serotonin, which can seep into our brain and produce a temporarily satisfied, feel-good effect when we, say, bit into a fresh, luscious strawberry. He made us to delight, to love, and to savor His creation.

But it is when we seek to satisfy our desires apart from God—without acknowledgment of God, union with God, or a recognition of the healthy boundaries that God has set—that we experience a diminishing life based on the satisfactions of Las Vegas-esque worldly pleasures, rather than an ultimate, deeply satisfying life based upon an obedient relationship with God that is the only satisfaction which can fill the eternal hole—the God-shaped abyss—in our hearts.

God created us with a desire of such magnitude that it can only be fulfilled in Him. This was not meant to be a cruel, tortuous trick, making us yearn for what we can never find in earthly goods and experiences, but rather, an opportunity to look above the earth—to look to God for our ultimate fulfillment, satiation, and satisfaction. As seventeenth-century English clergyman Thomas Traherne said, *"My desires are so august and insatiable that nothing less than a Deity can satisfy them."*

So that was likely one possible purpose of the existence of the tree of the knowledge of good and evil: to point to the true object of our desires, and to give us the opportunity and free will to seek fulfillment in a life with God, immersed in His joy, His love, and His peace, instead of fulfillment in the things of earth. When we succumb to the temptation and take that same free will and seek satisfaction apart from God, the consequences are devastating. We experience death, not so much in the immediate physical sense of the word, but rather, death in the sense that we are cut off from experiencing the complete fullness of life we were intended and created to experience, a separation from the very source of life itself, our Creator, and a banishing from the life of a paradise in Eden. Arguably, this separation is even more painful than physical death, because, while still breathing, standing, and walking, we are severed from the joyful, satisfied life for which we were created in the first place. We become like the walking dead, pursuing our own shallow pleasures in exchange for an existence without God, which, as I write about in Chapter 19 is really just the definition of hell.

Furthermore, the tree also offered an opportunity to display haughty and selfish self-dependence vs. humble and trusting dependence upon God, and acceptance of all His good gifts, almost as if you were, as a child, gifted with a host of wonderfully wrapped presents on Christmas morning, but your parents commanded that only one of those gifts was to remain under the tree, unopened. In such a situation, you would have the choice to either savor all the amazing gifts you'd just received or sit like a sulking toddler staring at the one remaining gift under the tree, throwing a tantrum because you can't open it, then eventually sneaking in and opening it anyways when nobody is watching. See, in prohibiting the eating of one tree out of a countless number of other trees, plants, leaves, vines, shrubs, fruits, nuts, and seeds, God was essentially saying, as John Piper writes about in a sermon about the tree that I'll link to on the resources webpage for this chapter:

> *"I have given you life. I have given you a world full of pleasure, pleasures of taste and sight and sound and smell and feel and nourishment. Only one tree is forbidden to you. And the point of that prohibition is to preserve the pleasures of the world, because if you eat of that one you will be saying to me, 'I'm smarter than you. I am more authoritative than you. I am wiser than you are. I think I can care for myself better than you care for me. You are not a very good Father. And so I am going to reject you.' So don't eat from the tree, because you will be rejecting me and all my good gifts and all my wisdom and all my care. Instead, keep on submitting to my will. Keep on affirming my wisdom. Keep on being thankful for my generosity. Keep on trusting me as a Father and keep on eating these trees as a way of enjoying me. There are 10,000 trees, every imaginable fruit. Just go eat. Be thankful. I have given them to you and see them as expressions of my goodness and savor them that way."*

So, despite all those "gifts under the Christmas tree," so to speak, that God gave us in the very beginning, Satan comes along and says, "God isn't generous. Ignore all these other amazing gifts, because God is selfish, stingy, and a skinflint. See, He's obviously not giving you *that* one." It's as though Satan portrayed the prohibition of one forbidden tree and treated it as a prohibition of *everything in* Eden, which of course really wasn't the case.

Instead, the tree of the knowledge of good and evil was a test for us, based on the free will that God gifted us with from the very beginning, to choose independence instead of God-dependence, and, as a result, to risk losing the pleasure of the entire garden and full union with God along with our choice to go it on our own and forsake supreme pleasure in God.

Finally, I'd be remiss not to give a head nod to one alternative, albeit much simpler suggestion for the existence of the tree: perhaps it really was just pure poison. No, really, perhaps the forbidden fruit did contain some kind of ancient variant of highly potent THC or psilocybin or DMT or some other mind-tweaking, brain-bending alkaloid or chemical that God knew would fry early human's neurochemical eggs to the extent to which they became incapable of savoring His creation or being in a state capable of fully honoring and worshipping Him, in the same way that God may also have warned against excess consumption of honey or trying to walk off the edge of a cliff and fly. He just knew that, although He made it for some purpose we just don't know about, it wasn't going to be a biologically beneficial thing to have as a staple in our diet.

In other words, maybe the tree and its fruit literally was poison—and although God had some good reason for creating it, such as some kind of built-in plant defense mechanism to keep a gorgeous sacred and ancient tree from getting consumed by birds and mammals or something like that—the Bible doesn't say exactly why it was there in the first place, but does indicate God was just giving a command rooted in "friendly gardener" advice. Maybe He knew that—very similar to the rampant effects excessive plant medicine and psychedelic compounds harvested from nature in modern-day times can potentially cause—the chemical soup such a plant might create in our brains could threaten to drive us away from Him and not *closer* to Him as we create some kind of God-like state within our own minds. Perhaps He didn't want Adam and Eve laying on their backs for three days drooling and staring off into space, or worse (for example, although I'm not against responsible uses of some plant medicines, I recently saw a video of a guy stumbling out of an Ayahuasca retreat, deciding he was "enlightened," and proceeding to cut off his own genitals with a pocketknife). So in the same way God put THC in cannabis but warns us to "stay sober," or put razor-like teeth in the mouth of a great white shark but gave us pain receptors and enough common sense to not stick our head into a set of giant shark jaws, perhaps his warning about the tree really was just practical advice designed to assist us with our own protection and preservation.

Based on this idea, maybe God *would* have let us eat of the forbidden fruit at some time later, in a more appropriate set and setting, and after He had taught Adam and Eve responsible use and the intended natural utility of the tree.

Or maybe the tree was necessary as some vital part of the ecosystem for nourishing creatures aside from humans, such as serving as some kind of food for ancient gods (as books like *The Unseen Realm* by Michael Heiser point out, we know there were other non-human, spiritually conscious beings who existed in addition to *the* God).

Or maybe it was a dwelling abode for beautiful, rare snakes, or pollen for some kind of insect that kept other plants and trees thriving, but was poison for humans.

Who knows?

SUMMARY

Obviously, one could weave down these hypothetical rabbit holes for quite some time. But ultimately, here's what we do know:

- *God created humans to glorify and worship Him by enjoying His magnificent creation while being fully satisfied in Him. He also made us non-robotic beings of free will.*

- *He told us something that was very important not to do—not to eat one thing— but based on our own free will and our desires for self-satisfaction, we rebelled, broke our trust with Him, and ate it anyway.*

- *As a result, we lost full union with God and visited a curse upon ourselves, but, quite beautifully when you really think about it, God gave us a merciful "out" through another tree—the* more powerful tree upon which Jesus Christ was crucified.

Because of that third fact listed above, I'm OK with the true nature of the tree of the knowledge of good and evil remaining perhaps a bit of a mystery, and I'm OK with continuing to be curious about it, but ultimately, in the end, it doesn't really matter because I have been given the grace to walk in full union with God and to eat of all the trees of all of Eden for the rest of all time with one simple act of faith, trust and belief in the deity, death, burial and resurrection of Jesus.

And one last thing—in case you find this whole tree theology thing to be interesting and want to take an even deeper dive.

I recently discovered the book *Reforesting Faith: What Trees Teach Us About the Nature of God and His Love for Us*. This intriguing walk through all way trees are woven into religion and the Bible, written by former physician and carpenter Dr.

Matthew Sleeth, makes the convincing case that trees reveal more about God and faith than I could have ever imagined. Any spiritually-minded person looking to reconnect to the natural world should read this book because they will find a passionate call to a more tree-aware stewardship of the Earth, and realize that the gospel story can be told through a trail of trees.

There's the trees you just read about on the first page of Genesis, but also in the first Psalm, on the first page of the New Testament, and on the last page of Revelation. The Bible's wisdom is even referred to as a tree of life. Every major biblical character and every major theological event has a tree marking the spot. A tree was the only thing that could kill Jesus (a wooden cross), and the only thing Jesus ever harmed (a fig tree). Once you discover the hidden language of trees, your walk through the woods or the Bible will never be the same, and if you enjoyed this chapter, I suspect you'll enjoy that book.

My favorite quote from the book is when the author asks his son what superpower he would want, and his son said he'd want to be able to grow as many trees as he could as fast as possible, reasoning, *"Think about it, Dad—you could plant mangrove trees and slow down a tsunami. A dense forest could stop an army. There'd be no more hunger. Everyone would have wood for houses and fires."*

Amen (and read the book for more—I'll link to it on the resources webpage for this chapter).

So, what do *you* think the tree of the knowledge of good and evil was, and why do you think it was created? Are there similar "trees" in your own life that you desire for satisfaction, rather than finding satisfaction in God alone?

For resources, references, links and additional reading and listening material for this chapter, visit GetEndure.com/Chapter4.

PART II

MASTERY OF PASSIONS & DESIRES

How to strike a balance between savoring God's creation and self-discipline.

CHAPTER V
HONEY

Ah...honey.

It's sweet, sticky, nutritionally dense, and a staple food of modern Western and indigenous hunter-gatherer cuisine alike.

It's one of the most energy-dense foods found in nature, and, as I learned when formulating a "clean energy bar" for my supplements and functional foods company, Kion, a perfect pure, blood-sugar stabilizing, probiotic-enriched, enzyme-packed sweetener.

In one fascinating article that I'll link to on the resources webpage for this chapter, author Cara Giazmo describes how Hadza, raw-game eating, persistence-hunting warriors will not only forsake an animal hunt if they stumble across a beehive full of honey, and opt to harvest the precious honey instead, but when wanting to find honey, *"they shout and whistle a special tune. If a "honeyguide bird" is around, it'll fly into the camp, chattering and fanning out its feathers. The Hadza, now on the hunt, chase it, grabbing their axes and torches and shouting "Wait!" They follow the honeyguide until it lands near its payload spot, pinpoint the correct tree, smoke out the bees, hack it open, and free the sweet combs from the nest. The honeyguide stays and watches."*

Even enthusiastic nose-to-tail, purely meat-eating disciples of the recently trendy carnivore diet have largely adopted honey as an "acceptable" animal-food based addition to their relatively strict nutritional regimen.

So, what's not to love?

The Problem With Honey

Recently, I was reading the book *Happiness* by Randy Alcorn. When speaking of honey, Randy says,

> "Consider this fatherly advice given in an ancient culture without refined sugar, in which nature's greatest treat was honey, 'My son, eat honey because it is good, And the honeycomb which is sweet to your taste.' The father doesn't want his son to stay away from honey because he might love honey more than God. If we're thinking biblically, we realize that God created bees to make honey not only for them but for us. He designed our taste buds to enjoy the sweetness of honey—it's a gift to the people He loves. To enjoy that gift is to enjoy the God who gives it to us. Could someone turn honey into a god? Of course. This proverb warns, 'If you find honey, eat just enough—too much of it, and you will vomit' (Proverbs 25:16, NIV). Enough honey makes us happy. Too much honey makes us sick. The father's advice to his son requires no explanation as to how it relates to God because that was self-evident to the original audience. The Hebrew worldview saw creation as the expression of the Creator's mind and heart. Therefore, to be happy with honey was to be happy with God's abundant gifts. And people's happiness with God's abundant gifts, they knew, made God happy too."

So naturally, after reading this part of Randy's book, I began thinking a bit more about honey.

Before I address the potential *problem* with honey, I'll first start here...

...God loves honey. He loves the stuff, sticky-sugary-syrupy and thick and creamy, all at the same time.

He also loves fat. Fat dripping with salty, savory greasy goodness.

And milk. Buttery, frothing, sweet milk, fresh milk.

Wine? You bet God adores a fine aged Bordeaux and a bold California cab accompanied by a moist slice of sourdough bread dipped in spicy, aromatic olive oil or salted and slathered in fresh blueberry preserves!

As a matter of fact, the richness and value of food and drink is all over the Bible.

Proverbs 24:13 gives sage advice from a father to a son, *"My son, eat honey because it is good, And the honeycomb which is sweet to your taste."*

The Song of Solomon 5:1 weaves honey, milk, spices, and wine into one of the greatest love poems of all time: *"I have come to my garden, my sister, my bride; I have gathered my myrrh with my spice. I have eaten my honeycomb with my honey; I have drunk my wine with my milk. Eat, O friends, and drink; drink freely, O beloved."*

In Deuteronomy 31:20, God blesses the Israelites as He, *"brought them to the land flowing with milk and honey, of which I swore to their fathers..."*

And Deuteronomy 32:13-14 reveals a similar blessing, with fruit, honey, oil, curds, milk, fat, wheat, and wine all woven in:

> *"He made him ride in the heights of the earth,*
> *That he might eat the produce of the fields;*
> *He made him draw honey from the rock,*
> *And oil from the flinty rock;*
> *Curds from the cattle, and milk of the flock,*
> *With fat of lambs;*
> *And rams of the breed of Bashan, and goats,*
> *With the choicest wheat;*
> *And you drank wine, the blood of the grapes."*

Nehemiah 9:25-26 describes how the Israelites *"...took strong cities, and a fat land, and possessed houses full of all goods, wells digged, vineyards, and oliveyards, and fruit trees in abundance: so they did eat, and were filled, and became fat, and delighted themselves in thy great goodness."*

Lest you wonder whether corn chips, polenta slathered with meatballs and cheese, a pint of beer, and a handful of salted almonds also fall under God's love and blessing, consider the words of James 1:17, which tells us that *"Every good gift is from God,"* and in John 3:1, we learn that *"All things were made by Him; and without Him was not anything made that was made."*

So yes, that means that an Almighty God formed and fashioned the cacao tree, the cannabis plant, the chickpea, and the catfish—and all this marvelous bounty is ours to enjoy in all of its intricacy, beauty, and tastiness—and even for its medicinal uses (1 Timothy 5:23, "Drink no

longer water, but use a little wine for thy stomach's sake and thine often infirmities.").

This, of course, includes honey.

Yet Proverbs 25:16 warns, *"Have you found honey? Eat only as much as you need, Lest you be filled with it and vomit."* and Proverbs 27:7, *"The soul that is full loathes honey, but to a hungry soul, any bitter thing is sweet."*

The principle behind wise King Solomon's advice in these verses is that over-indulgence, even of good things created and given to us by God, will surely make us sick. That's right: that same precious honey can quickly become poison in the hands of a fool or a glutton. And yes, you can consider honey to be a metaphor for any good thing from God that we wrongly abuse.

So, you may want to dwell upon a few questions, lest your hedonistic enjoyment of our magical planet has become too imbalanced. Some of these questions may hit home, and some may not. But read them nonetheless:

> *"Is your love of ribeye steak and a pour of fine wine depleting your ability to be able to give at least 10% of your income to the poor and needy?*
>
> *Is your need for a bit of weed at the end of the day to de-stress, relax, or sleep gradually pulling you away from lovemaking, deep reading, prayer, journaling, meditation, or any of the other spiritually enhancing and productive activities that occur even in the absence of the need for nighttime 'business work'?*
>
> *Is your regularly scheduled craving for, and subsequent indulgence in, dark chocolate-covered almonds and raw blueberry cheesecake an addiction to the dopamine-enhancing effects of sweet things and sugar that, twenty years from now, will leave you wracked with diabetes and unable to make maximum impact with your life on this planet?*
>
> *Is your constant, casual dining on commercially raised meat and snacking on bags of GMO soy crisps, Subway sandwiches, and Cheetos slowly destroying—via animal abuse, monocropping, pollution, and poison—the lovely Earth you've been blessed with and carry the responsibility to nourish and tend?*

Is your eighteenth Ayahuasca retreat creating a dependence upon reaping all your insight from a leaf and a vine rather than upon the promises, direction, wisdom, and word of a God who can speak profoundly to you even when you're not high?

Are you unable to feel as though you can fully function cognitively without coffee? Or a soda? Or an energy drink? Or a nootropic? Or a smart drug?"

Choose anything in your life that is a habit, enjoyment, staple, pleasure, pastime, or even necessity. Choose *any* of those "honeys" of life—even non-food items like cars, homes, money, golf, exercising, or even other people. If you cannot look at that object and say, *as Anthony DeMello so eloquently describes in his book Awareness:*

"I really do not need you to be happy. I'm only deluding myself in the belief that without you I will not be happy. But I really don't need you for my happiness; I can be happy without you. You are not my happiness, you are not my joy."

...then you risk that your blessing *from* God has *become* your God.

And that's the problem with honey.

Summary

So yes, eat honey, but not too much, and remember that ultimately, honey doesn't make you truly happy, in a deep, lasting sense of the word.

Enjoy an occasional nice steakhouse evening, but pay attention to your checkbook balance and make sure there's plenty of blessings to go around for others.

Smoke weed if you like, but not if it makes you lazy, gluttonous, or unable to do the very best job you can with everything God has placed upon your plate.

Eat your cake, but also eat mindfully, go for walks, lift heavy things, and sweat and get cold regularly to control your blood sugar.

Perhaps partake in plant medicine but only as a supplement to meditation and prayer founded on a holy and disciplined life, and not as an addiction or escape.

Drink wine if you can drink responsibly, but also think of the others around you, and whether they may stumble, and not be able to stop at two glasses or perhaps have a past history of abuse or trauma related to alcohol.

Savor your morning cup of coffee, whiff of tobacco, or boom-bang energy drink, but every once in a while stop stimulating yourself entirely just to make sure you haven't created a dependence.

You get the idea.

Ultimately, in my opinion (and perhaps this is fresh on my mind because I recently finished a five-day juice fast while simultaneously reading one of the best books on a spiritual approach to fasting that I've ever read, titled *A Hunger For God* by John Piper), if you do find yourself attached to any or all of the above, then a healthy dose of fasting can not only remind you of how much of a blessing that item is from God, but also allow you to forfeit any value or trust you may be placing upon that item to instead restore your value and trust in God alone.

As Piper says in the book, *"Fasting is a periodic—and sometimes decisive—declaration that we would rather feast at God's table in the kingdom of heaven than feed on the finest delicacies of this word."* Amen. Eat honey, but not too much. Honey doesn't make you truly happy. God does.

So how about you? Is there sweet honey you've been blessed with? If so, do you enjoy it, or do you idolize it? Do you agree that all that God created is good and for your enjoyment? I encourage you to leave your thoughts below, and to also list potential elements of God's creation that are good, but that you find yourself tempted to abuse.

For resources, references, links and additional reading and listening material for this chapter, visit GetEndure.com/Chapter5.

_____

_____

_____

_____

CHAPTER VI
MARSHMALLOWS

I've been thinking quite a bit lately about delayed gratification.

Perhaps it's that five-day fast I mentioned in the last chapter, which I was completing as I wrote this chapter, and was therefore heavily anticipating that giant ribeye steak waiting for me at the end of the whole thing.

Perhaps it's the fact I'm also currently, also as I work on this chapter you're reading right now, reading through a section of the Bible—namely the Gospel of Luke—that is jam-packed with parables of delayed gratification.

It's probably a bit of both.

Either way, it's a topic worth treating in this chapter, since delayed gratification has implications for everything from your health to your wealth to your happiness to the prospect of your eternal life. So, it's important for you to be aware of the importance of "the marshmallow test" and how it applies to crucial elements of your existence.

The Marshmallow Test

In human psychology, "deferred" or "delayed gratification" is defined as "the ability to wait patiently for something one wants or needs." It is generally acknowledged within the field of psychology that success in many areas of life demands the mental capacity and fortitude to delay something you may want in the moment, such as a bag of potato chips beckoning you from the pantry, driving straight home from work to collapse on the couch instead of stopping to visit the gym on the way home, or resisting the urge to hit the snooze button on the alarm clock.

You are no doubt are familiar with the physical rewards of delayed gratification if you've ever, say, resisted the circadian drive to eat breakfast while sitting to read e-mail and news and instead undertaken a morning fasted exercise protocol for the purposes of weight management, or taken a cold shower while resisting the constant temptation to turn the water to warm so that you can train your cellular and nervous system resilience. Compared to someone who wakes up, smells bacon, and eats it; or gets in the shower, grits their teeth at the cold, and immediately turns the handle to warm, you are likely going to have better body composition and better stress management and fortitude.

You are no doubt familiar with the marshmallow test experiment, also known as the Stanford marshmallow experiment.

The Stanford marshmallow experiment was a 1972 study on delayed gratification. In this study, about 650 four-year-old children were offered a choice between one small but immediate reward, or double the amount of that reward if they opted to wait for a period of time to receive their reward. During this time, the researcher left the room for about 15 minutes and then returned. The reward was either a marshmallow or pretzel stick (though nobody ever describes it as the Stanford pretzel experiment, for some reason), depending on the child's preference. In follow-up studies, the researchers found that children who were able to wait longer for their reward for the sake of a greater long-term reward tended to have better life outcomes, specifically as measured by SAT scores, educational attainment, body mass index (BMI), and other life measures, such as preparation or dealing with anxiety.

The majority of the kids lasted less than 3 minutes on average. However, about 30% waited for 15 minutes for the adult to return, who would then reward them with a second marshmallow. Based on the video camera the experimenters left in the room, all the kids appeared to wrestle with temptation but a few found a way to resist—even by covering their eyes so they couldn't see the treat, or by endlessly fidgeting in their chair.

I'd be remiss not to note that a replication attempt with a sample from a more diverse population, over 10 times larger than the original study, showed only half the effect of the original study. This replication suggested that economic background, rather than willpower, explained the other half. So yes, there may have been a few experimental errors in the study, but ultimately, it illustrates something that seems to be a built-in part of our existence…

...namely that delaying short-term pleasure can create a long-term reward that exceeds the reward of engaging in immediate gratification.

Delayed Gratification In The Bible

As I mentioned in the introduction to this chapter, I've been weaving through the Gospels with my family. Specifically, we are following a 260-day Bible reading and memorization plan called *"Foundations: New Testament"* from the YouBible app. (Incidentally, I'm personally using the Word On Fire Bible version of the Gospels, which I now—based on the epic illustrations, essays, and quotes spread throughout—consider to be my favorite Bible of all time and highly recommend you get if you want to enhance your Scripture experience—I'll link to the one I use on the resources webpage for this chapter.)

Lately, I've been struck by the magnitude of delayed gratification examples in Jesus's parables. It appears to be an essential part of an enlightened Christian existence and eternal happiness to set aside short-term pleasures for long-term gains.

For example, in Luke 16:19-31, there is a story of a rich man who clothed himself in purple and fine linen and fared sumptuously every day. But there was a certain beggar named Lazarus, full of sores, who was laid at his gate, desiring to be fed with the crumbs that fell from the rich man's table. Lazarus was in a state of almost no gratification at all. At that very gate, dogs came and licked his sores. So, it was that around the same time the beggar died and was carried by the angels to Abraham's bosom, the rich man also died and was buried. Being in torment in Hades, the rich man lifted up his eyes and saw the saint Abraham afar off, and Lazarus resting happily in his bosom.

> "Then the rich man cried and said, 'Father Abraham, have mercy on me, and send Lazarus that he may dip the tip of his finger in water and cool my tongue; for I am tormented in this flame.' But Abraham said, 'Son, remember that in your lifetime you received your good things, and likewise Lazarus evil things; but now he is comforted and you are tormented. And besides all this, between us and you there is

> *a great gulf fixed, so that those who want to pass from here to you cannot, nor can those from there pass to us.'*
>
> Then the rich man said, *'I beg you therefore, father, that you would send him (meaning Lazarus) to my father's house, for I have five brothers, that he may testify to them, lest they also come to this place of torment.' Abraham said to him, 'They have Moses and the prophets; let them hear them.' And he said, 'No, father Abraham; but if one goes to them from the dead, they will repent.' But he said to him, 'If they do not hear Moses and the prophets, neither will they be persuaded though one rises from the dead.'"*

Just imagine how that rich man felt. If only he had set aside some of his temporary pleasures in life, passed up a few marshmallows, and perhaps spread the wealth just a bit more to beggars like Lazarus. Now, he was stuck with eternal torment, traded for the relative short-term pleasure of a richly celebrated life on earth.

Next, in the very same book of Gospel, comes Luke 17:22-30, in which Jesus says to his disciples:

> *"The days will come when you will desire to see one of the days of the Son of Man, and you will not see it. And they will say to you, 'Look here!' or 'Look there!' Do not go after them or follow them. For as the lightning that flashes out of one part under heaven shines to the other part under heaven, so also the Son of Man will be in His day. But first He must suffer many things and be rejected by this generation. And as it was in the days of Noah, so it will be also in the days of the Son of Man: They ate, they drank, they married wives, they were given in marriage, until the day that Noah entered the ark, and the flood came and destroyed them all. Likewise as it was also in the days of Lot: They ate, they drank, they bought, they sold, they planted, they built; but on the day that Lot went out of Sodom it rained fire and brimstone from heaven and destroyed them all. Even so will it be on the day when the Son of Man is revealed."*

Once again, you can see that eating, drinking, and immersing oneself in all the temporary pleasures this earth has to offer—compared to following God's law and loving one's neighbor as oneself—results in eventual destruction and a state of eternal displeasure.

In Luke 18:18-23, you can find the well-known story of the rich young ruler. It goes like this:

> *"Now a certain ruler asked him, saying, 'Good Teacher, what shall I do to inherit eternal life?'*
>
> *So Jesus said to him, 'Why do you call me good? No one is good but One, that is, God. You know the commandments: 'Do not commit adultery,' 'Do not murder,' 'Do not steal,' 'Do not bear false witness,' 'Honor your father and your mother.'*
>
> *And he said, 'All these things I have kept from my youth.'*
>
> *So when Jesus heard these things, he said to him, 'You still lack one thing. Sell all that you have and distribute to the poor, and you will have treasure in heaven; and come, follow me.'*
>
> *But when he heard this, he became very sorrowful, for he was very rich."*

The rich man also had a difficult time wrapping his head around the concept of a treasure laid up in heaven waiting for him, should he opt to forego the temporary pleasure and instant gratification life here on earth has to offer.

Perhaps one of the most compelling tales of delayed gratification can be found not in the Gospel of Luke, but way back in Genesis 25:29-34, which tells the story of how Esau lost his birthright.

> *"Now Jacob cooked a stew; and Esau came in from the field, and he was weary. And Esau said to Jacob, 'Please feed me with that same red stew, for I am weary.' Therefore his name was called Edom.*
>
> *But Jacob said, 'Sell me your birthright as of this day.'*
>
> *And Esau said, 'Look, I am about to die; so what is this birthright to me?'*
>
> *Then Jacob said, 'Swear to me as of this day.'*
>
> *So he swore to him, and sold his birthright to Jacob. And Jacob gave Esau bread and stew of lentils; then he ate and drank, arose, and went his way. Thus Esau despised his birthright."*

Esau chose instant gratification and he paid for it dearly by trading all the allowances, heritage, and inheritances that were traditionally passed on to the firstborn son, along with the inheritance of God's eternal promise to Abraham to make him a great nation, and to bless all those who blessed him and curse all those who cursed him.

All for a marshmallow. A pretzel stick. A simple bowl of stew. Money. Purple linen clothes. Food. Drink. Planting. Building. Playing.

Now don't get me wrong: God doesn't mind us enjoying nice things. Heck, as my friend Ray Edwards writes in his new book *Permission to Prosper: How to be Rich Beyond Your Wildest Dreams*, God promises to bless us and does indeed bless us with money, clothing, houses, cars, honey, milk, fat, wine, meat (as I write about in Chapter 5), and all manner of fluffy, sweet marshmallows. But, if you've ever in your life heard a sermon about wealth before, then you know how the saying goes...

...God doesn't mind people owning nice things, but he minds nice things owning people.

So, allow me to ask you this...

...When was the last time you fasted not as an exercise of righteous self-denial or some kind of selfish anti-aging tactic, but as an exercise to delay gratification, bless others with a bit of extra food, money, or time, and pass up a marshmallow now for a reward in heaven later?

When was the last time you skipped dinner to free up an extra hour to go serve the homeless, and perhaps drop dinner off at the soup kitchen on your way?

When was the last time you pulled a big ol' ribeye steak from your freezer and a nice bottle of wine from the pantry, walked past your dinner table, put it into a padded cooler, and sauntered it down to your neighbor's mailbox instead?

When was the last time you took the same mental resilience, fortitude, and ability to engage in delayed gratification that you've used for so many years to "eat the frog," do the hardest task of the day first, squeeze in a morning workout or meditation session prior to jumping into e-mails, etc., and applied that same ability to simply forego a few pleasures to free up money, time, or resources to help others?

Summary

Ultimately, most people could do a better job striking a balance between enjoying and savoring the beauty of God's creation and self-denial or delayed gratification specifically for the purpose of helping and blessing others, and not necessarily for the purpose of self-improvement or self-growth.

Think about it this way: If a giant, booming trumpet sound were to emanate from somewhere up in the sky today, and the resounding voice of Jesus were to reverberate throughout the universe saying...

..."*I'm back! What have you been up to during my time away?*"

...would you be caught with your proverbial pants down? Would you be hunched over a steak stuffing your face, perhaps gathered with others sipping cocktails at a dinner party, or driving home from yet another movie outing, or out shopping for more shoes at the mall or playing yet another eighteen holes of golf?

...would you glance with guilt at your calendar and to-do list where you keep writing down your plans to help the homeless, or go serve in a soup kitchen, or donate time to a local pregnancy counseling center, realizing that you had a noble intention to get around to doing these things for months or even years on end, but by the time you got to the end of a busy day, there just wasn't enough time left (especially after you catch-up on making dinner and settling down in front of your must-see Netflix series?).

...would you be able to raise your hand as one who had actually passed God's great marshmallow test?

Consider the words of Keith Green in his moving song "The Sheep & The Goats," written and performed the very year I was born (1981). I still listen to it regularly to this day, and am deeply convicted every time I do. The lyrics are below, but I highly recommend you also check this song out on Spotify, YouTube or wherever else you digest music.

> *"And when the son of man comes, and all the holy angels with him,*
> *Then shall he sit on his glorious throne,*
> *And he will divide the nations before him, as a shepherd separates the sheep from the goats.*

And he shall put the sheep on his right and the goats on his left,
And he shall say to the sheep come ye, blessed of my father,
Inherit the kingdom I have prepared for you from the foundation of the world,
For I was hungry, and you gave me something to eat,
I was thirsty, and you gave me something to drink,
I was naked, and you clothed me,
I was a stranger, and you invited me in,
I was sick, and I was in prison, and you came to me.
Thank you! enter into your rest.
And they shall answer him, yes, they shall answer him,
And they'll say, lord, when?
When were you hungry lord, and we gave you something to eat?
Lord, when were you thirsty? I can't remember.
And we gave you drink?
Huh, when were you naked lord, and we clothed you?
And lord, when were you a stranger and we invited you in?
I mean, we invited lots of people in, lord. I could never forget that face.
And lord, when were you sick and we visited you?
Or in prison, and we came to you? lord, tell us?
In as much as you did it to the least of my brethren, you've done it unto me.
Oh yes, as much as you've done it to the very least of my brethren, you've done it,
You've done it unto me. Enter into your rest.
Then he shall turn to those on his left, the goats.
Depart from me, you cursed ones, into everlasting fire,
Prepared for the devil and his angels.
For I was hungry, and you gave me nothing to eat,
I was thirsty, and you gave me nothing to drink,
I was naked, out in the cold, in exposure, and you sent me away,
I was a stranger, and I knocked at your door,
But you didn't open, you told me to go away,
I was sick, racked in pain upon my bed,
And I begged, and prayed, and pleaded that you'd come, but you didn't,
I was in prison, and I rotted there,

I'd prayed that you'd come.
I heard your programs on the radio, I read your magazines, but you never came.
Depart from me!
Lord, there must be some mistake, when?
Lord, I mean, when were you hungry lord and we didn't give you something to eat?
And lord, when were you thirsty, and we didn't give you drink?
I mean, that's not fair, well, would you like something now?
Would one of the angels like to go out and get the lord a hamburger and a coke?
Oh, you're not hungry, yeah, I lost my appetite too.
Uh lord uh, lord, when were you naked,
I mean lord, that's not fair either lord,
We didn't know what size you wear.
Oh lord, when were you a stranger lord,
You weren't one of those creepy people who used to come to the door, were you?
Oh lord, that wasn't our ministry lord. we just didn't feel led, you know?
Lord, when were you sick? What did you have, anyway?
Well, at least it wasn't fatal, oh, it was?
I'm sorry lord, I would have sent you a card.
Lord, just one last thing we want to know,
When were you in prison lord? what were you in for anyway?
I had a friend in leavenworth
Enough!
In as much as you've not done it unto the least of my brethren,
You've not done it unto me.
In as much as you've not done it unto the least of my brethren,
You've not done it unto me. Depart from me.
And these shall go away into everlasting fire.
But the righteous into eternal life!
And my friends, the only difference between the sheep and the goats,
According to this scripture,
Is what they did, and didn't do!"

Just remember: When you die or when you lay dying on your deathbed, your cellar of wine, steak locker full of meat, garage full of cars, three extra fancy bicycles, and oodles of shiny extra shoes won't be impressive to God in the least—and are certainly unlikely to be redistributed to the poor, needy, and homeless. So, take care of that now instead.

And if you need a bit of extra help developing your own marshmallow test and delayed gratification skills, I can recommend nothing more powerful than a daily practice of service and self-examination (see the Spiritual Disciplines Journal at SpiritualDisciplinesJournal.com if you want a way to easily systematize that into your life) and also regularly fasting— fasting from food, fasting from booze, fasting from entertainment, fasting from fancy outings, or fasting from anything else that has become an imbalanced staple in your life—to remind you of the needs of others, and to take some of those extra things you're fasting from and spread them around to others. For that, my favorite recent book of late that highlights this specific importance of fasting is A Hunger for God: Desiring God through Fasting and Prayer, by John Piper.

How about you?

Based on that song by Keith Green, what *did* or *do* you currently do?

What *didn't* or *don't* you currently do?

What pleasures are you foregoing, or at least moderating now, for eternal glory later, and perhaps more importantly, to spread more widely the blessings you've been blessed with? How do you help others? What habits have enabled you to engage in delayed gratification and service to others? And finally, what *aren't* you delaying, and instead gratuitously consuming now, that may be detracting you from being able to fully love and serve others?

For resources, references, links and additional reading and listening material for this chapter, visit GetEndure.com/Chapter6.

CHAPTER VII
TEMPERATE

I've been enjoying my morning "time with God" quite a bit recently.

Perhaps that's because, at the time I'm writing this, it's almost summer.

So rather than being holed away in my basement flipping through the pages of God's Word (which there's absolutely nothing wrong with, of course, especially during the cold, dark mornings of fall and winter), I've of late been stepping out on my back patio as the bright morning sun peaks over the horizon, then reading the Bible and speaking and listening to God while bathed in the glory of His beautiful daytime star in the sky, surrounded by the lush, green forest and early morning birdsong.

You, too, will likely find that pairing nature with a morning spiritual practice, or, if time doesn't permit for that, an evening spiritual practice, say, under the stars, can prove even more meaningful or inspirational than reading, praying, meditating, or journaling indoors. After all, as Romans 1:20 tells us, God's invisible attributes, namely, his eternal power and divine nature, have been clearly perceived, ever since the creation of the world, in the things that have been made, which of course, seem to be most loudly and vigorously exclaimed in nature.

But I digress from the topic of this chapter, which is actually about something called *"temperancy."*

See, during one of these recent morning times with God, I was reading in my Bible, and came across a passage in 1 Corinthians 9:25-27, in which the Apostle Paul, one of the leaders of the first generation of Christians and a missionary, philosopher, and author who is often considered to be the most important person (after Jesus) in the history of Christianity, says,

> *"And everyone who competes for the prize is **temperate** in all things. Now they do it to obtain a perishable crown, but we for an*

> *imperishable crown. Therefore I run thus: not with uncertainty. Thus I fight: not as one who beats the air. But I discipline my body and bring it into subjection, lest, when I have preached to others, I myself should become disqualified."*

Paul seems to think of himself as being in something very much like a physical competition that requires focused and careful training, and, as a result, understands the importance of being "temperate in all things," just as an athlete who is striving for mastery. He, like many exercise enthusiasts you may run into these days, also emphasizes his priority placed upon disciplining his body and bringing it into subjection—literally pummeling his body and making it his slave, not in a masochistic, self-harming sense, but rather in the same way that you might imagine when you picture Apollo Creed preparing to fight Ricky Conlan in the recent Rocky film, or even Rocky himself preparing in the harsh Russian winter to fight the Russian fighting phenom Ivan Drago.

In the same way that getting hit in the face during a boxing match means that the stakes are significantly high in *that* scenario, Paul also knew the stakes were high in his scenario—an uphill operation to spread the message of salvation to a world that so desperately needed hope. At this point in his life, Paul had suffered much in his missionary journeys. He had been beaten, stoned, hated, mocked, shipwrecked, snake-bitten, and imprisoned. But yet he seemed to find a strange joy in each of these afflictions, because each trial strengthened his faith in leaps and bounds, and allowed him to become an even stronger missionary and champion for the message of salvation. In other passages of Scripture, Paul describes how he considers his body "as a living sacrifice" (Romans 12:1) for God's kingdom, and says that because he had faithfully run the race set before him (Hebrews 12:1) and that he knew God would be honored not only during his life but also at his death (Philippians 1:19–20).

Paul also knew if he opened himself up to temptation towards excesses of food, sex, money, and other worldly pleasures, if he did not practice self-control, self-discipline, and temperancy, and if he let his body get the upper hand, he was going to be lost, because he could not accomplish his epic journey in a broken, a lazy, an unfit, or an unhealthy body. He knew that he couldn't let his body simply "go to sleep," that to support his soul he must keep his flesh awake and watchful because, as Mark 14:38 says, *"The spirit indeed is willing, but the flesh is weak."*

Yet, this passage from 1 Corinthians also actually made me scratch my head a bit.

Why? Because in 1 Timothy 4:8, Paul says,

> *"For bodily exercise profits a **little**, but godliness is profitable for all things, having promise of the life that now is and of that which is to come."*

So which is it? Should you "discipline your body and bring it into subjection" or should you accept the fact that "bodily exercise profits a *little*" and prioritize godliness over self-care, self-control, and temperancy?

Let's dive in and answer this question, along with addressing what temperancy actually is, and why you should have a good understanding of it if you want to enable yourself to be fully impactful with your unique purpose and skillset in life.

What Is Temperancy?

So what is temperancy, exactly?

Temperancy is, simply put, a state of temperance. There. Now you know. Seriously, though, more specifically, according to Webster's 1828 dictionary (since I, of course, insist upon using very old, brown, and wrinkled reference texts), temperance itself is defined as:

1. *Moderation; particularly, habitual moderation in regard to the indulgence of the natural appetites and passions; restrained or moderate indulgence; as temperance in eating and drinking; temperance in the indulgence of joy or mirth. Temperance in eating and drinking is opposed to gluttony and drunkenness, and in other indulgences, to excess.*

2. *Patience; calmness; sedateness; moderation of passion.*

While you may be familiar with temperance as a reference to a late nineteenth- and early twentieth-century social movement that advocated the *moderate use of or— for some proponents—the total abstinence from the consumption of alcoholic beverages*, the concept has of course been a familiar component of human self-discipline long before that. For example, in the *Pocket Dictionary of Ethics*, temperancy is described as an ethical term that is used in two ways. First, the term denotes a virtue prevalent in both Greek and Christian ethical thought that is associated with moderation and self-control, especially with respect to *desires* and *appetites*, particularly related to the *restraint* of desires and the *mastery* of passions. The Greek philosopher Plato actually considered temperance to be one of four cardinal virtues and spoke of it as the virtue of *self-control*. He described temperance as the use of *reason* and *will* in the mastery of the appetites and the passions. Philosopher and theologian Thomas Aquinas viewed temperance as both a general and specific virtue. In the former sense, as a general virtue, temperance moderates the other moral virtues, whereas in the latter, as a specific virtue, it controls the bodily pleasures. So temperance is associated with both proportion and moral discernment.

Several quotes from notable religious figures in history highlight the importance of temperance related to the overall positive character of a human being, including:

Tyron Edwards, who said, *"Temperance is to the body what religion is to the soul—the foundation of health, strength, and peace."*

John Erskine, *"Temperance is the control of all the functions of our bodies. The man who refuses liquor, goes in for apple pie, and develops a paunch, is no ethical leader for me."*

St. Gregory I, *"If we give more to the flesh than we ought, we nourish our enemy; if we give not to her necessity what we ought, we destroy a citizen."*

C.S. Lewis, *"One great piece of mischief has been done by the modern restriction of the word temperance to the question of drink. It helps people to forget that you can be just as intemperate about lots of other things. A man who makes his gold or his motor bicycle the center of his life, or a woman who devotes all her thoughts to clothes or bridge or her dog, is being just as intemperate as someone who gets drunk every evening. Of course, it does not show on the outside so easily; bridge-mania or golf-mania do not make you fall down in the middle of the road. But God is not deceived by externals."*

William Temple, *"Temperance, that virtue without pride, and fortune without envy, that gives vigor of frame and tranquility of mind; the best guardian of youth and support of old age, the precept of reason as well as religion, the physician of the soul as well as the body, the tutelar goddess of health and universal medicine of life."*

The Apostle Peter, *"Add to your faith...knowledge; And to knowledge temperance: and to temperance patience." (2 Peter 1:5–6)*

And of course, the Apostle Paul, who wrote that, *"Those who sleep at night, and those who are drunk get drunk at night. But since we belong to the day let us be sober."* (1 Thessalonians 5:7–8) and also, *"Deacons must be respectable, not double-tongued, moderate in the amount of wine they drink... Similarly, women must be respectable, not gossips, but sober and wholly reliable."* (1 Timothy 3:8, 11)

The prevailing theme throughout each of these notable tributes to temperancy is a sharp contrast between temperancy and the opposite of temperancy: a lack of sobriety and self-control, not just in the realm of, say, substance abuse with a compound such as alcohol, but also A) abuse of one's body in general, including excesses of food or absences of physical exercise; and B) addiction or attachment to any object in life, both helpful or hurtful. And yes, not to throw any particular demographic under the bus, but this means that the fellas mowing down on Twinkies and Cheetos at a church potluck, their paunches rolling with laughter as they share a six-pack of Coke (in complete contrast to the type of muscular Christianity I introduce in Chapter 7 of *Fit Soul*), and the ladies who spent two hours in front of the mirror getting ready for the potluck are just as intemperate as the drunk stumbling down the sidewalk across the park from them.

This phenomenon of a lack of physical temperance, even amongst those who appear to practice a great deal of spiritual temperance, carries with it hints of *Gnosticism*, which is a philosophy originating in the late 1st century among Jewish and early Christians groups based upon a belief that the body is inherently *bad*, but the spirit is good—that all physical matter is basically *evil* and that only the *spiritual* matter is what demands primary care and attention.

But as Genesis 1 and beyond in the Bible points out, we humans are created as divine image-bearers of God. Our bodies—albeit broken from sin and far from the perfect state they will be restored to in heaven—are not nasty, brutish, evil, dirty things. Certainly, living only for the flesh with neglect of the spirit, which is the entire topic of my last book, *Fit Soul*, is a sinful practice—yet it's also important to understand, as Paul did, that the body is the house or the *temple* for the soul. For example, the Catechism of the Catholic Church says, *"It is a human body precisely because it is animated by a spiritual soul, and it is the whole human person that is intended to become, in the body of Christ, a temple of the Spirit."*

So we are a body and soul together. The body is not just a shell. As I write about in Chapter 18, the Bible does not describe eternity in the afterlife as some kind of disembodied existence in the heavens. Rather, as Romans 8:23 says, *"And not only they, but ourselves also, which have the firstfruits of the Spirit, even we ourselves groan within ourselves, waiting for the adoption, to wit, the redemption of our body."* This verse demonstrates the hope we have in the eventual redemption and resurrection of our physical bodies: the very bodies we live in now. God values these physical bodies and we are called to care for them. I'd even go so far as to say that because we are all made in the image and likeness of God, when we look at our body in the mirror, we are seeing an image of God Himself!

When Temperancy Is Good (& When It's Not)

But of course, temperancy and a prioritization placed upon physical self-care does have the potential to spiral out of control into selfishness and OCD-like tendencies.

For example, think about any category of a healthy life that may lend itself well to temperance, such as running for heart health, intermittent fasting for longevity, lifting heavy stuff to get strong, a yoga practice for mobility, or a strict diet of vegetables and chicken.

Those all sound like reasonable methods of passion-mastery, desire-restraint, and self-control, right?

But, as I tell you in Chapter 2, when habits and thoughts of temperancy spin out of control, becoming so intense and intrusive that they seem to take over against our will or what we know would be a more sane and normal approach to routine, they can turn into all-consuming rituals that are irrationally and often selfishly performed to rid us of an overwhelming sense of fear, dread, and anxiety. This signifies that we may be on a slow slide towards excessive control tendencies or obsessive-compulsive personality disorder.

In other words, *temperancy* can fast become an obsession that detracts from our spiritual health, and often even our physical health too, including:

That lunchtime run you insist on taking each day, so much so that when a co-worker who needs encouragement, compassion, empathy, or friendship asks if you can have lunch with them, you politely decline, because you know how crappy you'll feel about yourself if you don't run, even if you are tired and sore.

That insistence upon a strict daily 16-hour fast, dictating that when your daughter wants to go to breakfast with you, you watch as she awkwardly shoves forkfuls of eggs in her face, as you dutifully sip a black coffee, wishing inside that you could just share a nice meal with her, but not wanting to break your fasting "streak."

That weight training appointment or yoga class you have systematically planned each morning, causing you to cut your meditation, prayer time, journaling, and time with God quite short, or even occasionally cut it out altogether so that you can maintain the hypnotic rhythm of your morning workout.

That refusal to indulge in high-calorie meals or any dish served in rich, fattening foods such as butter, causing you to sit somewhat forlorn and sad at Thanksgiving dinner, munching on a stick of asparagus dipped in cranberry sauce while gazing wistfully at the coconut-creme pie on the table.

See, temperancy is not an act of prudish self-denial or holier-than-thou self-care or guilt-tripping yourself or others for not, say, exercising perfectly and eating perfectly, but rather, temperancy is the ability to moderate and self-control your desires and appetites, and specifically the ability to be able to *restrain* desires and *master* passions. So if you know that you possess the mastery to get up every morning to lift weights, then you also have the mastery to set the alarm clock fifteen minutes earlier to allow for more spiritual care prior to your physical care. If you can restrain yourself on the regular from eating a cinnamon roll slathered in bacon sauce each morning for breakfast as you stroll by the downtown cafe, then you also have the ability to be able to enjoy one of those same cinnamon rolls on a Saturday morning with your family, without fearing a fast, sticky slide into heart failure. If you have the fortitude to run every day at lunch, you also have the fortitude to trust God that skipping a couple of those runs so that you can be there for others more isn't going to suddenly transform you into a couch-lounging, Epicurean Jabba the Hutt.

So enjoy God's creation. Savor it. As I tell you in Chapter 5, eat the fat, drink the milk, eat the honey, lay on your back and gaze at the stars, sip a glass of wine while watching a sunset, and skip a stale gym workout to go for a stroll in green and lush nature.

But if there is any habit, enjoyment, staple, pleasure, pastime, or even necessity in life to which you can not say, as Anthony DeMello so eloquently describes in his book *Awareness*...

> ...."*I really do not need you to be happy. I'm only deluding myself in the belief that without you I will not be happy. But I really don't need you for my happiness; I can be happy without you. You are not my happiness, you are not my joy.*"

...then you risk that temperancy has become your god.

I don't know about you, but I personally enjoy the thought of being a temperate Christian hedonist: soaking up and savoring all of God's creation, with responsibility, self-control, moderation, and a noble and proud mastery of my desires and appetites because I know that my body is a divine image-bearer of God.

How To Be Temperate

One last thing is important to understand.

*When I throw around words such as "self-control," "moderation," and "mastery," there is a risk that I give you the impression that you can simply **will** yourself into temperancy, as the captain of your own ship and master of your own soul.*

There are certainly several effective means of equipping yourself to eat better, move more, break habits, or build new habits. The most effective, in my opinion, is the type of subconscious reprogramming taught in a book such as Joseph Murphy's *Power Of The Subconscious Mind*. The first step in that subconscious reprogramming process is making a purposeful decision to be temperate, very similar to Daniel in Daniel 1:8 who *"purposed in his heart that he would not defile himself with the portion of the king's meat, nor with the wine which he drank:*

therefore he requested of the prince of the eunuchs that he might not defile himself."

But the fact of the matter is that to build true and lasting temperance based upon a worldview perspective and life purpose of loving God and loving others, you cannot simply, as Benjamin Hardy describes in his book *Willpower Doesn't Work*, will yourself into temperance, nor can you "go it alone" with even the most powerful of mental habit-breaking or habit-building strategies.

Instead, you must:

1. **Eliminate those temptations in your life that draw you away from temperance.** Jesus, who I firmly believe was not only a deity but also the greatest philosopher that ever walked this planet, said in his epic Sermon On The Mount in Matthew 5:29-30: *"If your right eye causes you to sin, pluck it out and cast it from you; for it is more profitable for you that one of your members perish, than for your whole body to be cast into hell. And if your right hand causes you to sin, cut it off and cast it from you; for it is more profitable for you that one of your members perish, than for your whole body to be cast into hell."* This means that if you are snacking on too much chocolate-peanut butter ice cream after dinner, you should duct tape your mouth and also consider hunting down a hacksaw to lop off your ice cream-grabbing fingers. Just kidding. But it does mean that ice cream probably shouldn't be in your freezer until you've built adequate temperance to control that craving. That vape pen that you're hitting too hard at night for relaxation? Toss it in the trash if you really can't resist. Porn? Install blocking software (I'll give some good options on the resources webpage for this chapter) on your browser (and read Chapter 3). Prioritization of time in Scripture? Hide away any books by your bedside except the Bible. You get the idea.

2. **Understand that any ability to control your appetites, emotions, and attitudes is not based on your strength or will, but rather, is rooted in God's power—a topic I address when I teach you in Chapter 15 about the "atomic power" of tactics such as prayer and fasting.** Ephesians 5:18 says, *"And be not drunk with wine, wherein is excess; but be filled with the Spirit."* In other words, it is the power of the Holy Spirit that increases your capacity to resist sin and strengthens any resolution towards temperancy. No matter how hard you try, you can't work or will yourself into full mastery of your carnal desires. You will eventually crash and burn if you

attempt to fight sin based on your own strength. Think again to the words of Mark 14:38: *"The spirit indeed is willing, but the flesh is weak."* So temperance is not a skill you develop through blood, sweat, tears, and self-denial. It is instead a by-product of a Spirit-filled life. If you have accepted the simple message of salvation I outlined in this chapter and have cast all your heavy burdens, shame, guilt, and sin of the past at the foot of the cross, then allowed the fruits of love, joy, peace, patience, kindness, goodness, faithfulness, gentleness, and self-control to subsequently pour into your life, and finally, soaked yourself daily in the spiritual disciplines of devotions, prayer, meditation, gratitude, journaling, worship, love for God and love for others, temperance transforms from a teeth-grittingly difficult (and ultimately futile) attempt to fight against your own flesh, to a joyful process of responsibly caring for the divine body that houses your eternal soul so that your body, your brain, and your spirit are prepared to make maximum impact with the life you've been blessed with.

Does this mean that when you eliminate temptations that surround you and rely upon God's power that *everything* will be smooth sailing and that resistance to temptation will come effortlessly with pure ease and flow? Not exactly.

I personally still have to check myself and often find myself saying no, but with hesitation, when I'm at a steakhouse and the waiter asks if I want a second or third cocktail.

I still struggle when a scantily clad woman walks by me on the sidewalk and I'm tempted to mentally cheat on my wife.

When things get stressful on a long work day, I sometimes find myself around 4 or 5 pm thinking of ducking out for kava, or weed, or wine, or the soft lounger chair in the living room, rather than putting my nose to the grindstone and maintaining focus, productivity, and purpose-filled activities for the few remaining hours of the work day.

It's often hard to push myself away from the table when I want to keep stuffing my face, but know the health and temperancy values of the concept of Hara hachi bu (a Japanese term meaning "Eat until you're 80% full").

I still struggle, too, with selfish forms of temperancy, such as spending too much time focused on self-care, or squeezing in just a "few more minutes" at the gym, or spending a disproportionate amount of morning time on physical care vs.

TEMPERATE

spiritual care.

But ultimately, through 1.) intelligent elimination or hiding away of those temptations I know I'm most pulled towards—temptations that I know will pull me away from being impactful with my life's purpose—and 2.) reliance upon God and His power with deep focus placed upon the spiritual disciplines, I am slowly mastering the fine art of savoring and embracing God's creation while simultaneously being a "temperate Christian hedonist."

After all, as 1 Corinthians 10:13 says...

> ..."No temptation has overtaken you that is not common to man. God is faithful, and He will not let you be tempted beyond your ability, but with the temptation He will also provide the way of escape, that you may be able to endure it."

Summary

Look, God made *all* things good.

Yep, all of it, even those things we are tempted to abuse and even those things that threaten to rip us away from temperancy. If you haven't read it yet, then go back to Chapter 5 and read up on what I told about sticky-sugary-syrupy and thick and creamy honey, buttery, frothing, sweet and fresh milk, spicy aromatic olive oil, fine wine and more.

So be temperate, but check yourself regularly to ensure that you're not being intemperate with your temperancy.

> **Wine?** You bet God adores a fine aged Bordeaux and a bold California cab accompanied by a moist slice of sourdough bread dipped in spicy, aromatic olive oil or salted and slathered in fresh blueberry preserves!
>
> As a matter of fact, the richness and value of food and drink is all over the Bible...
>
> Proverbs 24:13 gives sage advice from a father to a son, *"My son, eat honey because it is good, And the honeycomb which is sweet to your*

taste."

The Song of Solomon 5:1 weaves honey, milk, spices, and wine into one of the greatest love poems of all time: *"I have come to my garden, my sister, my bride; I have gathered my myrrh with my spice. I have eaten my honeycomb with my honey; I have drunk my wine with my milk. Eat, O friends, and drink; drink freely, O beloved."*

In Deuteronomy 31:20, God blesses the Israelites as he, *"brought them to the land flowing with milk and honey, of which I swore to their fathers..."*

And Deuteronomy 32:13-14 reveals a similar blessing, with fruit, honey, oil, curds, milk, fat, wheat, and wine all woven in:

> *"He made him ride in the heights of the earth,*
> *That he might eat the produce of the fields;*
> *He made him draw honey from the rock,*
> *And oil from the flinty rock;*
> *Curds from the cattle, and milk of the flock,*
> *With fat of lambs;*
> *And rams of the breed of Bashan, and goats,*
> *With the choicest wheat;*
> *And you drank wine, the blood of the grapes."*

Nehemiah 9:25-26 describes how the Israelites *"...took strong cities, and a fat land, and possessed houses full of all goods, wells digged, vineyards, and oliveyards, and fruit trees in abundance: so they did eat, and were filled, and became fat, and delighted themselves in thy great goodness."*

Lest you wonder whether corn chips, polenta slathered with meatballs and cheese, a pint of beer, and a handful of salted almonds also fall under God's love and blessing, consider the words of James 1:17, which tells us that *"Every good gift is from God,"* and in John 3:1, we learn that *"All things were made by him; and without him was not anything made that was made."*

So yes, that means that an Almighty God formed and fashioned the cacao tree, the cannabis plant, the chickpea, and the catfish—and all this marvelous bounty is ours to enjoy in all of its intricacy, beauty, and tastiness—and even for its medicinal uses (1 Timothy 5:23, *"Drink no longer water, but use a little wine for thy stomach's sake and thine often infirmities."*).

Yet Proverbs 25:16 warns, *"Have you found honey? Eat only as much as you need, Lest you be filled with it and vomit,"* and Proverbs 27:7, *"The soul that is full loathes honey, but to a hungry soul, any bitter thing is sweet."*

The principle behind wise King Solomon's advice in these verses is that over-indulgence, even of good things created and given to us by God, will surely make us sick. That's right: that same precious honey can quickly become poison in the hands of a fool or a glutton. And yes, you can consider honey to be a metaphor for any good thing from God that we wrongly abuse.

Choose anything in your life that is a habit, enjoyment, staple, pleasure, pastime, or even necessity. Any of those "honeys" of life—even non-food items like cars, homes, money, golf, exercising, or even other people. If you cannot look at that object and say, as Anthony DeMello so eloquently describes in his book *Awareness*,

"I really do not need you to be happy. I'm only deluding myself in the belief that without you I will not be happy. But I really don't need you for my happiness; I can be happy without you. You are not my happiness, you are not my joy."

...then you risk that your blessing *from* God has *become* your God."

At the same time, enjoy God's creation and don't live a life saturated with glum self-denial.

Finally, understand that willpower is not going to grant you temperancy. Instead, a temperate life is achieved through the removal of temptations that you know you're drawn towards, combined with reliance upon the power of the Holy Spirit to provide you with *restraint* of desires and *mastery* of passions.

How about you? Are there areas in your life in which you have identified a need for greater temperance? If so, what are those areas and how do you plan to tackle temperancy? Do you find yourself

selfishly pulled towards excesses of temperancy, often manifested in imbalanced time placed upon self-care or health optimization? How do you deal with that, or plan on dealing with that?

For resources, references, links and additional reading and listening material for this chapter, visit GetEndure.com/Chapter7.

PART III

PURPOSE & PRODUCTIVITY

*Work deep, create beauty,
and experience rest and refreshment.*

CHAPTER VIII

SOUL

I very, very rarely watch movies and typically will only sit down to view a flick if it's been recommended to me at least half a dozen times, is "Certified Fresh" on Rotten Tomatoes with a 90% score or higher, and passes muster for "cleanliness" on websites such as CommonSenseMedia.org or ScreenIt.com. That's my general criteria at least, and based on that criteria, I wind up watching about three to four movies a year, tops.

Anyways, this rare occasion recently occurred, and so I watched the Pixar movie Soul, which is the story of a jazz pianist named Joe (voiced by the supremely talented Jamie Foxx) who has a near-death experience and gets stuck in the afterlife, subsequently contemplating his choices and regretting an existence that he mostly took for granted. I'll admit: I was initially a bit concerned that Soul could heavily conflict with my own personal, Christian views of the origin and destination of souls, the afterlife, near-death experiences, and how heaven and hell work; but ultimately—though it did indeed have several inaccuracies in that respect (read Randy Alcorn's book Heaven and read Chapter 18 for a more accurate perspective)—it did turn out to be what I was impressed with as a really, really great movie that resulted in three meaningful takeaways I'll share with you in this chapter.

Oh, and should you not yet have seen *Soul*, I promise no enormously significant spoilers.

Three Important Life Lessons From Pixar's Movie, Soul

1. Stop & Smell The Roses

Often, we're encouraged to pursue our passions in life and, to be fully self-actualized, to form our core purpose around those passions, which I discuss in my "How To Find Your Purpose" chapter in my book Fit Soul.

You'll find that if you're implementing this advice, it can become quite easy to get so immersed in your work and in tackling your life's purpose, that you occasionally forget to slow down and mindfully enjoy the smaller things in life. For example, I can personally become so completely immersed in and nearly obsessed with reading, writing, learning, and teaching—via activities such as working on articles, having podcast discussions with interesting people, consulting with clients, or reading and researching materials I'm fascinated with—that I fail to notice the majestic mountains just outside my office window, the flavor of the peppermint gum in my mouth, the aromas diffusing from the essential oil diffuser on my desktop, or the singsong of birds in my backyard.

In the movie, we see the character "22," a new soul on planet Earth, experience a deep sense of joy and wonder from seemingly mundane activities such as eating a pepperoni pizza, listening to a musician in the subway, or seeing a child. We also see souls who are so obsessed with their work and so immersed in "The Zone" while caught up in their passion that they become transported to an entirely new dimension that puts them into an out-of-body experience, which seems great, but also largely disconnects them from the wonders of their day-to-day physical existence.

So yes, possess a passion in life. But don't become so passionate and so caught up in an activity you enjoy that you forget to enjoy the small things in life. In other words, practice mindfulness. The little things are important, too. We live on a magical planet chock-full of the wonders of God's creation, and it'd be a shame to let them slip by because you're so focused on and obsessed with creating maximum impact with your life. As I write about in Chapter 9 living life to the fullest and experiencing what it truly means to be a human requires elegantly combining the *doing* with the *being*.

As with the other two important life lessons below, I'll include my favorite Bible verse on this matter.

> *Ecclesiastes 8:15: "And I commend joy, for man has nothing better under the sun but to eat and drink and be joyful, for this will go with him in his toil through the days of his life that God has given him under the sun."*

2. The Grass Is Always Greener

In one section of the movie, Joe lives his "dream moment" by experiencing the musical jazz performance of his life on stage. You'd think he would be absolutely over the moon and finally fulfilled by having checked that box. But as he wanders out of the nightclub, he turns to his companions and asks, *"What now?"* His saxophone-playing diva bandmate Dorothea Williams proceeds to tell Joe the story of a small fish swimming up to a bigger, older fish and asking where the ocean is. The fish elder explains that they are in the ocean. But the little fish replies, "No, this is just water, I want *the ocean*!"

So what's the moral of this tiny parable? In short, we often don't realize the satisfaction and meaning that already surrounds us because we're so caught up in trying to reach a destination or make it to the top of some Mount Everest we've painted in our heads as the perfect destination. We should perhaps stop and ponder whether, as we try to get out of the water to get into the ocean, we've actually already found and are immersed *in* the ocean.

For example, your quest for a job promotion may be sucking all the happiness out of your life because your current job may be exactly where you're supposed to be right now, and what you were meant to do. Your excess hard work for a better body may be wasting plenty of time you could instead be spending with friends, family, or engaged in other hobbies because your body is, well, just *fine* as it currently is. Your constant search for the perfect church, or social group, or team, or tribe may be blinding you to the fact that you're meant to bloom exactly where you've been planted, which is the field you're in right *now*. Perhaps you should consider that you've *already made it*, and the next best thing for you to do is to simply savor each moment of where you are with mindfulness, gratefulness, and enjoyment.

This shouldn't be used as an excuse to become passive and complacent in life, or to ditch the idea of constant improvement, but should instead be used as permission to become content with where you are right now, even if you have aspirations to become a better, more impactful person with each consecutive day. For more on being satisfied with seemingly mundane tasks you may do each day, rather than searching for the next big thing, read Chapter 11 and also consider beginning a daily gratitude practice, which I teach you how to do in Chapter 10 of *Fit Soul*.

> Philippians 4:11-13: *"Not that I speak from want, for I have learned to be content in whatever circumstances I am. I know how to get along with humble means, and I also know how to live in prosperity; in any and every circumstance I have learned the secret of being filled and going hungry, both of having abundance and suffering. I can do all things through Him who strengthens me."*

3. Find Your Spark.

Part of the film involves the concept of a "Great Before," where souls find their unique "spark" before venturing to Earth to be born as a baby and join the mortal coil. At first, as I was watching *Soul*, I thought, similar to Joe, that the special "spark" every soul was searching for was the same as their purpose in life. In other words, you must be fully self-actualized and working in your dream job to experience true meaning and happiness as a human. But it turns out that really isn't the case. As one character named Jerry in the movie says,

> *"A spark isn't a soul's purpose! Oh, you mentors and your passions. Your purposes, your meanings-of-life. So basic."*

The lesson here is *not* quite to give up on, say, pursuing your dream job. The lesson is to let go of the idea that having a dream job in which you are fully self-actualized and immersed in a magical marrying of your work and your passion is the *only* path to happiness and fulfillment. Instead, your spark can be simple. Your spark can be strumming the guitar after a long day at the office. Your spark can be nightly family dinners and evening storytime with your children. Your spark can be cooking yourself a fantastic meal when you've returned from your daily routine of chopping wood and carrying water. Your spark doesn't *have* to contribute to society. It doesn't *have* to earn you money. It doesn't *have* to be molded and contextualized within the idea of a life's purpose.

This is helpful for me personally. It means I can whip out my guitar after a day of writing, researching, consulting, coaching, podcasting, and doing all those other purposeful activities and simply play the guitar because it brings me joy, because I love how the wood and strings feel against my fingers, and because I adore the sensation as every sound wave of a plucked string vibrates every cell in my body. I can sing and play *not* so that I can someday "make it" on YouTube or step on stage in front of throngs of adoring fans to play my next hit single, but rather because it simply makes me happy. It's my spark.

Every meal I cook doesn't have to be an Instagram sensation or take me one step closer to competitive network cooking show fame.

Every kettlebell I swing doesn't have to get me that much closer to kicking someone's butt in a kettlebell swing competition.

Every time I get dressed up to go out to a fancy dinner, it can be just for me and my enjoyment of God's creation—from the variety of colors I choose, to the fabrics against my skin, to the scent of the fragrance I spray on my neck. It can be not to impress others or get noticed or strike the fancy of some businessperson who may want to do a deal with me because I'm dressed nicely, but rather, it can simply be for the pure sake of the action itself.

So sure, you absolutely do need to have clearly identified and be pursuing your purpose in life, your "Ikigai," as they say in Okinawa or your "Plan De Vida," as they say in Sardinia, but you can also have enjoyments in life that are simply your personal *spark*. The purpose is the doing, and the spark is the being. If both overlap, then great. You're blessed. But if not, that's OK, too. As Joe's mother tells him in the film, "Passion doesn't pay the bills." I agree, or at least I agree that your passion doesn't *have* to pay the bills.

> *Matthew 6:25-34: "Therefore I tell you, do not be anxious about your life, what you will eat or what you will drink, nor about your body, what you will put on. Is not life more than food, and the body more than clothing? Look at the birds of the air: they neither sow nor reap nor gather into barns, and yet your heavenly Father feeds them. Are you not of more value than they? And which of you by being anxious can add a single hour to his span of life? And why are you anxious about clothing? Consider the lilies of the field, how they grow: they neither toil nor spin, yet I tell you, even Solomon in all his glory was not arrayed like one of these. But if God so clothes the grass of the field, which today is alive and tomorrow is thrown into the oven, will he not much more clothe you, O you of little faith? Therefore do not be anxious, saying, 'What shall we eat?' or 'What shall we drink?' or 'What shall we wear?' For the Gentiles seek after all these things, and your heavenly Father knows that you need them all. But seek first the*

kingdom of God and his righteousness, and all these things will be added to you."

Summary

So the message is quite simple, and there are really just three big takeaways from the film that I thought valuable to share with you:

- *Stop and smell the roses. Enjoy the smaller things in life. Don't let the simple pleasures pass you by. God loves for us to be joyful as we enjoy His creation.*

- *The grass is always going to be greener. Consider the fact that you may have already "made it" and now your job is to simply do the very best you can each day and savor God's blessings.*

- *Find your spark. Your spark doesn't have to be your life's purpose or something that is part of your career. It can simply involve engaging in activities that feed your soul and make you happy, even if those activities seem trite or don't "advance your career" in some way. Don't worry about doing so much: God will take care of you.*

How about you? What is your approach to digesting media such as movies and gleaning valuable life information from the story woven into the cinema? Just as importantly, do you stop to smell the roses, get up in the morning and do the very best job you can with whatever God has placed upon your plate for the day, and include frequent little sparks in life that feed your soul? If not, what do you plan to change?

For resources, references, links and additional reading and listening material for this chapter, visit GetEndure.com/Chapter8.

CHAPTER IX

CREATE

I pride myself on getting things done.

Heck, people often congratulate and compliment me about how hard I hustle.

Yep, I'm productive. I'm a "do-er." I make sh*t happen. I check off just about every box one would expect to have checked off as a metric of corporate and professional success in life. I'm like a friggin' robot—I wake, I buffet my body, I crush the day, I digest a massive amount of information, and I produce a ton o' content.

Yin  Yang

Yin	Yang
Dark	Light
Hidden	Obvious
Wavering	Direct
Feminine	Masculine
Round	Straight
Flexible	Solid
Night	Day
Moon	Sun
Passive	Active
Ice	Fire
Shade	Light
Wet	Dry
Slow	Fast
Tired	Lively
Soft	Hard
Earth	Sky
Internal	Eternal
Winter/Fall	Summer/Spring
Left	Right
Interior	Exterior
Negative Charge	Positive Charge
Intuition	Logic
Rest	Movement
Calm	Energetic
Soothing	Vibrant
Tiger	Dragon
Storage	Usage
Quiet	Loud
Receptive	Creative
Death	Life
Closed Space	Open Space

Not only that, but I'm a *man's man*. That's right: I'm hardcore, I'm macho and I'm muscular. I can brag about a bio that champions me as a guy who has traveled the globe for decades proving my manhood in some of the most masochistic events known to humankind. I can post flex shots to Instagram that publicly portray my chiseled body in all its fleshly glory. I swing heavy kettlebells, swim in icy cold water, and "defy aging." Heck, in a display of skills that society deems highly noble and honorable, I've shown that—from bowhunting to spearfishing to barbecuing to lovemaking—I can protect, provide, and procreate with the best of 'em.

Oh yeah, by all definitions of the word, I'm yang, baby.

Yay me, right?

You'd never have guessed that I grew up as president of the chess club, a violin virtuoso, a watercolor painting enthusiast, a devourer of every fantasy fiction book I could get my hands on, and a kid whose idea of a fantastic Sunday afternoon was to get symphony tickets and go sit in the balcony with my eyes closed making up princess and dragon stories inside my head while smiling and tapping my feet to the reverberating orchestral tunes.

Screw that. Long ago, in my teenage years, I left all *that* tomfoolery behind. After all, artsy-fartsy boys don't get the girls, aren't hard to kill, and bear no resemblance to the Rocky Balboa macho warrior I spent hours watching in my bedroom while pumping iron and flexing in the mirror—all the while quietly convincing myself *that's* the hero the world needed, wanted, and expected me to be.

So yep: I traded in my violin for the electric guitar, my watercolor brushes for a barbell, and all my fiction books for hardcore science manuals. Rigid, rational, logical, unemotional, productive, take-no-prisoners mentality ruled the day, and served to fuel my seemingly successful rise to the top that I describe in my book Fit Soul.

But along the way, I lost something—something very important and something that, as I look around me at all the other "successful" men and women, I think that many others have lost, too. In this chapter, I'll tell you exactly what that is and how to become a more complete and happy human by rediscovering and reclaiming that missing element.

When Did You Stop Dreaming, Singing & Dancing?

My friend, and former podcast guest Paul Chek, has a little song that he likes to sing to his patients when he is doing emotional healing work with them. It goes like this:

> *"I am happy*
> *I am healthy*
> *I am Whole*
> *I take my love wherever I go."*

Thing is, as Paul details in an article that I'll link to on the resources webpage for this chapter, when he asks his clients to sing along, many seem held back due to some kind of internal fear or blocking factor. The three questions he then proceeds to ask them are:

1. When did you stop dreaming?

2. When did you stop singing?

3. When did you stop dancing?

Interestingly, the time that a person stops dreaming (*and this could include elements such as, say, reading fiction, storytelling, or even watching funny movies instead of all, say, non-fiction and documentaries*), singing (*including sacrificing podcast and audiobook time to instead listen to a heart-warming or soul-exciting new album from your favorite band, or perhaps nostalgic songs from your youth*), and dancing (*which does not necessarily mean taking formal ballroom dance classes or playing Dance Dance Revolution in the basement, but could arguably include everything from ecstatic raving to wild acts of lovemaking*)...

...often correlates to a specific time and/or event(s) that disrupted that person's natural state of inner-harmony and led to the injury or illness they are experiencing.

Paul says:

> *"When we grow to the point that we finally realize that our body and*

relationships mirror our mind, we can look back, and typically we see that it was during stressful and often unresolved transition points in our lives that we lost our authentic harmony and creative impulse."

Paul then encourages those of his clients who feel blocked in their ability to join in his little ditty because the voices in their head are judging, or telling them how silly this is, to be brave enough to give this harmless practice a try, citing the old saying: "Being happy may not make you sing, but singing will make you happy!"

And while I fully agree with Paul that the absence of dreaming, singing, dancing (and any other element of creative, free, artistic flow) in one's life does indeed often manifest in an overall unharmonious imbalance and eventually an injury or illness, I'm not quite convinced there needs to be a single factor such as an intense trauma, a broken relationship, or a horrific accident that sparks that loss of creativity. I instead think that for many people, including myself, the fading away of our youthful, happy, and carefree dreaming, singing, and dancing can occur gradually over an extended period of time as we become more and more mindful of fulfilling the basic survival elements of Maslow's hierarchy of needs (find food, make money, start a family, get a home, etc.) and more and more obsessed with and satisfied with doing, accomplishing, and producing to the ultimate and sad sacrifice of being, savoring, and creating.

THE HYPNOTIC RHYTHM

So, in addition to our gradual tendency as we become full-fledged "grown-ups" to shove free, artistic, creative flow and elements such as dreaming, singing, and dancing to the side in our relentless pursuit to instead climb the mountain of success (which, as outlined so well in the book *The Second Mountain* we often tend to look down from to realize we weren't really climbing the most fulfilling mountain in the first place)...

...what else keeps us from dreaming, singing, and dancing?

I would argue that it is the "hypnotic rhythm."

The *what?*

That's right: the hypnotic rhythm. Although he's perhaps better known for his book *Think & Grow Rich*, American self-help author Napoleon Hill (born October 26, 1883, died November 8, 1970) also wrote a lesser-known but, in my opinion, just as life-changing a book titled *Outwitting The Devil*. In the book, Hill describes what he calls the hypnotic rhythm, which is a law of subconscious human nature that tends to slowly solidify our habits and make them a permanent part of our lives, often without us even noticing how powerful and addictive those habits may have become.

These rhythms are the things we do that we don't even tend to think about: the daily automatic actions we take that are built into our existence—everything from brushing our teeth to checking our e-mail to scrolling through a set number of social media feeds (e.g. the vicious loop of Instagram to Twitter to Facebook to Slack to the e-mail inbox and then 20 minutes later back through again) to even more time-consuming OCD-like tendencies I describe in Chapter 2 such as performing a set, specific workout on a designated day of the week (come hell or high water), eating a specific way no matter *what*, or becoming locked into a certain manner of living, working, or interacting with people—that can indeed become long-lasting habits that lend to the structure and order that can create success. But, these habits can also bring about misery and permanent failure or unfulfillment, particularly as we become resistant to any semblance of change or the ability to be able to embrace free, creative flow that rips us out of the rhythm we've grown to associate with control, safety and survival.

In other words, it is the hypnotic rhythm that dictates you *must* listen to that 30-minute financial news podcast on your daily commute, even though every shred of your soul is craving is to crank up the radio with rock music like you did when you were a carefree teenager; you *must* hit the weights at the gym even though all those guys and girls out playing noon basketball look like they're having way more fun and that's what you would have done in college; or you *must* be the responsible person at the party engaged in polite conversation in the corner instead of ripping moves on the dance floor like nobody's watching.

Hill describes how this hypnotic rhythm becomes a built-in, automated part of our lives via a three-step process of *1) action; 2) habit; 3) rhythm*. Actions, including our thoughts, are the things we do that we have complete control over. We consciously decide whether or not these actions come into being. When we repeat the actions long enough, they become *habits*, the things that we do to give us our daily momentum and help us feel safe and comfortable as we navigate life. It's possible for us to stray from these habits, but as they become more and more solidified in our lives, we tend to repeatedly return to them.

If those habits are repeated long enough, they then become—you guessed it—a hypnotic *rhythm*. This is when the habit becomes a part of what is called our "phenomenological level." In other words, those habits become linked to our identity and how we define ourselves. For example, I simply *am* that person who gets up at 6 am to go on a morning jog, vs., God forbid, occasionally staying in bed and making love to my spouse. I *am* that person who drinks black coffee every morning so that I maintain my strict intermittent fasting protocol day-in and day-out, though that matcha green tea with coconut oil and stevia recipe looks like a fun little change-up. I *am* that person who slips away after dinner to read a book in my office, though my kids really want to go outside and stargaze. These habits eventually get put on subconscious autopilot, and at that point, the actions associated with each habit require basically no willpower at all. At this stage, we may find that we have almost no control over those very actions, whether they produce good or bad fruit in our lives.

Related to Hill's ideas of the development of a scarcity mindset and our tendency to be able to think and manifest what it is that we eventually become—whether that be abundance or scarcity—a concept Hill explores in *Think & Grow Rich*, he says:

> "Nature uses hypnotic rhythm to make one's dominating thoughts and one's thought-habits permanent. That is why poverty is disease. Nature makes it so by fixing permanently the thought-habits of all who accept poverty as an unavoidable circumstance."

In this instance, Hill is referring to us being able to think our way into poverty by allowing thoughts of scarcity to become our dominant thought pattern. However, I would propose that in the same way you can think yourself into being poor (again, you can read the entire book *Think & Grow Rich* to fully grasp this concept, and I'll link to it and the other books I mention in this chapter on the resources webpage), you can think yourself into an automatic habit loop (a hypnotic rhythm) of constantly *doing* instead of *being*, and thus think yourself into a habit loop that gradually pulls you out of all the fun, creative things you may have enjoyed to do as a child, such as dreaming, singing, and dancing.

In the book *Denial Of Death* by Ernest Becker, this type of controlled action that eventually becomes an automated habit is described as a way for us to escape the stressors of life. For instance, many people overwork during periods of anxiety and stress. This habitual pattern of overworking not only distracts us from impending anxious thoughts, but it can reinstill in us a lost sense of control, functioning as a kind of safety net that not only protects us from fear of death, but from fear of life as well. To avoid the uncontrollable lows and the irrepressible highs often experienced during creative free flow or stepping outside our controlled comfort zone, we tend to stick to what we know, burrowing ourselves in routine and complacency.

Danish theologian and philosopher Søren Kierkegaard describes this type of person as an "automatic cultural man," someone who accepts the reality that culture provides, seeking to actualize their identity within the carefully sketched lines of society—what the world expects them to be (rather than their true, authentic self). Struck by the horror of creative freedom and its multitude of possibilities, we can experience overwhelming anxiety and loss of control, and thus suppress most semblances of freedom whatsoever, eventually descending into—you guessed it—our predictable, controllable hypnotic rhythm. Painting with watercolor is messy and sometimes unpredictable, but reading science is predictable. Dancing is expressive, flowing, and also sometimes unpredictable, but our daily visit to the gym involves a series of rote exercises fully within our control. Dreaming, fantasizing, reading fiction, singing, learning new recipes, and other forms of creative expression, though often what we *really want to do* in the moment, suddenly pull us out of being able to control or experience predictable outcomes, and it becomes so much less anxiety-inducing or bothersome to instead bury ourselves in checklists of work.

Flow Vs. Function

And now, having just turned 39 years old at the time of this writing, as I approach what could very well be the halfway point of my life, I've realized that I've reached that very point myself: often stuck in a daily hypnotic rhythm of control and predictability, operating as an automatic cultural man who is much like what the world expects me to be and indeed congratulates me upon being (a functional hard-charging, hardcore, high-achiever) and much less like what my internal soul at many times craves to be (a flowing, creative, soft, romantic lover of art, fiction, and music).

I give you the full details on exactly how this gradual slide from creativity happened to me in Chapter 2 but I'll add one additional thought here regarding the common formation of hypnotic rhythm, because much of this process is neurologically based.

As a guy who works, consults, advises, and writes in the realm of health and fitness, I'll give you an example from that specific world, because I tend to see the pattern I'm going to describe to you repeatedly in clients I coach. Take the hypnotic rhythm of a daily exercise routine for example, which is a somewhat laudable effort (the Apostle Paul says in 1 Timothy 4:8 that physical training is of *"some value"*), but an effort that can nonetheless lead to selfishness, sacrificing other more important activities for the holy workout, or even ignoring a pull towards creative activities such as painting or playing a musical instrument because the gym must be hit at all costs.

Often, this rhythm begins with *food*. This train to eat/eat to train cycle can easily pull one into what, from a neurological standpoint, can be a highly hypnotic rhythm.

Allow me to illustrate.

Let's say that you—the privileged modern human living in an environment surrounded by a calorie-rich, highly-palatable abundance of foods—swings open the refrigerator in the evening and are struck with pangs of guilt over the cornucopia of food that spilleth forth, often in addition to the reams of energy bars and superfood powders filling the nearby pantry. So you gorge yourself on a fantastic, tasty, nourishing, calorie and nutrient-dense, rich dinner (after all, it's not like it's fried chicken, pizza, and ice cream for crying out loud—just a bunch of wild-caught fish, sweet potato fries and dark chocolate), then perhaps make yourself a nighttime post-dinner treat of some kind of ketogenic fat bomb recipe comprised of coconut milk, chocolate collagen, and maybe some raw honey. Before you know it, you've stuffed yourself with over a thousand calories, but that's OK because you have a grand, soul-punishing, body-buffeting workout planned for the next morning. In addition, from a neurological standpoint, this feel-good meal has charged you up with a massive hit of dopamine and serotonin.

You get up the next morning, perhaps *briefly* (but ever-so-briefly, because the workout awaits) glance at some kind of devotional or spiritually uplifting book, jot for a few moments in a gratitude journal, then head out to do what you *really* want to do: burn all those calories that are fresh on your mind from the night before and pat yourself on the back for making your body stronger, fitter, and harder to kill. After all, we've already established that the world deems that type of yang-method of starting the morning to be a quite noble and laudable way to launch one's day off to a good start.

So off you rush to the health club or home gym to throw down your daily workout, which fills you with another big surge of dopamine and serotonin—not only for having "checked something off" your to-do list for the day, but also because exercise in and of itself is a positively addicting effort and, as my friend and neuroscientist Dr. Andrew Huberman teaches, any type of physical forward movement or progress can serve as a potent remedy for fear, stress, anxiety, depression, etc. Incidentally, this is why one of the more common forms of exercise for people who are trying to A) excessively control their lives; B) escape pain; or C) both A and B tend to love things like treadmills or jogging, stationary or real bicycles, frequent walking, swimming, or any other forms of chronic repetitive motion. (Dr. Huberman explains that this is because when you face adversity, forward progress suppresses the amygdala and you subsequently secrete dopamine as a response to making steps forward.)

But of course, gosh-darn-it, you must now eat again to refuel. So you rush back to the kitchen or cafeteria to prepare yourself an 800-calorie superfoods smoothie, which satisfies two burning needs: 1) to make a dent in all that food you bought that you don't want to go to waste; 2) to top up your body's energy stores in preparation for the next day's or afternoon's dopamine-surging workout.

Then it's off to work, where you can escape for a while, make some money, check off your checklists, and do a whole lot more "doing." The next day, and the next, and the next, you do the same thing. After all, God forbid you miss your streak of physical activity you've kept up so well the past several months, or allow your scarcity mindset to allow you to take a break from work.

Do, do, do.

Workout, eat, work, workout, eat, work, workout, eat, work.

Train-to-eat, eat-to-train. Make money. It's great, right? You're staying healthy, paying the bills, and simultaneously enjoying oodles of lovely, calorie-dense, highly palatable food that in any other circumstance would probably make you, well, fat.

Problem is, by relying upon food and exercise and work as your three primary modes of sparking up rewarding neurotransmitters, you're essentially keeping your brain "satisfied" within a relatively narrow band of the full spectral experience of life—in this case, that narrow band being eating, exercising, and checking off your checklists while making money in your business or place of employment in between all the eating and exercising. Now don't get me wrong: Neither eating, nor exercising, nor making money are inherently *bad*, nor should you feel *guilty* about these activities, but I have repeatedly witnessed in both myself and in others (particularly within the fitness and health industry) the tendency to become so myopically obsessed with these three activities that very little character growth or neurotransmitter-sparking occurs outside the context of eating, exercise, and business. Folks seem to get so consumed with nutrition and fitness and work that there's simply little or no time remaining for painting, music, singing, dancing, dreaming, or just lying around reading a thrilling fiction book.

It's a hard cycle to break, too.

After all, even if you do, say, sacrifice some or all of your planned afternoon workout to instead paint a butterfly, based on your hypnotic rhythm, you still probably swing open the refrigerator an hour later and consume your massive workout-fueling dinner, which makes you feel guilty and/or fat and/or lazy and/or unhealthy immediately after, and so you plan for the next afternoon to skip the painting nonsense and go crush the gym instead. That, or you stay up late at night catching up on all that extra work you "missed" to instead paint. Or you do both the exercise punishment and the work to make up for the lost time spent in creativity.

This can create a quite yang, hardcore, do-do-do scenario that continually pulls you away from anything that can produce a pleasurable response besides eating and exercising. But, nobody lies on their deathbed with the satisfying feeling that they were a good exerciser, or managed to eat quite a few calories in their lifetime. The more rewarding deathbed moments come from reflecting upon activities such as meaningful friendships and relationships, good acts done for the world, meaningful experiences often enjoyed with others, or masterful works of art or music one may have created.

Perhaps the example above doesn't resonate with you.

Perhaps it's a completely foreign concept for you to imagine a person who enjoys eating weird foods and exercising a lot.

But your hypnotic rhythm may be something else. It may be that endless cycle of social-media-feed-checking or online-news-website-monitoring that you find yourself sucked into each day and every day, unable to break your streak of "check-ins." It may be a constant consumption of non-fiction podcasts and audiobooks, with absolutely no room allowed for music or fiction. It may be the slot machines or the poker table. It may be the full hour you spend every morning on beauty and self-care. It may be golfing. It may simply be slipping away to work and getting things off your checklist whenever you have a free moment, even in the wee hours of the evening.

As a matter of fact, you get the same rewarding neurotransmitter release from any of the activities I've just listed as you do from a vicious cycle of excessively eating and exercising or overworking. And, if any of these items are near-automatic, built-in, subconscious, rote activities that require very little creativity, loss-of-control, challenge, discomfort, or even the perception of danger—and if they also do not result in some meaningful act of beautiful, creative creation that requires conscious thought applied to mindfulness, beauty, or the more delicate elements of yin—then it is very likely you have found yourself caught up in a hypnotic rhythm that is keeping you from "dreaming, singing, and dancing" in a way that would ultimately bring more happiness and fulfillment to your life.

For me personally, being a very yang, hardcore, hard-charging, high achiever who works hard, exercises hard, eats hard, and *does* hard (then rinses-washes-repeats daily) has created a very yang scenario that has pulled me away from alternative activities that can spark a similar pleasurable neurotransmitter response. These alternative activities can also result in highly meaningful acts of creation, a more mindful enjoyment of beauty, or allowing myself to simply engage with *being*. This includes activities such as painting, making music, lying on the living room floor playing games with my kids, more time in nature, and even engaging in right-brained creative flow to pen the type of "slightly dangerous" writing you're reading right now—instead of focusing on pure, left-brained hard science or biohacking. I know deep down inside that these types of activities that pull me out of my hypnotic rhythm are highly rewarding and personally fulfilling, but it hasn't been until quite lately that I've really made a concerted attempt to get out of that rhythm and engage more of my yin side.

And I'll admit: It's been somewhat difficult, primarily because I've been defined, and have *defined myself*, by functional hardcore doing, macho-esque fitness and competitive exercise for so long that it's taking time to "shake that off" and release—as my friend Lewis Howes writes about in his book *The Mask Of Masculinity*—the "athlete mask" to instead enter into a more flowing, relaxed approach to life in general, particularly one that embraces creativity.

CREATION

Truly, I believe that it's that very act of embracing creativity that can serve as a potent tactic to pull us out of the hypnotic rhythm of constantly doing.

Free expression of art and creativity—especially in a spirit that loves others and loves God by both creating things ourselves while simultaneously celebrating His creation—is something we not only derive a great deal of pleasure and fulfillment from, but something that we are actually called to do and something that God, having designed us in the image of Himself the Creator, takes great pleasure in. Indeed, our unique human impulse to create reflects the fact that we were created in the image of a Creator God. As Francis Schaeffer says in his book *Art & The Bible*, "The lordship of Christ should include an interest in the arts...a Christian should use these arts to the glory of God, not just as tracts, mind you, but as things of beauty to the praise of God...the Christian is the one whose imagination should fly beyond the stars."

As I read Francis Schaeffer's quote above, and am inspired to allow my own imagination to fly beyond the stars, I am also reminded of reformer and theologian John Calvin who, despite being a man one might not think of as an ecologist, has a general philosophy on environmentalism, the goodness of labor, creation care, and the duties of cultivating the earth that really resonates with me—particularly the section in the quote below from his commentary on Genesis 2:15 in which he advocates "stewardship" of the planet as something we are called to engage in, rather than simply "consuming life in eating, drinking, and sleeping." (For more on this topic, listen to my Christian environmentalism podcast with Gordon Wilson, which I'll link to on the resources webpage for this chapter.) Calvin explains:

> "And the Lord God took the man Moses now adds, that the earth was given to man, with this condition, that he should occupy himself in its cultivation. Whence it follows that men were created to employ themselves in some work, and not to lie down in inactivity and idleness. This labor, truly, was pleasant, and full of delight, entirely exempt from all trouble and weariness; since however God ordained that man should be exercised in the culture of the ground, he condemned in his person, all indolent repose. Wherefore, nothing is more contrary to the order of nature, than to consume life in eating, drinking, and sleeping, while in the meantime we propose nothing to ourselves to do. Moses adds, that the custody of the garden was given in charge to Adam, to show that we possess the things which God has committed to our hands, on the condition, that being content with a frugal and moderate use of them, we should take care of what shall remain. Let him who possesses a field, so partake of its yearly fruits, that he may not suffer the ground to be injured by his negligence; but let him endeavor to hand it down to posterity as he received it, or even better cultivated. Let him so feed on its fruits that he neither dissipates it by luxury, nor permits to be marred or ruined by neglect. Moreover, that this economy, and this diligence, with respect to those good things which God has given us to enjoy, may flourish among us; let every one regard himself as the steward of God in all things which he possesses. Then he will neither conduct himself dissolutely, nor corrupt by abuse those things which God requires to be preserved."

How about you? Are you "consuming life" by eating, drinking, and sleeping? Or perhaps you could throw into that self-obsessed mix a bit of over-exercising and over-working? Or are you tilling the field of a garden, or a musical instrument, or an art canvas in an act of creation and stewardship that brings a smile to God's face and makes this world a better place?

Sure, if you're a man reading this who has already read Chapter 7 in my book *Fit Soul*, then you know that being a good father, husband, or contributor to society does indeed incorporate hardcore elements that allow us men to provide and protect. I respect guys who can work hard, lift heavy weights, and withstand physical discomfort. At the risk of being sexist (which I define as merely recognizing that males and females are *different*, both anatomically and psychologically), I would propose that many women seem to, in my subjective opinion, do a little bit *better* job embracing their artistic, creative, yin side. But, I also think that if you're a woman reading this book—particularly if you're a woman caught up in the fitness craze of training-to-eat and eating-to-train, or only engaged in business and making money, or denying and suppressing any creative urges that you may have—that you, too, would benefit from more creation.

After all, what would it feel like to have more *flow instead of function*? To have more *being instead of doing*? I often ask myself who I want my twin boys to be, both now and when they grow up. Perhaps they can hunt a deer with grit and precision, but also sit in the forest and decide to simply paint or photograph that deer, too. Perhaps they can carry a heavy sandbag up the driveway and swing a kettlebell, but also sit quietly at the top of the driveway in prayer and meditation. Perhaps they can run their fledgling cooking podcast business and create an income for themselves, but also lounge in the music room for hours playing with their piano, guitar, and drums, without a thought of business or money. I don't know about you, but those are the type of kids I want to raise and *that's* the type of human being I want to be.

Don't you think the world needs more men and women who can wake up, exercise, eat, and put in a hard day of work, but also spend time in the evening painting or strumming a ukulele? Don't we need more parents who can spontaneously erupt into initiating a pre-dinner dance party with the family? I doubt you'd deny that our world is enriched by the hopeless romantics, the artists, the stargazers, and the dreamers, but don't you have just a little bit of that inside yourself right now, just waiting to be allowed to spring forth?

Isn't part of being a fully functioning human also being a fully flowing human who sings, dances, dreams and creates art and beauty?

At this point, you may be asking yourself...

...but isn't sitting at my desk computer programming or writing a science paper or engaged in an engineering project an act of creation? Isn't making my morning smoothie, or even perhaps sculpting my body also an act of creation? Isn't posting a beautiful photo to Instagram an act of creation? Yes, perhaps to a small extent, but I'd argue that in most cases for most people these activities are *rote, repetitive, automated, subconscious and rhythmic,* as opposed to what I am encouraging you to do...

...which is to engage in acts of creation and spontaneous, free and flowing singing, dancing and dreaming that actually *feels* different, non-rhythmic, embarrassing, uncomfortable or even dangerous. These are the kind of acts that engage entirely different neural pathways than those you are triggering with activities that have become subconscious, hypnotically rhythmic components of your routine day-to-day activity. For the watercolor artist, this may very well be woodworking; for the violinist, reading science; for the writer, gardening; or for the Crossfitter, learning the violin. Most of the time, you'll *know* when you're breaking the rhythm, or just making an excuse to yourself that you're being creative or creating art and beauty, or singing, or dancing, or dreaming, when you're really not.

Love God & Love People

Finally, remember to *love others* with your acts of creation. As I wrote in my article about how to find your purpose in life, a key component of finding your purpose in life is not just creating a single, succinct purpose statement for your life but also going forth and executing that purpose statement in a fully mindful spirit of loving God and loving others, which are the two greatest commandments in the Bible.

Why is this "loving others" caveat to creation important?

Because creation doesn't simply have to be about painting a watercolor portrait or writing a song. Creation can also involve arguably more complex and potentially world-changing or life-altering activities such as inventing new freeway systems, building jet planes, programming complex software or designing vaccines. And thus, if your ability to create also incorporates an ability to be able to drastically affect the world around you for better or worse, you must have some sort of filter to decide whether or not your act of creation is *good or harmful.*

In other words...

...*is the watercolor portrait a nude female objectification painting that may cause a young boy to lustfully ogle as he sees it in a museum?*

...*is the song you've written chock-full of lyrics that are rhyming and entertaining, but also rife with violence or worldly angst?*

...*does the new freeway cut through the fields of three different hundred-year old farms and disrupt the income of multiple small farmers?*

...*does the jet plane pollute the atmosphere due to a poorly thought out fueling system?*

...*does the software enable millions worldwide to be able to spy on each other or access confidential information that violates privacy?*

...*does the vaccine have the potential to cause more harm than good, or perhaps require abortion of babies or violation of personal freedom rights to produce and administer?*

You probably see where I'm going with this. Don't just launch into an act of creation without considering the consequences. Instead, ask yourself if, through your act of creation, you are fully loving God and loving others. Sure, the same software that runs a small church charitable giving platform might also be used to host transactions for a porn website, or an air filtration system you've designed might be used to keep the air clean for greater customer comfort in a casino or brothel. But that's more of an issue of *others* twisting your creation for potentially sinful activities, and not necessarily *your* fault, in the same way it's not God's fault that some people enjoy a nice Bordeaux (made from the grape that He has created) with their family dinner, while others get sloshed and engage in domestic violence after drinking two full bottles of the stuff. Ultimately, if, as you create, you foresee potential for your creation to cause harm, then my advice to you is to assess *your motives* for creating it. If your motive in creating is to love God and love others, and not to make money, make your creation as popular as possible, gain power and prestige from your creation, get someone to like you because of your creation, etc., then I say, go forth and create.

And sing. And dance. And dream.

Then thank God for creating you in His image with the ability to create, to savor life to the fullest, and for giving you the grace to be able to leave the entire burden of your hypnotic rhythms at the foot of Christ's cross.

Summary

Last night, our family prepared and ate a holiday dinner together, then gathered for our annual Christmas tradition of "puff-painting" Christmas shirt.. We then snuggled on the couch for an hour and a half to watch a cartoon about elves. Afterwards, we went up to the boys' bedroom and I read the family a Christmas story entitled *A Boy Called Christmas* (one of the best modern holiday tales I've read in quite some time). I played guitar. My wife and I made love. Over the course of those five hours, I did quite a fair bit of being and it felt *wonderful*.

I commented to my wife as we were falling asleep that for me to devote that much time to simply "chillaxing" is something that would have driven me bat-sh*t crazy as much as a few months ago. After all, I wasn't producing. I wasn't "helping all the people." I wasn't getting stuff done in hardcore, high-achieving mode. I wasn't producing, helping to make the world turn, or doing, doing, doing.

But you know what else I told her?

I'm learning to be. To simply savor life. To release the reins on control and production to embrace more free, artistic, creativity. To go on a walk and listen to music instead of a podcast or audiobook. Or listen to nothing at all but God's music of birdsong and wind. It's a slow process. And I'm still working on it. But it feels so, so good.

Anyways, when I told her that, Jessa smiled, kissed me on the forehead, and we fell asleep in a lover's embrace. I'm pretty sure an evening like that one I described above is the way God intended for us to spend many evenings, and I personally plan on plenty more evenings like that in the future, along with more time devoted to fasting and fiction, meditation and music, and prayer and painting—even if it does mean those kettlebells out in the cold garage occasionally get neglected.

How about you? Are you learning to be and not just to do? When did you stop dreaming, singing, and dancing? More importantly, when are you going to start again? Perhaps you can start simple: such as a pre-dinner family dance party to your childrens' favorite song, or going to a music store to treat yourself to that random instrument you've always wanted to play, or teaching yourself to draw a cartoon dog, or simply turning off the podcast or audiobook on your next commute and instead singing along with the radio at the top of your lungs. Just try it. Try creating. Try being. It's transformative, and I have a strong hunch that it makes our Creator smile and will make you smile a bit more too. Imagine how you'll do it in the personal reflection section below. In the meantime, I'm off to strum the guitar.

For resources, references, links and additional reading and listening material for this chapter, visit GetEndure.com/Chapter9.

CHAPTER X

Chop Wood, Carry Water

A mentor once told me that one of his primary keys to success in life was to simply wake up and do the most extraordinary job he could with whatever God had put on his plate for that day.

As a matter of fact, I've always been the kind of guy who simply wakes each morning, does the best job I personally can with whatever opportunities God has brought my way, then sits back and just kind of enjoys the adventures in life that this approach seems to bring me (which has certainly resulted in the many interesting and unexpected directions that you can read about in Fit Soul).

Another way to think about this concept is that the most important work to be done is the work of the day.

Speaking of this idea of waking up, rolling up one's sleeves, and just "plodding along" and doing the work for the day, Doug Wilson writes in his book *Ploductivity: A Practical Theology of Work & Wealth*, "So my responsibility is, so to speak, whatever is in front of me, there on my workbench or desk or counter. I should do a first-rate job with that, and other things will fall into place."

In the book *Every Good Endeavor*, author Timothy Keller writes similarly, *"If God's purpose for your job is that you serve the human community, then the way to serve God best is to do the job as well as it can be done."*

In other words: Wake up, chop wood, carry water—rinse, wash, repeat. And do it all to the glory of God, with as much excellence as you possibly can.

So, since I, in the last chapter, may have given you the impression that life is all about traipsing naked through a pastoral field with a flower tucked into your hair, and doesn't really involve any grit or hard work, I'd like to explore in this chapter the concept of how I approach the working and the doing bits of life—beginning with two examples of

chopping wood, carrying water, and accomplishing the "work of the day," then moving on to a couple of important sieves through which to filter this philosophy.

Two Stories

I really have no clue where I originally heard this first story—the so-called "parable of the trucker"—but it highlights the importance of putting your nose to the grindstone and doing your work to the very best of your ability.

The story, from my approximate remembrance and with apologies to anyone who knows the actual tale well and may grimace over my bastardization of it, goes something like this...

...there is a trucker who is driving along his usual route, and, as he drives, he is asking himself over and over again: *Why am I here? What is my purpose? What am I meant to do?* Then, suddenly, as he rounds a corner, he slams on his brakes as there is a giant tree that has fallen across the road. Naturally, being a gritty trucker, he gets out, fires up his electric chainsaw, and carves enough of the tree up to be able to manhandle it out of the road and clear the path.

He then hops in his truck and keeps driving, continuing to ask himself over and over again: *Why am I here? What is my purpose? What am I meant to do?*

All the while, a stream of cars behind him pass through the unblocked road successfully, and thousands of happy citizens make it to work on time and enjoy their daily commute without having to hassle with a giant tree in the road.

See, the trucker's "purpose" was right there in front of him the whole time, and he didn't really even know—by doing his job of "chopping wood" (in this case, in the literal sense) and "carrying water"—how much he was positively impacting the world around him. The work to be done was simply the work of the day.

Next, there's the tale of one boy's journey to achieve his lifelong goal of becoming a samurai warrior, as told by author Joshua Medcalf in the book *Chop Wood Carry*

Water: How to Fall in Love with the Process of Becoming Great.

In the book, the primary protagonist, a boy named John, is in love with samurai culture and possesses a relentless desire to become a samurai archer. All the seemingly mundane tasks assigned to him by his wise sensei that John must complete in order to achieve his goal are similar to the mundane tasks you too may experience in your "daily grind," such as making your bed, doing the dishes, weeding the garden, sweeping the floor, putting away the groceries, paying the bills, replying to e-mails, making 50 cold calls, doing 20 pushups every hour, or perhaps just writing 200 words a day (my own minimum requirement, which technically allows me to write the equivalent of an entire novel yearly with that minimum amount of words, though I often exceed that word count).

Joshua explains in the book that it seems everyone wants to build the next Apple or Facebook, but nobody wants to sell matches door to door. Everyone wants to become a samurai warrior, but few are willing to faithfully chop wood and carry water like the boy John—until their sensei graduates them to shooting arrows, swinging swords, and other forms of samurai training.

After all, it isn't sexy to chop wood and carry water every single day. People instead dream of easy, instant success. Winning the lottery. Getting noticed by a talent recruiter. Hitting it big on Instagram. Getting retweeted by a celebrity. Few, however, are willing to chop wood and carry water. As Joshua writes, *"Everyone wants to be great, until it's time to do what greatness requires."* He explains that for many years it might feel as if nothing is happening, but you must trust the process and continue to chop wood and carry water, day in, day out, regardless of what is happening around you.

At the risk of "tooting my own horn," I will use my own personal success as an example of chopping wood, carrying water, and simply waking up each day to do the most extraordinary job I can with whatever God has placed upon my plate for the day.

- In high school, I'd rise at 4 am to work on medical insurance claims for my Dad's ambulance service, then go deliver newspapers, then bust butt to finish all my studies (I was homeschooled) by 11 am, after which I coached tennis for 3-4 hours to save up money for college, and finally operated an evening babysitting service for our neighborhood and friends.

- During my university studies, I took 28-32 credits a semester for 5 years in a

- row while simultaneously waking at 5 am to work at a bakery, moonlit as a personal trainer in the evening, taught kids' sports camps and wellness classes in between my regular classes, managed a coffee shop, and continued to teach tennis lessons.

- Once I graduated and began to open a series of personal training studios and gyms, I'd wake at 4 am, ride my bike 12 miles through rain, sleet, and snow to train clients the entire day, then return home around 7 pm, eat a quick bowl of food, then stay up until 2 or 3 am programming websites and teaching myself to code so that I could launch an online personal training business.

- Over the next several years, while traveling the world and competing in Ironman triathlon—while still managing and operating all my personal training studios—I sat hunched over a laptop in tiny taxis in Thailand and airport coffeeshops jamming away on my word processor while writing my first New York Times bestselling book *Beyond Training*.

- In between writing books, training clients, and training myself, I published a daily newsletter from my website, wrote 1-2 articles a week, and launched a weekly podcast in an effort to establish the fitness media "empire" I now operate, which really began with me and the best tiny video camera I could afford from the local Best Buy.

Ultimately, I chopped a lot of wood and carried a lot of water. Things eventually snowballed, but kind of like a snowball one rolls up a hill one single sweaty roll at a time, and not a snowball one easily pushes from the top of a hill.

As an example of the slow snowball effect, I remember my first monthly "affiliate" check from Amazon in 2009, which was the fruits of publishing half a dozen articles a month that I disseminated about the internets. The check amounted to one dollar and thirty-seven cents. But in 2021, my monthly affiliate check from Amazon was around twenty thousand dollars.

My first book royalty payment was about seventeen dollars. My last book royalty payment was well over a quarter-million dollars.

I began posting instructional videos to Instagram a few years ago with next to zero followers. Last I checked, followers were well over 350,000.

Granted, none of these examples are metrics of my worth as a human being. But they do highlight the fruits I've experienced by simply

waking up each day, putting my nose to the grindstone, and doing the very best job I can with whatever God has placed upon my plate for the day. This success has come slowly, but has been built upon a solid foundation of blood, sweat, and even sometimes tears, and not a shaky foundation of "getting lucky" or taking a shortcut. Of course, the entire journey itself has been character-building and allowed me to learn plenty of valuable life lessons I can now teach to my children and teach to others in the form of books such as the one you're reading right now.

SERENDIPITY

As you engage in your own process of chopping wood and carrying water, there is another important consideration you should be aware of, something I wish I'd come to a realization about earlier in my life.

If your life has been anything like mine, you may occasionally be presented with opportunities of a so-called "serendipitous" nature. Serendipity is defined as "the faculty or phenomenon of finding valuable or agreeable things not sought for."

These often refreshing, welcome, and sometimes fortunate breaks from your monotonous or mundane tasks of doing the daily grind may be marked by a pleasant level of surprise and spontaneity when they occur. Some call them luck, some call them happenstance, some good fortune, but I call them God's providence. After all, random good things don't just *happen*. Instead, God delights in occasionally surprising us, and gives us a seemingly random passing moment of unexpected meaning or importance, such as meeting someone in a coffee shop you haven't seen in years, receiving a random call about the chance for a new book deal or insight into a problem you've been trying to solve, getting a raise or a promotion, or receiving a networked introduction that turns out to be exactly the person you need in your life at that moment for a project you've been working on.

Ultimately, if you've been doing your daily work of chopping wood and carrying water, these serendipitous opportunities are far more likely to be sent your way by God. You've no doubt heard this wise perspective on luck before...

...*chance favors the prepared mind*...

...diligence is the mother of good luck...

...the winds and waves are always on the side of the ablest navigators...

...luck occurs when smart, prepared people are in the right place at the right time...

...you get the idea. What's important for you to understand is to *not* shrug these seemingly random occurrences off as "luck," but as meaningful opportunities that may very well materialize into something big for you. So pay close attention to all of these occurrences, both large and small. They aren't accidents.

I spent much of my life shrugging off the idea that "nothing happens by accident" as woo and weird superstition and a view that might cause one to waste too much time looking for meaning in relatively meaningless chance happenings, but I've realized in the past several years that I couldn't have been more wrong. For example, when someone randomly pops into my head, I don't shrug it off as my brain simply firing off a few random neurotransmitters, but I now call that person, or e-mail them, or text them. When I'm trying to solve a problem and I accidentally knock a book off my bookshelf, I pop the book open and immediately start thumbing through it for the answer to my problem. If I'm creating a new recipe and I hear a song that names a random spice or herb ("it's thyme to part; every rose has its thorn; pour some sugar on me"...), I'll fumble around for that ingredient. Call me weird and superstitious, but I do indeed now pay very close and mindful attention every moment to what some would say what "the universe" is telling me, but what I say *God* is telling me. Even if it does occasionally result in rose petals on the roast chicken.

Of course, what we often consider to be serendipity is simply the result of the manifestation of bringing something tangible into our lives through attraction and belief. You've no doubt also heard of this concept before couched within phrases such as "if you think it, it will come;" "ask and your prayers shall be answered;" or "think and grow rich." Manifestation simply involves making everything you want to feel and experience a reality via your thoughts, actions, beliefs, and emotions. So, if you're working on a book, you not only write your daily word count, but you tell others you are working on a New York Times Best Seller. If you're launching a new company, you not only set your alarm for 5 am every morning to work, but you create a vision board of your big, hairy, audacious company goals in your office. If you're trying to lose 100 pounds and race an Ironman triathlon, you sign up for the race and buy your Ironman race suit in the exact size you need it to be in, long before the actual event occurs.

See, in the Bible, Jeremiah 29:11-13 says that God knows the very plans he has for you: plans to prosper you and not to harm you, plans to give you hope and a future. He tells you to call on Him and come and pray to Him, and He will listen to you. In addition, Psalm 139 says:

> "For you formed my inward parts;
> you knitted me together in my mother's womb.
> I praise you, for I am fearfully and wonderfully made.
> ...My frame was not hidden from you,
> when I was being made in secret,
> intricately woven in the depths of the earth.
> Your eyes saw my unformed substance;
> in your book were written, every one of them,
> the days that were formed for me,
> when as yet there was none of them."

That's right: God planned everything out for you before you were even born. All you need to do is wake up each day, do the hard work of chopping wood and carrying water, and pay close attention to every opportunity (even the seemingly random ones) He sends your way, tackling each of those opportunities with wisdom and discernment. Ultimately, every moment of your life was meant to be.

Hell Yes Or No?

Finally, I'm often asked how—by keeping myself open to opportunities (even the seemingly serendipitous ones), somewhat flexible with a "life plan," and focused on attending primarily to the work of the day (including all those new opportunities that come my way)—I assess whether an opportunity is a true fit.

After all, I'd be overloaded with work in addition to constantly "having coffee" with every random person who asked me to coffee (as an aside, I never do coffee meetings), doing quick calls with everyone who wants to "pick my brain" (I also *allow for zero brain-picking), investing in every new startup that comes my way (hint: I invest in about 0.1% of the companies that contact me daily) and reading every book that's recommended to me (if I don't get through the first 10 pages without highlighting something in a book, it gets shelved).*

Related to these kinds of decisions, the wise modern day philosopher Naval Ravikant says, *"If you can't decide, the answer is no."*

The equally wise modern day entrepreneur Derek Sivers says, *"If it's not a hell yes, it's a no."* (I would even modify that to say *"If it's not a full body hell yes, it's a no."*)

But I would add two clarifications and considerations…

First, sometimes an opportunity arises and you're not in the correct state of mind (which usually means you are in a tired or stressed state of mind) to properly assess whether the opportunity is a fit. So don't react with a blanket yes or no. Pray on it, walk on it, and sleep on it. Come back refreshed and undistracted. Then decide.

Second, have rules through which you filter new opportunities. For example, I know that 99% of "coffee meetings" have turned out to be a complete waste of my time, random phone calls to answer "quick questions" often turn into an enormous time suck of me explaining to someone something they could have found on Google for free, most new startups fail, and a book that doesn't intrigue and enchant me within the first chapter will usually not deliver anything extraordinary in later chapters. Hence, the "rules" for these types of opportunities that I described above.

In other words, do indeed stay open to new opportunities, but also be wise, be discerning, and don't be a "say yes to everything because ya never know" type of person.

Summary

So let's review the most important parts of having this daily philosophy of chopping wood and carrying water.

- *Work hard, to the best of your ability, and in full excellence to the glory of God, chopping wood and carrying water every day and doing the very best job with whatever God has put on your plate for the day.*

- *Understand that the seemingly "random" so-called serendipitous opportunities, meetings, and networked introductions that may arise are not random, but planned by God, and manifested by your actions, words, and thoughts. So pay attention to each with wisdom and discernment.*

- *Regarding those random opportunities, only say yes to the hell yeses, but remember that you do need to set boundaries and rules and that the yes or no doesn't need to be an immediate gut response. Sometimes a hell yes or hell no may take a bit of praying, walking, and sleeping on to materialize.*

And should you be tempted to think your work is too small, or to glance with envy at the size of your neighbor's garage, Instagram follower size, or monthly paycheck, consider the words of 1 Corinthians 15:58. Paul writes that, *"In the Lord, your labor is not in vain."* He was speaking of Christian ministry, but this can ultimately be true of all work. As Doug Wilson notes in *Ploductivity*...

> ..."*remembering the finitude of your labors will keep you humble. Recognizing that your labors have a place in God's cosmic intentions for the universe will keep you from thinking that your tiny labors are stupid labors. They are nothing of the kind.*"

Finally, I highly recommend you read two books: read *Ploductivity*, a book that considers the theology behind technology, work, and mission and advice on how to be productive—and to think about productivity—in the digital age. Also read *Every Good Endeavor* (I'll link to both books on the resources webpage for this chapter), which addresses the following three questions:

Why do you want to work? (That is, why do we need to work in order to lead a fulfilled life?)

Why is it so hard to work? (That is, why is it so often fruitless, pointless, and difficult?)

How can we overcome the daily difficulties and find satisfaction in our work?

As a matter of fact, let's finish with a quote by author Timothy Keller from his book *Every Good Endeavor*. In it, Keller says,

> "*...all human work (especially excellent work), done by all people, as*

a channel of God's love for his world. They will be able to appreciate and rejoice in their own work, whether it is prestigious or not, as well as in the skillful work of all other people, whether they believe or not. So this biblical conception of work—as a vehicle for God's loving provision for the world."

How about you and your approach to work? Do you view it as a way to love others, no matter how small or how much of a daily grind your work may be? Do you wake up in the morning and stack each brick you've been handed one by one, knowing that someday, even if you're perhaps not personally around to see it finished, a great and glorious mansion will be the eventual result? Do you chop wood and carry water, with a giant, satisfied, stupid grin on your face, doing so to the glory of God, no matter how mundane the work may seem to be? If not, how do you plan to start based on what you've learned in this chapter?

For resources, references, links and additional reading and listening material for this chapter, visit GetEndure.com/Chapter10.

CHAPTER XI
SEATBELTS & SENTRIES

God helps those who help themselves.

So trust God, but put on your seatbelt.

Trust God, but strap on your life jacket.

Trust God, but wear your bicycle helmet.

Trust God, but lock up your house at night.

Trust God, but don't eat crap all day.

Trust God, but don't lick the hospital room floor.

I'm pretty sure none of the phrases above actually appear in the Bible, but they're prudent sayings nonetheless. They all relate to the idea that a trust and belief in a higher power and a faith that there is a story written for your life must be yoked to actual conscious and responsible action that you take based on your own free will—and not couched in a *que sera sera* approach to life in which you smoke weed and binge watch Netflix while waiting for God to magically deposit money into your bank account.

I've written elsewhere on trust, particularly the fruits that can pour forth into your relationships with others when you trust God that you will have enough time to create transformational relationships, which is a concept I explore in Chapter 4 of *Fit Soul*. But in this chapter, I'd like to unpack the topic of trust just a bit more, particularly when it comes to marrying deep faith in God that you will be protected, cared for, and kept safe with actual action on your part to ensure you aren't the spiritual fool who plays frogger every time you jaywalk across a busy road because—well—God's in ultimate control and what will happen will happen no matter what you do differently because it's deterministically destined to happen that way, right?

Sentries

What got me thinking about this whole topic was when I was reading in the book of Nehemiah in the Bible and noted that Nehemiah prayed to God for protection over the building project that he was working on, but then simultaneously planted armed sentries on the wall. In other words, he put his trust in God's protection, then took massive action to ensure that protection actually manifested.

Who was Nehemiah?

I'll quickly give a historical clarification for you if you are unfamiliar with his story.

Nehemiah was a Jewish leader who supervised the rebuilding of Jerusalem in the mid-5th century BC after his release from captivity by the Persian king Artaxerxes I. He had been a cupbearer to Artaxerxes when Judah in Palestine was partly repopulated by Jews released from their exile in Babylonia. Distressed at the news of the desolate and despairing condition of Jerusalem at the time, Nehemiah received permission from Artaxerxes to travel to Palestine to help rebuild Jerusalem's ruined structures. Artaxerxes provided Nehemiah with an escort and with documents that guaranteed assistance from Judah's Persian officials. Around 444 BC, Nehemiah traveled to Jerusalem and raised up people there to begin repopulating the city and rebuilding its walls. Nehemiah encountered some hostility from the local officials in nearby districts, but in just 52 days, the Jews under his direction did indeed succeed in rebuilding Jerusalem's walls.

The book of Nehemiah is a strong reminder to the followers of God of how He worked to bring the people he loved back to their land to rebuild the city of Jerusalem. Throughout the book of Nehemiah, there are constant reminders of how God orchestrates historical events to provide for His children.

In acknowledgment of the orchestration of God, at one point in the story, in Nehemiah 1:5, Nehemiah utters a powerful prayer in which he proclaims:

> *"I pray, God of heaven, O great and awesome God, You who keep Your covenant and mercy with those who love You and observe Your commandments, please let Your ear be attentive and Your eyes open, that You may hear the prayer of Your servant which I pray before You now, day and night, for the children of Israel Your servants, and confess the sins of the children of Israel which we have sinned*

against You. Both my father's house and I have sinned. We have acted very corruptly against You, and have not kept the commandments, the statutes, nor the ordinances which You commanded Your servant Moses. Remember, I pray, the word that You commanded Your servant Moses, saying, 'If you are unfaithful, I will scatter you among the nations; but if you return to Me, and keep My commandments and do them, though some of you were cast out to the farthest part of the heavens, yet I will gather them from there, and bring them to the place which I have chosen as a dwelling for My name.' Now these are Your servants and Your people, whom You have redeemed by Your great power, and by Your strong hand. O Lord, I pray, please let Your ear be attentive to the prayer of Your servant, and to the prayer of Your servants who desire to fear Your name; and let Your servant prosper this day, I pray, and grant him mercy in the sight of this man."

Now of course, after pouring his heart out to God like that, Nehemiah could have simply trusted that God the Almighty orchestrator would look down favorably on the building project and proceed to grant prosperity, mercy, and protection. But Nehemiah didn't *stop* with prayer.

He prayed, then he *planted sentries*. He stationed half of the workers as sentries with swords, spears, and bows to guard the walls. The rest of the workers, including those who were carrying the building materials, were also required to keep their weapons close by. In Nehemiah 4, you can see that the laborers who carried materials worked with one hand and held a weapon with the other, and each of the builders worked with his sword strapped to his side. Nehemiah 7:3 says, *"And even while the gatekeepers are on duty, have them shut and bar the doors. Appoint the residents of Jerusalem to act as guards, everyone on a regular watch. Some will serve at sentry posts and some in front of their own homes."* But in implementing these kinds of protective measures, Nehemiah wasn't diluting his confidence in God. He knew where his protection was coming from. "Our God will fight for us," he told the people.

FAITH WITHOUT WORKS

See, faith is laudable and praiseworthy, but faith without works is dead.

In other words, trust in God isn't going to get you very far if you don't take action. God feeds the tiny sparrows, but they flitter and peck like crazy to get those worms He provides. He clothes the lilies of the field, but there's an ample of photosynthesis those little plants are engaged in to be able to harness the sunlight He provides for this clothing. And He'll take care of you, too, provided you take care of yourself.

James 2:14-26 says:

> "What does it profit, my brethren, if someone says he has faith but does not have works? Can faith save him? If a brother or sister is naked and destitute of daily food, and one of you says to them, 'Depart in peace, be warmed and filled,' but you do not give them the things which are needed for the body, what does it profit? Thus also faith by itself, if it does not have works, is dead.
>
> But someone will say, 'You have faith, and I have works.' Show me your faith without your works, and I will show you my faith by my works. You believe that there is one God. You do well. Even the demons believe—and tremble! But do you want to know, O foolish man, that faith without works is dead? Was not Abraham our father justified by works when he offered Isaac his son on the altar? Do you see that faith was working together with his works, and by works faith was made perfect? And the Scripture was fulfilled which says, 'Abraham believed God, and it was accounted to him for righteousness.' And he was called the friend of God. You see then that a man is justified by works, and not by faith only.
>
> Likewise, was not Rahab the harlot also justified by works when she received the messengers and sent them out another way?
>
> For as the body without the spirit is dead, so faith without works is dead also."

Verses 15 and 16 above are quite relevant to what I've talked about in Chapters 6 and 15. It's easy to kneel by your bedside and say a quick prayer for the homeless. It's quite another thing to put yourself in their shoes, show you actually care, and bring a man or woman laying in a sleeping bag by the sidewalk on a cold winter's night a warm plate of food. That, also, appears to me to be trusting God by putting on your seatbelt.

JUST. DO. SOMETHING.

"But wait!" you might be thinking…

"…if God is a great orchestrator and, say, has pre-destined and pre-ordained all deaths including my own, then why bother wearing my seatbelt?"

Ultimately, this all comes down to free will vs. determinism. Free will is a term that postulates that we as rational people are free to choose the courses of our actions, often from amongst a variety of alternatives. Meanwhile, determinism is the idea that God determines all that we humans will ever do, and both knows and decrees our actions in advance. In our own tiny human logical and rational minds, it seems the two are completely contraindicated: either we choose our actions, or we don't. Now obviously, from a deterministic standpoint, we can't have free will because God has determined all our actions beforehand and they cannot be changed.

This conundrum has spun-off a host of theories, such as the idea that perhaps we have the *illusion* of free will and we think we're making our own decisions, but really, God is making them for us. Or perhaps we live a choose-your-own-adventure style storybook in which we reach choices in the book of our life and make a decision about which page we are going to turn to, but God has already written the next pages of the story for either choice we make, so it's all mapped out either way. Or perhaps God fully empowers us with tools such as the Bible and prayer to enable us to make the right decisions in life (such as—at the risk of opening up a giant mask mandate debate—submitting to our local authorities while simultaneously doing as we would want our loved ones to also do, and wearing our seatbelt), God has created a universe that operates on specific principles, rules, and consequences based upon whether we use those tools wisely or not, and God knows exactly what's going to happen and what choices we are going to make. Or, and I tend to think this way, God has created a universe that operates on specific principles, rules, and consequences based upon whether we use those tools wisely or not, and God knows exactly what's going to happen and what choices we are going to make.

As you can imagine, this entire "free will vs. determinism" debate has been argued in theological circles for eons, creating quite a bit of angst, and understandably so. After all, it centers around a core issue of morality: *"Am I responsible for my actions or not?"*

First, *yes*, you're responsible. You have a choice. I'm in full agreement with Doug Wilson on this topic when he points out in an excellent, short treatise on the matter that I'll link to on the resources webpage for this chapter, while speaking of the idea that we can be free from external compulsion and consequently at liberty to do what our heart desires:

> *"This is a natural liberty, and all men are in possession of it. It is the only kind of liberty possible for us, and it is a gift to us from God. Under the superintendence of God, all men, Christian and non-Christian, have the freedom to turn left or right, to choose chocolate or vanilla, or to move to this city or that one—depending entirely upon what they want to do."*

Doug ultimately concludes that we are free to do as we please. We have this freedom only because God grants and sustains it—and perfectly controls it. I fully agree.

Second, before we get any more into the free will vs. determinism weeds, we actually aren't going to, because *the purpose of this short chapter is not to prove or disprove free will or determinism, but rather to point out the fact that we are to trust God and then take massive action, just as Nehemiah did when rebuilding the city of Jerusalem.*

Trusting God means listening to His wisdom, then allowing Him to work through you to accomplish His actions.

Trusting God means exercising character traits such as prudence, preparation, and caution because, in a book like Proverbs, He repeatedly tells us to incorporate such values.

Trusting God means handing Him your business success dreams, then marching out to attend the conferences, make the phone calls and write the e-mails that *allow that to happen.*

Trusting God means seeing a pretty girl across the room, telling God it'd be your absolute pleasure to get to know her, then mustering up the courage to actually go walk across the room and meet her.

Trusting God means asking Him to remove some health "thorn in your side," then hunting down the doctors, books, knowledge, and connections who can practice the right type of medicine on you. It doesn't mean praying for 6 months for your headaches to go away while you continue to watch TV until midnight and eat junk food.

Trusting God means preparing for a competition by telling yourself you can do all things through Christ who strengthens you, then putting in the sets, reps, sweat, blood, and tears that allow you to actually cross the finish line.

Trusting God means asking for financial blessings, then working hard in your career, buying insurance, saving, investing, trading, and not just burying a pile of cash in the ground.

Trusting God means seeing injustice and evil happening around you and actually taking action to stop it, not just saying a prayer that God would "change stuff" as you fall asleep in bed at night, looking for the cold side of the pillow.

Trusting God means, as Steve Jobs once said, picking up the phone: "Most people never pick up the phone. Most people never call and ask. And that's what separates sometimes the people who do things from those who just dream about them. You gotta act. You gotta be willing to fail. You gotta be willing to crash and burn. With people on the phone or starting a company, if you're afraid you'll fail, you won't get very far."

In my own life, I've observed that the most fruit seems to pour into one's life when one steeps themselves in prayer, Scripture reading, devotions, meditation, and all the spiritual disciplines I systematize at SpiritualDisciplinesJournal.com—while simultaneously planning, preparing, saving, investing, and staying wise, organized, pursuing excellence and, yes, even crashing and burning and failing as they become more equipped every day to live out the life God has planned for them to His full glory.

In other words, much to the chagrin of any English editorial sticklers out there, I can sum things up in just six words...

...Trust. God.

Then...

Just. Do. Something.

Summary

So trust God, but put on your seatbelt. Pray to God, and—as Nehemiah did—plant sentries on your walls and keep your sword at your side.

Understand that God does indeed help those who help themselves, provided their self-helping is pursued in a spirit of trust and faith in Him, and not in their own works and power. Furthermore, you have free will and if you continually embark upon a path towards enriching your life with wisdom from Scripture and seeking discernment and direction from God, you'll make the right choices, which will be in full alignment with what God has already planned for you and already knows you are going to choose.

How about you? What's your take on striking a balance between trusting God but taking action? Where have you found yourself praying but not taking action or vice versa?

For resources, references, links and additional reading and listening material for this chapter, visit GetEndure.com/Chapter11.

CHAPTER XII

FLOW

I recently read Greg McKeown's book *Effortless*. Greg's first book (also quite good) *Essentialism*, was about doing the right things, but his newer book *Effortless* is about doing these things in the right way.

In the book, Greg writes that you've likely been conditioned to believe that the path to success is paved with relentless work and that if you want to overachieve, you have to overexert, overthink, and overdo. If you aren't perpetually exhausted from the hustle, you're not doing enough.

But lately, working hard is more exhausting than ever. And the more depleted we get, the harder it is to make progress. Stuck in an endless loop of "Zoom, eat, sleep, repeat," we're often working twice as hard to achieve half as much. Greg explains that getting ahead doesn't have to be as hard as we tend to make it. No matter what challenges or obstacles we face, there can be a better way: instead of pushing ourselves harder, we can find an easier path. In other words, although not every hard thing in life can be made easy, we can make it easier to do more of what matters most...

...and Greg refers to the ability to be able to do that as an "effortless state": an experience many of us have had when we are physically rested, emotionally unburdened, and mentally energized, while completely aware, alert, present, attentive, and focused on what's important at this moment, able to focus with ease on what matters most. He describes how in Eastern philosophy this effortless sweet spot is referred to as *wu wei* (pronounced "Oo-Way"). Wu means "not have" or "without." Wei means "do," "act," or "effort." So wu wei means "without action," "without effort," "trying without trying," "action without action," or "effortless doing." The goal in being effortless is to accomplish what matters by trying less, not more, and to achieve your purpose in life with bridled intention, not overexertion.

If you're curious whether you happen to be one of those people who might be pushing harder instead of working easier and making things effortless, then you can go take the helpful "Effortless" Quiz (GregMcKeown.com/quiz), in which he presents helpful thought exercises such as:

When I feel overwhelmed by all the work I have to do, I tend to:

1. Think about it more than actually get it done
2. Grit my teeth, and try to work as efficiently as possible
3. Dive into it immediately, and keep pushing myself until every last thing is done

My job often makes me feel:

1. Stressed and anxious
2. Burnt out and exhausted
3. Motivated but sometimes bored

I go the extra mile in everything I do:

1. Always
2. Only when there's a payoff
3. Never

I tend to focus most on:

- The past
- The present
- The future

My motto is "An assignment is not done until _____:"

1. It's perfect
2. I'm up against the deadline
3. It meets the required criteria

When I hit a wall on a task or project, I tend to:

1. Take a short break, and wish it were longer
2. Power through anyway
3. Spin my wheels and eventually give up

When someone I care about makes me feel angry or hurt, I usually:

1. Replay the incident over and over, and silently hold a grudge

2. Complain about it to anyone who will listen
3. Try not to think about it. I have too many other things to focus on

For me, the hardest part of a big project is:

1. Getting started
2. Knowing when to quit
3. The tedium of the work

When I have to get something done, my typical pace is:

1. Slow and steady
2. Sprint until I drop
3. Lots of starts and stops

I think relaxation is:

1. A waste of time
2. Hard to do without thoughts of work getting in the way
3. Something I enjoy when I'm not too busy

Again, you can take the quiz on Greg's website to see where you fall on the effortless scale. Greg's book actually reminded me a bit of what I've also heard repeatedly from my friend Tim Ferriss. Tim not only allows himself to engage in work and productivity "flow" by allowing things that are easy to be easy, but also often asks himself *"what if this were easy?"* or *"what would it look like if this were easy?"* Confronted with extreme anxiety and overwhelm in the process of writing a book, Tim developed this easy questioning philosophy and says that it led him to some very specific insight and the answer to many of the problems in life he was confronting, along with deep personal and professional growth, new connections with several mentors, and the ultimate culmination of the publishing of his wildly successful book *Tribe of Mentors*.

So what does it mean exactly to ask yourself "what if this were easy?" And why was it so powerful for Tim? How can your work and life be more flowing and effortless? In this chapter, I'm going to explain to you why a focus on effortlessness, flow, and ease may indeed allow you to approach life and life's difficulties through an entirely new lens, especially when paired with the time and trust principles I talk about in Chapter 4 of *Fit Soul*.

WHAT WOULD THIS LOOK LIKE IF IT WERE EASY?

The question *"What would this look like if it were easy?"* is based on the same idea that Greg presents in *Effortless*: it's easy to convince yourself that things need to be hard and that if you're not redlining, working your fingers to the bone, burning the candles at both ends, have smoke coming out your ears during any particular mental task for the day, can't do a workout without two pre-workout drinks and a breathe-up session because you know how masochistic it has to be, pull your hair out planning family vacations or time with friends, and need a great deal of complexity to even do something as simple as meditating (as I write about in Chapter 21), you're simply not trying hard enough. This mentality leads any human to eventually seek the path of most resistance, creating unnecessary hardship in the process.

If you're anything like me, then for you, this idea of working less hard may feel uncomfortable, lazy, and nearly guilt-inducing, perhaps because you're stricken by the Puritanical idea that the act of doing hard things carries with it some kind of inherent value. This Puritanical viewpoint not only embraces the hard but tends to distrust the easy. When paired with Bible verses such as Genesis 3:19, which says "In the sweat of your face you shall eat bread, Till you return to the ground," we can almost feel as though we are "letting God down" as some kind of Proverbial sluggard if we aren't mopping sweat off our face during a day of toil.

Don't get me wrong: many of the meaningful or successful accomplishments I've had in life have indeed been accompanied by blood, sweat, and tears, but in looking back, I have spent many wasted hours micro-managing projects, avoiding outsourcing because I wanted to know how to do everything myself, trying to convince myself that working harder would eventually solve a problem, and procrastinating everything from work to spiritual disciplines to exercise simply because I hadn't considered what it would look like if that task or the steps leading up to that task were easier. I'm pretty confident that the Almighty Creator didn't intend for us to simply work hard, but to also use our God-given creative powers to work smart, and I would even argue that working hard and working smart while being fully self-actualized and immersed in a vocation that implements your God-given talents can actually feel quite effortless much of the time, or at least *fun*, in the same way that I've found a Spartan race, marathon, or Ironman triathlon can be brutal, hot, and energetically draining, yet simultaneously thrilling and smile-inducing.

Tim Ferriss hypothesized, in his development of the "easy" question mentioned above, that better results might come if he used a tactic of "inversion" to frame his own work in terms of elegance instead of strain, and he eventually solved his authorship conundrums by reframing them to seek the easiest solution instead of the most stressful, time-consuming, hard-working, unending-labor-in-the-salt-mines solution (despite the societal veneration that seems to be placed on the latter approach).

This philosophy reflects the same philosophy of author Dr. Wayne Dyer, who has written that...

..."When you change the way you see things, the things you see change."

As he was figuring out how he was going to write his next big book, Tim decided one morning to spend a week test-driving the path of least resistance. That morning, by journaling the question "*What would this look like if it were easy?*" an idea presented itself.

Tim's idea, as he describes in more detail here on a good blog post and also in a brief YouTube snippet from an interview with James Altucher, both of which I'll link to on the resources webpage for this chapter, was this: *"What if I assembled a tribe of mentors to help me?"*

More specifically, related to his book *Tribe of Mentors*, Tim eventually developed this question into: *"What if I asked 100+ brilliant people the very questions I want to answer myself? Or somehow got them to guide me in the right direction?"*

And voila! The result of Tim's outside-the-box, approach-the-problem-from-an-easy-angle question culminated in the ultimate choose-your-own-adventure book, a compilation of tools, tactics, and habits from 130+ of the world's top performers, from iconic entrepreneurs to elite athletes, from artists to billionaire investors, who all, basically, wrote the book *for* Tim (and as an additional upside, promoted the book for him and often appeared on his podcast afterward).

So let's say that you, like Tim, want to approach a problem, a habit, a routine, or any desired outcome with similar effortlessness and ease. Here are a few additional questions that will help you determine what the path of least resistance might be:

- Why am I doing this activity in the first place? What am I trying to accomplish? What's the ultimate goal?

- What does the project or task look like once it's done? In *Effortless*, Greg describes how getting the outcome clear can provide massive focus to your efforts as all of your resources shift into gear to bring that outcome to fruition. Examples include...
    - *Vague Goal:* "Lose weight."
    - *What "Done" Looks Like:* I look down at the scale and see the number 177 pounds staring back at me.
    - *Vague Goal:* "Walk more."
    - *What "Done" Looks Like:* Reach ten thousand steps a day on my Fitbit for fourteen days in a row.
    - *Vague Goal:* "Read more books."
    - *What "Done" Looks Like:* On my digital book reader it will say, "Finished," next to War and Peace.
    - *Vague Goal:* "Turn in the big report."
    - *What "Done" Looks Like:* Type up twelve pages full of concrete examples and actionable advice and be able to picture the customer saying, "It's terrific!"
    - *Vague Goal:* "Launch my product."
    - *What "Done" Looks Like:* Have ten beta users try the app for a week and give feedback.
    - *Vague Goal:* "Complete podcast episode."
    - *What "Done" Looks Like:* The podcast is recorded and the file is uploaded.

- Where are the obstacles, barriers, and bottlenecks? What's slowing me down or keeping me from getting started in the first place? At what stage do I experience a sense of dread, resistance, or temptation to procrastinate?

- What steps could I eliminate? If I cut out step x, y, or z, what would happen? Would it really destroy the process, or simply result in a new and potentially easier way to do things?

- What steps could I accomplish differently? If I can't eliminate a step, can I execute it in a different way or reframe how I think about it?

- Does this all need to be done at once, or can I creatively split it up? For *example, Greg also describes the concept of utilizing "microbursts," which are ten-minute surges of focused activity that can have an immediate effect on your essential project, providing a burst of motivation and energy from taking that first obvious action, such as:*

- *Essential Project: Remove the clutter from the garage.*
- *First Obvious Action: Find the broom.*
- *Microburst: Sweep out the shed and move the bikes into the shed.*
- *Essential Project: Launch a product.*
- *First Obvious Action: Open a cloud-based document to put ideas in.*
- *Microburst: Brainstorm product features.*
- *Essential Project: Complete a large report.*
- *First Obvious Action: Pick up a pen and a piece of paper.*
- *Microburst: Draft an outline for the report.*

For example, let's say that I have an incredibly busy day chock full of meetings and phone calls, but I know I want to jumpstart that day with a workout so that I feel good and am energized for the entire day. Setting the alarm clock back an hour will inevitably result in less productivity due to a sleep-deprived, brain-foggy haze, so that's not an option. But rescheduling some of my work so that I can take those first few phone calls while walking briskly outdoors in the sunshine, perhaps increasing intensity by wearing blood flow restriction bands or a weighted backpack could actually be an option. Or, I can come to the realization that mini "micro-workouts" spread through the day can be just as effective as a dedicated gym session, and I can navigate the entire busy day by stopping every 50 minutes for five minutes of air squats, push-ups, and burpees, allowing me another five minutes to recover and move on to my next task. Or perhaps I can eliminate any commute to the gym by equipping my garage with a few inexpensive kettlebells and a fancy exercise bike from Craigslist (where rich folks often list workout equipment for amazing prices because they bought something super cool then realized they never use it).

Perhaps I'm struggling to find time for Bible reading in the morning and also be able to meditate, journal, get ready for work and spend time with the family. So I could instead use an app such as YouBible to *listen* to the Bible while I'm up and around washing my face, preparing coffee, and stretching, then gather my family to meditate and journal along *with* me. It can be the same with prayer. How can I find time to pray when I also want to squeeze in a bit of morning movement, sunlight exposure, sauna, and cold? Couldn't I wake up, go on a sunrise walk while I talk to

God, come back, hit the sauna while I listen to a sermon, then finish with another prayer while I take a cold shower or soak in the cold pool?

Maybe I have a host of recipes I've always wanted to try to cook, but simply don't seem to have the time for all the prepping, chopping, soaking, marinating, and the like. What would it look like if this were easy? Well, I'd have all those ingredients prepped and ready for me so I can focus on nailing the recipe. On my way home from work, could I swing by the dollar store, get my kids a cool, nifty gift, then "employ" them in trade for the gift to do all the prepping and chopping while I create the meal?

Perhaps I want to spend more time with my family in the evening, but feel guilt-tripped over it not being a giant, crazy adventure, a trip to a trampoline park, or a night out at a fancy restaurant. Couldn't I instead surf over to Amazon, spend 100 dollars on enough fun card games and board games to last nearly an entire year, then host a family game night for five nights of the week (incidentally, as I write about in Chapter 5 of *Fit Soul*, your kids love that type of experience just as much as an overpriced vacation to an exotic locale)?

Let's say my wife and I want to have more sex but feel like we always run out of time at the end of the day or have no energy by the time we finally collapse into bed. Why not get some fancy mint or cinnamon-infused breath spray (my wife and I actually do this, and we use a brand called "Dirt" spray), keep an incense stick and lighter next to our bed, set a smartphone alarm for a beautiful playlist that allows us to greet the morning with fully activated senses, and instead make love in the morning?

What if I want to make a bunch of headway on a new book but simply don't have the time or desire to be hunkered over my keyboard all morning long? Could I buy a simple digital recording device or use the voice dictation app on my phone to speak my book ideas and chapter outlines to myself while I'm out walking, then come back and upload that to a virtual transcriptionist or an online transcription service like those I'll link to on the resources webpage for this chapter, thus resulting in all my chapters mapped out for me to easily fill in the blanks once I do have the time to edit and write?

As one final example, suppose I keep getting asked to speak at conferences, but the organizers either A) can't afford my keynote fees or B) I can't free up the time to travel to the event. Could I instead offer to appear virtually via Zoom or Skype, cut my fees in half, and give the presentation from my home office wearing a nice shirt and otherwise clothed in nothing but my boxer shorts? That's certainly a viable, simple option, and one that I actually adopted a great deal during the travel-restricted COVID pandemic.

These may seem like silly or random examples, but they're all elements I've struggled with in my own personal routine—such as finding time for spiritual disciplines, being with family more, cooking more, making love, writing book chapters, or being able to speak at conferences without oodles of travel—and I have successfully used the "what if this were easy?" approach to actually solve these problems.

FLOW, TRUST & RELEASING CONTROL

The entire concept of effortlessness and ease is also highly related to the concept of "flow" and can even be further amplified by getting into flow, which, also known colloquially as being in the zone, is a mental state in which a person performing an activity is fully immersed in a feeling of energized focus, full involvement, and enjoyment in the process of the activity. This flow state often includes releasing control and attachments, trusting, surrendering, and being relaxed and accepting of a situation, rather than trying to micromanage, alter, or control every situation, especially big tasks, projects, or goals.

While there are entire books—most notably Steven Kotler's books *The Art Of Impossible* and *The Rise Of Superman*—written about how to attain and perfect a state of flow, getting into flow as you approach a difficult task isn't really quite as hard and complex as it may seem (heh, sound familiar?). In a sense, to attain this state of ease, you simply 1) invert a situation by asking yourself the questions listed above; 2) let those things that are easy be easy; 3) then relax, trust, and surrender, releasing attachments and control.

Number three can be the most difficult step for most people.

Especially me.

I personally struggle quite often with destressing, relaxing, and accepting a situation, rather than trying to micromanage, alter, or control that situation.

I also struggle with, as Anthony DeMello says in his book *Awareness* and as I mentioned several times throughout this book, detachment and saying to any difficult task I may be attempting to "conquer:"

> *"I really do not need you to be happy. I'm only deluding myself in the belief that without you I will not be happy. But I really don't need you for my happiness; I can be happy without you. You are not my happiness, you are not my joy."*

I struggle with frequent temptations to change or alter or modify a situation that seems near-perfect already, often asking myself whether there's a *better* workout or a *better* diet, or a better Bible reading plan, or a *better* game I could play with the family on family dinner game night, or a *better* restaurant to take my wife on a date to, or a *better* title for an article or paragraph I could add to an article, or a *better* supplement to help me with energy or sleep, or a *better* walk than my daily afternoon farm road trek. But often, if what you're doing is already working, these kinds of temptations simply arise from a "grass is always greener" syndrome—a constant questioning of whether there might be something better out there or a constant comparison of us or our work to others and their work. But, while this type of thought pattern can indeed result in greater drive, personal discoveries, and breakthroughs, or attaining new heights of excellence, it can often threaten to constantly derail us from something that's good enough and working just fine. In other words, you sometimes just need to stay the course because what is working is working.

I struggle with control. I reveal my OCD-like tendencies (and what I've managed to do about them) in Chapter 2, yet when working on any project I still have that nagging tug at the back of my mind to want to ensure I have 100% complete clarity, knowledge of every possible future outcome, the ability to supervise each small step that occurs along the way, and the reluctance to "hand over the reins" to others who may be able to help me and achieve an even better, more efficient outcome than I could achieve myself—all desires that are technically *impossible* to attain if the end goal truly is effortlessness and ease.

I struggle with surrender, which, as David Hawkins writes in his excellent book *Letting Go: The Pathway To Surrender* and as Michael Singer recognizes in his book *The Surrender Experiment*, is synonymous with simply letting go. David says, *"Letting go involves being aware of a feeling, letting it come up, staying with it, and letting it run its course without wanting to make it different or do anything about it. It means simply to let the feeling be there and to focus on letting out the energy behind it."* Yet though I know this, I still become pulled to obsessing over feelings, judging those feelings, and attempting to steer the ship of my life in exactly the direction I want, which often results in a sensation of paddling upstream, rather than floating downstream, reacting to every situation with a sense of acceptance and gratefulness, and then proceeding to do the very best job I can with whatever God has placed upon my plate for the day, accepting and trusting that complete acceptance of what is can be paired with a faith and trust that all will be well, even without my fingers white-knuckling the steering wheel.

As you are hopefully beginning to realize, each of these tendencies—stress, attachment, envy, control, and failure to surrender—all of which threaten to impede flow and ease, are intimately linked to the emotion of *fear*, which, as you'll discover in David Hawkins' books, is one of the lowest, most draining emotions one can experience.

And fear arises from a lack of *trust*.

We try to control things because of what we think will happen if we don't. Control is rooted in fear.

Control is a result of being attached to a specific outcome, even if it may seem that we need to micromanage the entire universe to make that outcome happen.

Control is that feeling you have when your awareness fades, your vision becomes very narrow and focused, your breath becomes shallow, your adrenaline is pumping, and your heart rate increases—all in complete opposition to the biological sensations you would experience when in a state of flow.

Control, ironically, can create a state in which you become *less* able to positively contribute to your work because you feel less in control, begin to micromanage and obsess over details, and get in your own way of being able to see or accept an easier path.

But *trust* enables you to surrender.

In surrender mode, you become calm and peaceful. Breathing deeply, you become present in the moment. You see more clearly and your vision extends out around you, allowing you to see the bigger picture.

When you have surrendered, you have stopped fighting with yourself, fighting with the universe, and fighting with God; you have placed your trust in God; you have accepted the natural flow of things that the Almighty Creator has designed. You have stopped resisting and pushing against reality. You have accepted that, as Matthew 6 says, that *"the birds of the air neither sow nor reap nor gather into barns, yet your heavenly Father feeds them,"* and that you, of much more value than they to your heavenly Father, will all the more be fed, clothed and cared for. Therefore do not worry about tomorrow, for tomorrow will worry about itself. Each day has enough trouble of its own.

Ultimately, you have accepted what is, not in a spirit of helplessness, inaction, or laziness, but in a state of taking wise, flowing, effortless, and easy action, fueled by surrender energy and your knowledge and awareness to be able to ask yourself not only...

...what would it look like if this were easy...

...but also...

...do I trust God that if I release control and surrender to His plan, everything is going to be OK?

When you elegantly combine this level of *trust* paired with asking the easy question and seeking the effortless route, then jumping in with joy and gratitude and getting the job done (as I write about in Chapter 11), life does indeed become a process of *flowing*.

Summary

Look, I'm not saying that life should be easy. Frankly, I don't believe that's the case.

After all, just look at the Apostle Paul, arguably one of the most influential historical figures of all time, and a man responsible for the early massive growth of Christendom and the entire Western culture built upon that foundation. Was his life easy? Let's consider that.

In 2 Corinthians 6:4-10, Paul described his ministry this way:

> *"...as ministers of God: in much patience, in tribulations, in needs, in distresses, in stripes, in imprisonments, in tumults, in labors, in sleeplessness, in fastings; by purity, by knowledge, by longsuffering, by kindness, by the Holy Spirit, by sincere love, by the word of truth, by the power of God, by the armor of righteousness on the right hand and on the left, by honor and dishonor, by evil report and good report; as deceivers, and yet true; as unknown, and yet well known; as dying, and behold we live; as chastened, and yet not killed; as sorrowful, yet always rejoicing; as poor, yet making many rich; as having nothing, and yet possessing all things."*

And in 2 Corinthians 11:23-29:

> *"...in labors more abundant, in stripes above measure, in prisons more frequently, in deaths often. From the Jews five times I received forty stripes minus one. Three times I was beaten with rods; once I was stoned; three times I was shipwrecked; a night and a day I have been in the deep; in journeys often, in perils of waters, in perils of robbers, in perils of my own countrymen, in perils of the Gentiles, in perils in the city, in perils in the wilderness, in perils in the sea, in perils among false brethren; in weariness and toil, in sleeplessness often, in hunger and thirst, in fastings often, in cold and nakedness— besides the other things, what comes upon me daily: my deep concern for all the churches. Who is weak, and I am not weak? Who is made to stumble, and I do not burn with indignation?"*

Elsewhere, even Jesus himself, in Matthew 7:14 says *"...narrow is the gate and difficult is the way which leads to life, and there are few who find it."*

Yet Matthew 11:30 says, *"For my yoke is easy, and my burden is light."*

So yes, while in the case of eternal salvation (a topic I tackle in Chapter 21)—which is the most important aspect of all our existence—forsaking the world's temptations and passing the so-called marshmallow test I describe in Chapter 6 can be a test of perseverance and a road fraught with difficulties and challenges, this doesn't mean that as 1 Corinthians 10:13 says, *"there is no temptation that has overtaken us that God has not provided a way of "effortless escape" from."* Furthermore, despite very few finding and passing through that narrow gate to salvation, the deep peace, love, and joy derived from a daily walk in union with God does actually seem to make living according to His commandments more and more effortless with time and more and more like a "flow state" each day as one flourishes and grows into becoming a new creation.

And from an entirely practical standpoint, though *life* may be fraught with difficulties, certain habits, rituals, routines, tasks, and goals in that life can be tackled with more effortlessness and ease than most people realize, especially when one is in a state of flow, has released attachments and controls, and inverts the scenario to ask themselves the "easy" question. For example, I suspect the Apostle Paul would have leaped at the chance to preach the gospel via a Zoom call to Ethiopia, rather than trekking south for days on a hot and dusty trail to travel to Ethiopia itself, or, as an easier thought exercise, since he *actually* did this, would have dictated to a scribe many of the letters he wrote that later formed significant parts of the New Testament, rather than writing those letters himself. Working smarter, not working harder, is certainly not to be synonymized with lazy shortcuts or taking the easy way out.

Let's finish by summarizing Greg's ideas from *Effortless*.

- *Begin by inverting. When faced with a seemingly difficult task, instead of asking, "Why is this so hard?," invert the question by asking, "What if this could be effortless or easy?"*

- *Next, challenge the assumption that the "right" way is, inevitably, the harder way. Make the impossible possible by finding a more indirect approach. When faced with work that feels overwhelming, ask, "How am I making this harder than it needs to be?"*

- *Have fun. Try to pair your most essential activities with the most enjoyable ones. Accept that work and play can co-exist. Turn tedious tasks into meaningful rituals. Allow laughter and fun to lighten more of your moments.*

- *Release, surrender, and let go of emotional burdens or added stress that you don't need to keep carrying. Focus on what you can control, and accept with joy and gratitude that which you cannot control, relaxing and accepting a situation, rather than trying to alter or control it.*

How about you? What's an activity you do regularly, or an activity, task, or project you find daunting, and what would it look like if it were effortless and easy? Are you willing to surrender complete control, place your trust in God, and enter into the flow, without fussing and

stressing about your entire day? How do you plan on doing that?

For resources, references, links and additional reading and listening material for this chapter, visit GetEndure.com/Chapter12.

CHAPTER XIII

ANALOG

One May, my wife and I were on a morning walk, and chatting about how "big" of a month that was for our thirteen-year-old twin sons.

See, that month was their official "Rite Of Passage" month.

Working in close conjunction with my former podcast guest Tim Corcoran and his Twin Eagles Wilderness School, our sons had been preparing for a rite of passage into adolescence for several years, primarily via immersion in wilderness survival training, plant foraging, nature awareness, and an overall unique but refreshingly ancestral approach to discovering how to creatively co-exist with the giant, magical garden upon which we humans were placed. The month of May culminated in a solo, ego-dissolving excursion into the wilderness, followed afterward by a ceremonial "cutting of the cord" and recognition of each of them taking one more giant step towards becoming a man who can protect, provide, survive, and doing so in a spirit of full love for and presence with others.

Yet, on that same walk with my wife, we simultaneously discussed our observation that because of the boys' daily and constant immersion in an "analog" world chock full of unschooling (I'll link to multiple resources for that topic on the resources webpage for this chapter), real-life experiences, time in nature, being with other people, tennis, jiu-jitsu, sauna, breathwork, cold pools, and trampoline parks...

...they're not very well-versed in the ins and outs of the *digital* world.

They don't have a smartphone.

They don't have a video gaming system.

They don't own any virtual reality (VR) technology.

Though they each own a Macbook for school, they're not really very good at using computers, at least compared to other kids their age, or, as you'll learn shortly, me at their same age.

They have social media accounts and a website for their online healthy cooking show "GoGreenfields," but have chosen to outsource any work on those platforms to a virtual assistant and business manager who they hired (with income they received from sponsorship advertisements and affiliate sales) so that they would have more time to, well, go outside and throw snowballs.

So yeah, they're kind of mini-Luddites.

Me?

I was raised in a highly digital world. One of my first memories is of playing Memory (ironic, I know) on one of the first personal computers that Apple developed (the 1984 Macintosh, to be precise), which my family promptly bought, along with purchasing just about every new fancy personal computer system that ever appeared in Costco, accompanied by high-end graphics cards, new modems (a smokin' 28.8K, baby!), multi-function joysticks, and all the latest games released by Wizard, ESPN Sports, Microsoft, and beyond to support our family's robust video gaming habits.

For most of my teenage years, I spent 2-3 hours on a computer each morning filing insurance claims for my father's non-emergency medical ambulance service, then another 2-3 hours each evening playing a cornucopia of video games, writing stories on a word processor, learning programming languages, and even tinkering with and taking apart my entire computer just to see what the insides looked like. When my father shifted to the telecommunications industry and began to sell the very first cell phones, along with pagers, modems, answering machines, and other hot new digital devices, our family vehicles were suddenly equipped with giant brick-sized cell phones and massive antennas on the roof of each vehicle. Our friends were absolutely astonished that we could make phone calls, *while moving, from a car.*

We also always upgraded to the fastest internet in town as soon as it was released, we were the first in the neighborhood to get caller ID (you mean we can actually see who is calling us on the phone?), and perhaps most comically, my two brothers and I were required to wear personal pagers *everywhere*, basically looking like little drug dealers when really all the pagers were for was so that mom could keep tabs on us and remind us to "pick up the milk" (my older brother eventually hurled his pager out the window of his truck during one particularly stressful grocery shopping list request from mom).

From Tetris and Frogger to World of Warcraft and World of Starcraft to SimCity and DOOM, I was not only an avid video game enthusiast, but even had a private tutor in computer programming to support the technology aspect of my homeschooling curriculum, and had my sights set in high school on being a computer programmer and video game designer. I wasn't half-bad at *playing* strategy-based video games either, but became pretty disillusioned with the entire world of gaming when "cheat codes" got around (it always annoyed me when people didn't play by the rules), so I quit, which I'm sure is the only reason I'm not an e-gaming billionaire YouTube sensation now. 20-20 hindsight, I s'pose.

As a result of growing up in a digital, hyper-connected environment, I've certainly faced an uphill battle in my adult years to develop a true appreciation for the arguably *far more real, palatable, enjoyable, meaningful, and natural analog world*.

But slowly over the years (and ironically through the use of YouTube videos, phone apps, podcasts, and audiobooks), I've discovered how to identify edible and medicinal plants in my backyard.

I've learned how to shoot a bow and hunt small and large game.

I've learned how to navigate and interact with my environment using my senses of smell, touch, taste, and feel.

I've learned how to see trees as actual living entities that I can know by name rather than as one big patch of a giant green somewhat foreign and difficult-to-understand forest. Heck, I can't even walk down a nature trail now without taking my eyes off the dozen or so plants I can actually identify and appreciate. Currently, I'm learning elk language with my sons (they are also learning bird language, but if I have to choose one animal language I have the time to learn, I'll choose an animal that I can also barbecue).

Although I certainly also have a high amount of daily interaction with the digital world—such as owning cryptocurrency, operating multiple websites, blogging, podcasting, audiobook-ing, Clubhousing, Instagram-storying, and even "biohacking" with a dizzying array of self-optimization tools and toys—I also raise goats and chickens, store gold, silver, guns, and ammo, live on solar panels, well water and buried gas tanks, have pantries full of food for years, and spend anywhere from 3-5 hours every day *living outdoors* and embracing an escape from anything remotely digital except, admittedly, the audiobooks I'm constantly listening to on my smartphone, which to me, doesn't feel very digital at all, and more like somebody following me around and peacefully reading a book to me while I'm working out, walking, shopping for groceries, etc.

And I have to admit that despite my continued heavy reliance upon the digital world to operate my health "empire" of podcasting, blogging, speaking on Zoom, consulting on the phone and internet with clients, researching and interacting with a virtual team of contractors and employees (you could probably play a drinking game out of the number of times on my podcast I've said that I "blend ancient science with modern wisdom"), I actually now *like* the analog world a whole lot better than I like the *digital* world.

Long term, I think I'm better for slowly embracing a bit of fully analog Luddite-ism and making a concerted attempt not to be one of those who live in the Digital Matrix.

The Matrix

Yes, I said it: the Matrix.

OK, I'll briefly assume you may not be familiar with the film "The Matrix." If you are, feel free to skip this somewhat spoiler-alert-free paragraph. It goes like this: in the early 21st century, a war between humanity and intelligent machines broke out, which humanity lost, after which all surviving humans were subsequently captured and pacified in a "Matrix," which was basically a shared alternate reality designed to simulate the world as it existed in 1999. Folks could just live their whole little, pleasant lives happily plugged into the Matrix, blissfully unaware they were floating naked in a glass human pod with IV vitamins and calories being pumped into their bodies to sustain their brains and bodies in what was actually a purely digital existence.

Of course, films like "Blade Runner 2049," "V for Vendetta," and "Minority Report" feature similar dystopian futures.

Quite concerningly (to me at least), we don't seem to currently be that far behind these films. Allow me to give you a few examples of what the future of humans living digitally (and virtually) could look like if we remain on a path of nature-distancing, technology-infused, analog-obsolete existences—examples that we all would perhaps have heartily laughed at twenty years ago but that now seem to be inching their way towards becoming a very real part of our everyday life.

Sex...

...not that I endorse sex before marriage (I don't, for a *variety of important reasons I describe in Chapter 3*), but you can just Google *"Youth Having Less Sex"* to see examples of what rampant internet access to pornography, virtual reality headsets, haptic suits, and decreased levels of hormones due to a relatively sedentary, digital lifestyle are doing to young humans. *Supposedly in Japan*, "love dolls" or "sex dolls" are evolving into highly advanced beings capable of giving a man or woman all the carnal pleasure they might desire from intercourse with an actual, real human being. Doug Wilson's book *Ride, Sally, Ride* (which at the time I'm writing this will soon be made into a movie, and I bet it'll be good) describes quite hilariously the slippery slope we are sliding down as identity culture and sex doll advancement results in these little love robots being legally classified as actual artificially intelligent humans. Should us fellas desire to conceive in the future, perhaps we'll be able to just pop a bit of sperm off over to the local sperm bank, swipe left or swipe right to select the perfect mother we desire from our Instafamily phone app, and grow us a little baby from that mother (who may or may not be a robot equipped with a digitally functioning uterus), or perhaps we can just buy a stored embryo with a bit of bitcoin that we can sprinkle our seed on when the time comes. Of course, this birth of new life will only be permitted so long as our environment, home, and banking sensors detect that we have a low enough carbon footprint, adequate amounts of cryptocurrency, and enough food in the refrigerator to responsibly introduce a new carbon-consuming human parasite into the world.

Food...

...why undertake the laborious measures necessary to harvest, grow, prepare, chew, and digest food, when the food of the future can simply be a symmetrical brownish-orange block of perfectly comprised carbon molecules with a customizable and highly engineered protein, fat, and carbohydrate composition? This sustenance will not only match your exact biological needs but when paired with your VR goggles and a haptic headset that triggers neurons responsible for taste sensations of food will allow you to experience all the bliss of happily mowing down a prime rib roast and Bordeaux, blissfully unaware you are just eating brown soy mush and drinking tap water. Fortunately, you will be able to engage in family dinners as your children eat their virtual macaroni and cheese, your spouse their special diet of digital spinach and blueberries, and your entire family plays a rollicking round of Battleship, inside your personal VR headsets.

Fitness…

…soon there will be no need for a gym, health club, backyard, park, or garage workout space. All you'll need to do is pull on your electrical muscle stimulation suit lined with haptic sensors, pair the suit with a virtual reality boxing, tennis, or Himalayan hike workout (the hike will of course be synced with synthetic essential oil diffusers that mimic a walk in the forest), and voila! We can all stumble—pale, clammy, electrocuted and sore—out of our basement from our six-mile trek up to a pristine mountain peak, just in time to refuel with a post-workout meal: two purple pods of engineered meat and a fabricated chain of maltodextrin beads blended in the perfect protein to carbohydrate ratio, containing as a pleasant bonus (when paired with our haptic tasting headset), the addictively succulent flavor of roast chicken and dark chocolate. Beat that, Rocky Balboa, with your stupid jogging suit, freezing cold Russian snow workouts, and raw eggs in a blender.

Hunting…

…reminiscent of the old-school Duck Hunt Nintendo game, you will be able to take your bow with the fake rubber-tipped arrows to a virtual hunting range, shoot at digitized animals of your choice, take part in online hunting competitions, and have your supper that night be comprised of a virtual meatapalooza that allows you to track, hunt, shoot, and subsequently eat elk (soy elk, that is) in the span of a pre-dinner hour. For those of us with ample acreage, our virtual hunting headsets may possibly blind us to the fact that our entire backyard garden has been eaten by a recent infestation of whitetail deer (a quite common occurrence now that hunting land doesn't need to be managed quite as intensively anymore) but it sure beats having to get up at 4 am and trudge through the hills to find food, and at least it wasn't the stray wolf pack who ate your neighbor's dog last week while he was in the same state of blinded indoor digital hunting oblivion.

Plant medicine…

...why embark upon an expensive and time-consuming trip to Peru for an Ayahuasca immersion when you will be able to simply strap on an Oculus Rift and use a software system like Tripp paired perhaps with a carbon dioxide Carbogen-like or xenon gas inhalation device (yes, I have friends who are already doing this very thing) to create a virtual reality, highly psychedelic, and hallucinogenic experience in which you can dissolve ego, simulate death, and release trauma—all with none of the plane tickets, the mosquitoes, or the puking. Heck, if you get to be a really good psychonaut perhaps you can, while nestled in the comfort of your basement couch, or perhaps while floating in a Matrix-esque tube with electrodes attached to your head, be utilized and employed by a high-ranking government agency who can take your medicinalized ramblings and use your thoughts and ideas to create an oracle-like scenario in which you help them predict the future, brainstorm difficult problems, or solve crimes, somewhat reminiscent of the CIA's secret MK-ULTRA program (a 1950's search for a mind-control drug like LSD that could be weaponized against enemies).

Sheesh, even if, 50 years from now, some global governmental entity *isn't* planting us in giant tubes at birth and feeding us baby food through an umbilical cord we never got cut off so that they can harvest our mitochondrial ATP energy to build new servers, our neural firing patterns and brainwaves to design better AI, or our blood cells to develop new vaccines, sometimes I wonder if A) we will eventually get to the point where we gladly volunteer ourselves and our children for that flavor of digital living because, well, it's paid for, we're fed, and get to play video games in our head all day, and B) if we're simply repeating the Tower Of Babel scenario again.

Yeah, the Tower Of Babel.

The Tower of Babel story—as told in the Genesis 11:1–9 narrative—describes a united human race in the generations following the Great Flood, around 1285 BC, who spoke a single language and eventually migrated eastward, where they then agreed to build a city and a tower tall enough to reach heaven, saying,

> *"Come, let us build ourselves a city, with a tower that reaches to the heavens, so that we may make a name for ourselves; otherwise we will be scattered over the face of the whole earth."*

But God came down to see the city and the tower the people were building, and He said:

"If as one people speaking the same language they have begun to do this, then nothing they plan to do will be impossible for them. Come, let us go down and confuse their language so they will not understand each other."

So God confounds their speech so that they can no longer understand each other, and subsequently scatters them from there over all the earth, and they stopped building the city and the Tower Of Babel.

But isn't an attempt to create a digital living scenario in which we have safety and complete control over each and every possible outcome—as opposed to the unpredictability, chaos, and actual danger we may encounter when in a less controlled environment such as nature—an attempt to *be* a sort of god, or worse yet, to be *God*, just like the folks building the Tower of Babel seemed to want to be?

I don't know about you, but I'd personally rather exist in a slightly dangerous, unpredictable, and chaotic analog world in which I know everything is *real* and in which I could get along just-fine-thank-you without so much as a single smartphone, compared to a safe, clean, predictable, yet ultimately fake and relatively unimpactful digital world. Hopefully, I'll never have to choose between the two and can simply continue to embrace the analog while responsibly utilizing the digital.

The Hows of An Analog World

Right then, so, how does one embrace analog in a world gone digital? Here's a few tips:

1. **Connect to nature.** No, I mean *really* connect to it, in a sensual way. Go outside, gather a handful of dirt up into your cupped palms, and take a giant whiff of that rich, earthy smell. Go for walks in the wind and the rain and embrace those elements, too. Next time you've got some privacy to yourself, lay outside naked in the sunshine in your backyard. Every time you step outside, think of yourself as a newborn baby and curiously, fearlessly soak in something new every time.

2. **Create real stuff you can feel, touch and smell.** Yes, yes, I know that new digital creations such as NFT's are *digitally* attractive, but deep down in your soul, don't you *know* that it's more meaningful to get a framed, analog photograph or piece of art from your loved one, as opposed to a digitally SMS'd snapshot? Humans built with the ability to see, touch, taste, and smell created art, so despite how simple it can be to pride yourself upon an epically-edited Instagram gallery, perhaps instead try to dust off your physical creativity and take hands-on moments (with your opposable thumbs and all) in life to paint a watercolor postcard, carve a wooden spoon, learn how to repair a bicycle, or even take a pottery or glass-blowing class, and to embrace the flaws, imperfections, and slight chaos that arises when building with objects other than 0s and 1s. For inspiration, check out the books *Why We Make Things and Why It Matters: The Education of a Craftsman* and *Making Good: An Inspirational Guide to Being an Artist Craftsman*.

3. **Know the dangers.** Educate yourself on the massive amount of unnatural EMFs you're likely exposed to if your digital life far outbalances your analog life. On the resources webpage for this chapter I'll link to my favorite three podcasts I've recorded about these so-called "non-native electromagnetic fields," and what to do about them.

Dr. Joseph Mercola's book *EMF'd* is also a fantastic overview of exactly how to choose wisely when selecting things like wearables, smart appliances, and home electronics, and how to protect your cells from the ever-increasing volley of electronics exposure. Trust me: it's so much easier to place your phone in airplane mode and trade the VR headset in for a bicycling helmet when you understand that your cells have a surprisingly finite capability to be able to withstand 24-7 bombardment with manmade electricity.

4. **Learn to survive in an analog world.** Really, if you're following tip #1, you'll ideally also want to learn basic skills such as how to start a simple fire, how to identify edible or medicinal plants in your own backyard, how to negotiate with or even defend yourself against threatening people or animals, and how to be prepared for the inevitable unpredictability of the analog world. Neil Strauss's book *Emergency*, in which Neil lives "off-grid" in the middle of LA for several months, could be an inspiring read for you to get started. You can also Google "NAME OF YOUR TOWN wilderness survival," take a local hunter's education course, or even sign up for something like a Sheepdog Course, which my wife and I have both taken, to learn how to engage in close-quarter combat,

identify potential threats or escape routes in areas such as parking lots or theatres, and how to handle basic weaponry (I'll link to an entire podcast I recorded about this experience on the resources webpage for this chapter). You don't have to necessarily earn a "Hard-To-Kill" or "Badass" badge, but generally, I don't think there's much wrong with having that moniker floating around in the back of your mind, or at least committing to having some sort of dependable chops that allow you to thrive even without a computer, a smartphone or a grocery store.

5. **Use your memory.** Look, I'll readily admit that by digitally outsourcing the rote memorization tasks we normally would have struggled with for much of human history, such as "what are the step-by-step directions to Grandma's house" or "what's my phone number," "what's the square root of 1000," we likely have freed up our brain to engage in more creative or meaningful tasks. In other words, that brain surgeon whose job was replaced by a fully automated, AI-driven robot may be a physician who instead goes on to cure cancer, or develop a safer drug, or discover a better vaccine and that New York taxi cab driver who can now outsource to Google Maps may have just a bit more creative steam left upon arriving home from work to paint something inspiring for a local gallery. But science has also repeatedly demonstrated that memorizing facts and skills does indeed keep the brain young, so you shouldn't assume you should just use Google and Siri everything. For example, I personally memorize chords on the guitar, memorize Bible verses, memorize card game and board game rules, and memorize names of plants, trees, and even physiological mechanisms I may need to describe on a podcast or in a speech. Build memory into your life, somehow. For me, that's generally with music, nature, and facts that I find myself frequently needing to recall anyways. Author Arlene Taylor's website and writings, which I'll link to on the resources webpage for this chapter, is good for getting practical, fun quick tips and games for memory development and maintenance, as is Jim Kwik's book *Limitless*.

6. **Go analog with entertainment.** Entertaining yourself with non-technology options can be an entirely different, multi-sensorial experience, especially when compared with digital entertainment immersion. So while you don't need to completely eschew your Kindle, you should also read paper books and feel those pages turning in your hands or feel your pen scratching in the margins on the paper. Get a turntable and play a few records. Get a Polaroid camera and print out some real photos (ironically, those cameras seem to be gaining in popularity once again, anyways). Go to a live concert or play. Sure, you can't quite so easily

fast forward or quickly scroll to get to the parts you want, but this can force a sort of mindful attention that is often difficult to come by in a scroll-and-click type of existence.

7. **Play a ball or balance sport.** I'll admit that Peloton bikes, Tonal cable machines, Mirror workouts, Ergatta rowing, Fightclub boxing, Katalyst electrostimulation, and other forms of relatively digital fitness are convenient and can even be highly efficient "hacks'" for getting fitter faster, but none involve the same level of the personal interaction, social environment, hand-eye coordination, balance and unpredictability of playing an analog sport, particularly a ball or balance sport that fully engages your senses, such as pickleball, tennis, volleyball, ping-pong, pick-up basketball, tossing a pigskin at the park, kicking a soccer ball with your kids, throwing a paddleboard in the river, or finding a new mountain bike trail.

8. **Learn to navigate.** Despite the nervousness and mild panic that may ensue if you try to so much as leave to shop for groceries without your precious phone navigation system, you really should try to rely just a bit less on the little voice in the phone to tell you where to turn next and actually pay mindful attention to where you are in the world, and how your city and neighborhood is generally laid out. As I discuss in detail in a podcast that I'll link to on the resources webpage for this chapter, in a manner quite similar to birds, bees, and sharks, human beings are equipped with a bit of the mineral magnetite in our "snouts" that actually allows us to sense directions such as north, south, east, and west magnetically. Most humans, save for a few Aboriginal tribes, have lost touch with this capability due to its modern lack of necessity in an era of GPS and Google Maps, but that doesn't mean that you shouldn't at least have a rough understanding of basic navigation skills. Know where the sun rises and sets. Know the major constellations and their positions in the night sky. Take a quick way-finding, map, and compass course, such as at your local REI or even online via YouTube (yes, I get the irony), to learn daytime and nighttime navigation. Ask a real, human, flesh-and-blood person for directions (trust me, they won't bite). I guarantee you'll find it slightly empowering and confidence-instilling to know how to find your way from Point A to Point B without the use of digital technology.

9. **Live with people, in a culture.** Knowledge, beliefs, arts, laws, customs, capabilities, habits, and traditions are a crucial part of family, legacy, and community-building. While there's nothing inherently wrong with working

from your laptop on an isolated beach in Thailand via a digital nomadic lifestyle, you may also want to think about actually setting up roots somewhere and a place you call home—a place with neighbors you frequently see, a coffee shop you visit each day, or the same set of friends your children might play with each week. Take your family out on the town to restaurants and tennis outings and farmer's markets. Go to a local church. Throw dinner parties. Plant a garden. Mow your lawn. Volunteer in the community. Go pick up trash somewhere along the road. Engage in activities like this that constantly remind you that you are a real human, living a remarkable life and culturally evangelizing those around you with the peace, love and joy that comes from loving others, loving God, and savoring His creation.

Ultimately, technology isn't bad. I use it every day. More than most, actually.

In our digital world, it is easy for us to believe that technology must always take the form of tools such as digital smartphones and computers. But even crude tools such as cooking knives, shovels, rakes, hoes, hammers, nails, and saws are all technological innovations. Arguably, one of the most important pieces of technology in all of human history is the printing press, which revolutionized the world, allowing books and other printed materials to be mass-produced cheaply and efficiently, and making them available for mass distribution, not just for the wealthy or those with high societal status. Just imagine how much good has been done in the world now that everyone can own their own copy of a Bible, and have access to libraries of other knowledge that kings of old would never have possessed in their wildest dreams. Similarly, social media, despite its increasingly common vilification, can be used to encourage others, bring together neighborhoods, spread news, rally community volunteers, share inspiring photographs, and communicate in ways that can be largely positive and even world-changing.

So technology itself isn't evil, but it can be used by broken and sinful people for nefarious and evil purposes. As Paul writes in 1 Corinthians 10:23, *"All things are lawful for me, but not all things are helpful; all things are lawful for me, but not all things edify."* Just watch a documentary like "The Social Dilemma" to see what I mean. Technology, especially digital technology, can also take us so far away from savoring God's creation that we can slip into a pitiable existence in which we aren't fully tapping into the wondrous body, brain, and senses that God has blessed us with because we are simply too immersed in a somewhat fake digital world. Even

AI, as described in the book *The Age of AI: Artificial Intelligence and the Future of Humanity* is being used in countries like China, Russia, North Korea, and Egypt to demean certain people or deny them fundamental human rights. But this same AI technology can also be used ethically to identify criminals, stop terrorist threats, or allow you to pay for a meal at a restaurant by simply smiling at a camera.

If we are in union with God and acting in a full spirit of loving others, we can redeem just about any human invention—including technology—for noble and righteous use, especially if we resist the temptation to become so attached to that technology that in its absence we cannot fully function as a human being, or at least cannot walk ten steps without imagining that our phone is vibrating like a biological implant in our pockets so we had better check it.

Summary

Look, barring a solar flare or some other kind of natural or manmade disaster, we'll likely continue to experience an onslaught of new technologies and digital infiltration into nearly every crook and cranny of our lives. AI and VR, extreme automation, sex dolls, and smartphone addictions may very well become the status quo in society.

But you can *choose* to live analog in an increasingly digital world.

You can develop a deeper connection to nature in your own backyard and beyond. Go dig up some dandelion greens and toss them in your salad. It's OK. Even if UberEats didn't deliver it, you won't die. You can engage and train your senses by foraging plants like this, and also by growing your own vegetables and barbecuing your own meat.

You can create real stuff that is more tangible and meaningful than 0s and 1s, like cartoons, drawings, carvings, paintings, musical compositions, and handcrafted gifts. Nobody cares if it sucks. They care that it's coming from you and that it's *real*.

You can look people in the eye (even if you can't see the rest of their face because of some darn virus protection mask) and see them as real human beings. Do that, as much as you can.

You can play tennis and golf and volleyball and badminton on a real lawn with real friends, no devices required.

Yes, you can continue to live a remarkable analog life, *while still being grateful for and retaining a responsible use of the conveniences of the digital world.*

...while still being grateful for and retaining a responsible use of the conveniences of the digital world.

After all, God made us His divine image-bearers, and as tiny creators who are inspired by our Creator, as I describe in Chapter 9, we humans have learned to forge earth's elements to fashion technology and computers and phones and circuit boards and all other manners of other digital magic, and it is *all* a gift from God. But any gift from God can become a sin, an idol, and a curse, particularly when we grow so attached to that gift that it becomes a god from which we are incapable of detaching ourselves.

So know how to detach from digital, and embrace analog. Your life will be more full as a human because of it.

How about you? Do you prefer the analog world and eschew the digital world? Do you try to elegantly blend both with responsibility? Do you think, based upon our extreme reliance, addiction to, and seeming irrational embrace of every new technology, we're all going to hell in a handbasket?

For resources, references, links and additional reading and listening material for this chapter, visit GetEndure.com/Chapter13.

CHAPTER XIV

BOOKENDS

Anyone who has struggled with organizing their personal library, or any random bookshelf in a house, knows how handy a decent set of bookends can be. Bookends are simply some type of tall, sturdy, and heavy enough item that, when placed at either end of a row of upright books, supports or buttresses the books so that they don't topple over, especially when there's a long line of books, books of varying sizes, or no other good way to support all those precious books.

I like to think of my own morning and evening journaling, meditation, prayer and spiritual disciplines practice as a bit of a bookend approach to my day: a helpful support and buttressing process that serves as a reliable and positivity-infusing habit that makes each day better and—just like a workout routine that consists of, say, a morning sunshine walk and an evening weight training session - allows for a gradual build-up of increase in spiritual stamina and endurance.

For this bookends process, I use my handy Spiritual Disciplines Journal. But I have a very unique approach that I've honed over the years to get the most out of the journal. I detail the thought and theory behind actual disciplines in the journal (namely: gratitude, service, self-examination and purpose) in my book Fit Soul, and also explain them all in more detail in the pages of the journal, but the purpose of this chapter is to give you insight into my own practical usage of the journal.

So in the comprehensive walk-through video that I'll link to on the resources webpage for this chapter, and in the written description below, I'll fill you in on how I personally combine spiritually strengthening strategies such as meditation, breathwork, visualization, tapping, prayer, gratitude, service, self-examination, and purpose into my morning and evening journaling practice.

Bookend #1:
The Morning Spiritual Disciplines Journal Practice

For your morning journaling practice, I recommend that you find or create a "sacred space" that you can go to each time you journal. This can be a comfortable meditation cushion placed in a quiet area of the house, a favorite spot in your backyard or a nearby location in nature, inside a peaceful sauna if you happen to have one, or, if you're the type of person who knows that once the day's busy-ness gets going you'll be more likely to skip your journaling practice, simply laying in bed each morning.

Once you've found a good spot, here's what to do if you want to simulate my own practice, which seems to work quite well.

Morning:

1. Download the free Insight Timer app. Set the timer for a 7-minute meditation (I use Angel Choir as my background music of choice) and then also set a timer to chime at the beginning of the meditation, then the first 2-minute mark, the second 2-minute mark, and the third 2-minute mark.

2. Begin to breathe with a 6 count in and a 6 count out, using a long, slow, and deep breath, and preferably a breath through the nose, generated from deep in your belly.

3. Read the verse at the top of your page in the *Spiritual Disciplines Journal*, then start the timer. For the first 2 minutes, meditate upon that verse. What does it mean to you? Ask God for clarity. Tell Him *"I am here."* Open your eyes and read the verse again if you'd like. These first 2 minutes are for you to connect to that truth you just read, connect to yourself, and the way your body is feeling, and connect to God.

4. When the bell chimes at the first 2-minute mark, begin to dwell upon what you are grateful for that day. Visualize someone or something you are grateful for and bring it to life in your mind's eye. See it. Feel it. Sense it. Breathe the gratefulness into your heart's center (a technique called "quick coherence," which you can learn more about at HeartMath.com/quick-coherence-technique). When you're ready, write down what it is you are grateful for in your

journal, and if you finish before the next bell chimes, close your eyes and return back to dwelling on the gratefulness as you continue your deep breathing pattern.

5. When the bell chimes at the 4-minute mark, begin to think about who you can pray for, help, or serve on that day. Ask God to bring someone to mind if you can't think of anyone. Write the name of that person in your journal, then close your eyes and begin to plan how you can go out of your way to serve them, help them, or even simply pray for them. In that very moment, begin to send that person positive emotions and pray for them, though you'll want to commit to continuing to do so throughout the rest of the day as well.

6. When the bell chimes at the 6-minute mark, raise your hand to your chest and begin to tap over your heart's center, about fifteen to twenty times. This is a process of setting an "anchor" for the feeling of peace you are experiencing as you approach the end of your 7-minute meditation. Anytime you are stressed later in the day, you can return to that same feeling of peace instantly, without a 7-minute meditation, by simply tapping in that same location. As you are tapping, listen to God, continue to pray, continue to breathe long, deep, and slow, and enjoy the feeling of peace, love, and joy.

7. At the very end of my own meditation, right at the 7-minute mark after I've finished my tapping, I like to finish by taking one final deep breath in through the nose, then release a long, audible sign through the mouth, and finally, recite the The Lord's Prayer. Why this prayer? Frankly, Jesus said it was how we are to pray, it provides good structure and prayer training for other prayers you might say throughout the rest of the day, and it's quite easy to memorize and recite, which means you can rely upon it even when you don't know what to say or don't know how to pray.

Although a mere seven minutes may seem like quite a brief amount of time for your morning practice, if you're anything like me, you'll find that this do-able chunk of time allows for greater consistency, a low barrier-to-entry, and greater conduciveness to gathering loved ones, friends or family members who may want to join you, without having to "herd cats" for some kind of epic but time-consuming morning meditation. This is the same reason most of my workouts don't last much longer than around thirty minutes. I know that a brief workout that I'll do every day of the year is much better than a long, brutal multi-hour marathon-esque workout that I grit my teeth to even get started and am more prone to skip or to only squeeze in one or two days of the week.

Evening:

For your evening journaling practice, you can return to your sacred space, or (and I've found this works because the evening practice tends to be quite relaxing), you can do it in bed as the very last thing you do before you fall asleep each night.

1. You will not really need the Insight Timer app for evening journaling and meditation, but you can use it if you would like.

2. To begin, I simply close my eyes, and settle into a 4:8 breathwork pattern, which is slightly more calming than the 6 in/6 out breath from the morning, and is simply a 4 count in and an 8 count out, preferably through the nose. The process of exhaling for a longer period of time than you inhale will naturally activate your rest-and-digest parasympathetic nervous system, and prepare your body for restful, refreshing sleep.

3. As you breathe, for anywhere from 3 to 6 minutes, begin to visualize the day that's just passed by. During this time, I recommend you replay your entire day in your mind like a movie, watching yourself in the third person and identifying what you have done well, what you could have done better, and where you felt most self-actualized and connected to your purpose statement. Watching the character of yourself in your mind, in the third person, ask yourself what you *aren't* rooting for the character to do, or wishing they'd done differently, or where they failed and learned. Ask yourself what you are proud of that character doing and how you really see them acting their best or, in that movie, where you're really rooting for them as a laudable hero. Finally, ask yourself where that person seemed most "in the flow" and doing exactly what seems to be the very reason they are in the movie in the first place. Where are they most purpose-filled? As you play the movie in your mind, stop when necessary and write down in the journal what you have done well, what you could have done better, and when or where you lived your life's purpose.

4. I like to finish with a prayer of gratitude and a request to God for a refreshing night of sleep and an impactful day on the morrow, then I smile, open my eyes, finish and tuck away my journal to have it ready for the following morning!

Like the morning meditation, this practice is brief, with a low barrier-to-entry but a great deal of value packed into a short period of time. I've personally found the process of self-examination to be particularly impactful for learning from each day and making the next day even better, more purpose-filled, more productive and more connected to God. I enable myself to learn from my failures, see how certain elements of my day were structured to allow me to do good, and identify the sections of my day that seem most impactful and purpose-filled. As a result, every day gets just a little bit better, and these gradually better and better days tend to "stack" throughout the entire year, and provide for a veritable renewing of the mind and spirit that allows you to grow more like Christ with each consecutive day.

Surrender

Finally, I'd like to leave this chapter with a word of encouragement for you, especially if you still find yourself struggling to prioritize or to carve out the time for the practice I've just described, or for breaks to pray and remain in union with God throughout the day.

I was recently reading Andrew Murray's provoking book Absolute Surrender. It's a good book and well worth a read.

Regarding union with God, he says:

> *"The keeping is to be continuous. Every morning, God will meet you as you wake. It is not a question: If I forget to wake in the morning with the thought of Him, what will come of it? If you trust your waking to God, God will meet you in the mornings as you wake with His divine sunshine and life. He will give you the consciousness that through the day you have got God to continually take charge of you with His almighty power. And God will meet you the next day and every day. Never mind if, in the practice of fellowship, failure sometimes comes. If you maintain your position—and say: 'Lord, I am going to expect You to do Your utmost, and I am going to trust You day by day to keep me absolutely,' your faith will grow stronger and stronger. You will know the keeping power of God in unbrokenness."*

This statement resonated with me...

...because that daily, specifically morning, keeping of union with God is *hard*.

I don't know about you, but it's hard for me to wake and suppress the urge to leap from bed (especially since clearly identifying my life's purpose)—and instead actually take the time to breathe, read my Bible, and complete my spiritual disciplines journaling.

It's even *harder* when I'm traveling and I went to bed later than planned due to late-night dinner obligations, or had a crappy night of sleep because I'm outside my home environment; and then I wake knowing I'm supposed to be at a conference or meeting in an hour and I have so much to do to get ready, yet I know that the very *best* thing I can do is greet the day by greeting God.

Heck, even if I set aside for a moment any thoughts of stopping for a meditation later in the morning, or squeezing in an AM workout, or having a few quality moments with the family...

...the mere act of praying, cracking open the Bible, and spending time in God's Word before my feet hit the floor is just...

...hard.

It takes time. Admittedly, not a ton of time—as ten to fifteen minutes usually suffices for me—but it's time nonetheless.

And it takes trust. Trust that God will provide for me even if I don't bang out those twenty e-mails that I really want to get off my chest or out of my mind before I start my "real" workday; trust that God will put food on the table even if I don't get those extra precious few minutes of work in; and trust that God will help me remember all those jumbling thoughts marching through my head that I woke up with and I want to act upon right away.

Is it the same for you?

Fortunately, Andrew presents a solution within the pages of the book, and based on the book's title, the solution comes as no surprise: absolute surrender.

He says...

..."*When God has begun the work of absolute surrender in you, and when God has accepted your surrender, then God holds Himself bound to care for it and to keep it. Will you believe that?*"

He then goes on to write:

> *"Oh, we find the Christian life so difficult because we seek for God's blessing while we live in our own will. We should be glad to live the Christian life according to our own liking. We make our own plans and choose our own work, and then we ask the Lord Jesus to come in and take care that sin shall not conquer us too much, and that we shall not go too far wrong; we ask Him to come in and give us so much of His blessing. But our relationship to Jesus ought to be such that we are entirely at His disposal, and every day come to Him humbly and straightforwardly and say: 'Lord, is there anything in me that is not according to Thy will, that has not been ordered by You, or that is not entirely given up to You?' Oh, if we would wait and wait patiently, I tell you what the result would be. There would spring up a relationship between us and Christ so close and so tender that we should afterward be amazed at how we formerly could have lived with the idea: 'I am surrendered to Christ.' We should feel how far distant our intercourse with Him had previously been, and that He can, and does indeed, come and take actual possession of us, and gives unbroken fellowship all the day. The branch calls us to absolute surrender."*

So what does all this mean?

When we *truly* love God and have a true desire to live a Christian life, when we have truly surrendered all to God that He will care for our each and every need, when we come to God daily and pray—yes, earnestly pray—that we would have the fortitude and trust to surrender *all* worries, work, racing thoughts, lack of time, stress, pressure, scarcity, and doubt upon Him, then we will stay in bed to greet God each morning and read that Bible not because we *have* to, but because every last shred of our being *wants* to and *loves* to.

So I pray each day that as I grow in grace and grow in God that He would make every morning in bed reading the Bible something I look forward to just as much as a juicy ribeye steak, a glorious sip of a fine Bordeaux, a beautiful hike with my family, a luxurious date with my wife, or a game of family tennis at the park.

Summary

In the same way that a good set of bookends will keep your library from toppling, a good routine that begins and ends each day can serve to keep you calm, peaceful, grateful, purpose-filled, impactful and infused with a spirit of loving God and loving others throughout the hours between each morning and evening. I can't recommend this practice highly enough, and hope I've now equipped you with all the knowledge, direction and tools you need to implement it.

How about you?

Do you currently have a morning or evening meditation or journaling practice? Do you trust that God will create the time to do so, and care for you even if you feel like you just can't squeeze it in? Is there anything else that is keeping you from beginning, and if not, how and when do you plan to start?

For resources, references, links and additional reading and listening material for this chapter, visit *GetEndure.com/Chapter14.*

CHAPTER XV

PRAYER

Prayer has been on my mind quite a bit lately.

I suppose my desire to explore prayer and focus more on the practical aspects of tapping more deeply into the power of prayer was partially sparked when I was engaged in a bit of deep research and writing about union with God for my book Fit Soul. In Chapter 19 of that book, I included the following anecdote:

> *"...magically, this same all-powerful God continues to walk among us mere humans. And we can actually talk to him. To me, this concept is simultaneously breathtaking and humbling. Don't take for granted the ability to be in daily union with the mightiest King that has ever existed—to walk with Him, talk with Him, and share his joy...*
>
> *...I have three simple suggestions for you to maintain your union with God.*
>
> *First, take everything to God in prayer. He will grant you wisdom and discernment if you ask for it. He will give you answers. All you need to do is ask (as the words of Matthew 7:7 say, 'Ask, and it shall be given you; seek, and ye shall find; knock, and it shall be opened unto you.') So this week, every day, even with the smallest of decisions, consider coming to God with questions such as 'What should I eat?,' 'Who should I ask about this problem?,' 'What task should I tackle first?' Then simply stop, breathe, and listen for His still, small voice in the silence. He will give you direction.*
>
> *Second, stop at a few points during your busy day, once again breathe, and simply survey the wonders of Creation around you and speak to God a simple phrase: 'I am here,' and you can even add to that phrase, 'Speak to me and show me what You want to teach me.'*

Then, once again, be silent and listen. God's words to you will once again come in the still, small silence.

Finally, be grateful and stop to thank God multiple times during the day. In my article on breathwork, I told you:

> *'...each night, as I fall asleep to the gentle diaphragmatic lull of my own '4-count-in-8-count-out' breathwork pattern, I'm silently thanking God and trusting God that there will be yet more oxygen available for me for my next inhale. Indeed, the mere act of mindful breathing combined with a silent gratefulness to God for each and every breath is a wonderful practice, and one I recommend you try the next time you're stuck in twenty minutes of traffic. After all, our great Creator smiles when we worship Him, and I certainly think that no king would complain of a subject entering their throne room for several minutes and saying with the deepest gratitude with each breath... Thank you...thank you...thank you...'*

But don't just thank Him with your breath. Thank Him before a meal. Thank Him when you see a bald eagle soaring overhead. Thank Him when you're stuck in traffic. Thank Him when you get a good e-mail. Thank Him when you get a bad e-mail. Thank Him when a loved one hugs you. Thank Him when a loved one is sick. Thank Him in all things."

Since writing that chapter, and discovering the deep meaning and fulfillment I've derived from my daily Scripture reading practice and the bookends habit I described in the last chapter, all while continuing to focus on building my union with God, I've continued to study prayer while pondering questions such as...

...How can I practically implement prayer into my life more often, without it seeming like a formal, dry, or intellectual affair, which it often seems to be for me?

...What happens to my psychology and mood when I pray?

...How did great leaders and inspirational figures from history pray?

In my own personal exploration of prayer, I think I've found some pretty good answers to these questions, and so, I want to share those

answers about prayer with you in this chapter.

The Power Of Prayer

Before delving into the practical aspects of how we can and should pray, it's important to understand how powerful prayer really can be. In his thought-provoking book, The Way of the Heart: Connecting with God Through Prayer, Wisdom, and Silence, Henri J.M. Nouven writes:

> "Prayer is standing in the presence of God with the mind in the heart; that is, at that point of our being where there are no divisions or distinctions and where we are totally one. There, God's Spirit dwells and there the great encounter takes place. There, heart speaks to heart, because there we stand before the face of the Lord, all-seeing, with us."

Thomas Merton, a twentieth-century American Trappist monk and social activist, was known as a great thinker, philosopher, and a devout man of God. One of Merton's most notable accomplishments was sharing his views of the transformative experience of what he described as a "mystical union with God." Merton considered prayer to be the most worthy of all activities in which a human can engage, with rewards that are twofold: contact with God, and the attainment of the most elevated expression and highest actualization of one's own self.

I fully agree with Nouven and Merton. There is something very special that happens during prayer—something that goes beyond what you may experience while reading Scripture, meditating, journaling, singing, or any of the other spiritual disciplines.

Perhaps part of the power of prayer is related to what actually occurs on a biological level when we pray. In the book *Miracles Every Day: The Story of One Physician's Inspiring Faith and the Healing Power of Prayer* you can read about a new field of science and faith study called "neurotheology," which blends the existing fields of biology, neurology, psychology, and theology.

At the University of Pennsylvania, Dr. Andrew Newberg directs the Center for Spirituality and the Mind, where he has conducted studies of people who meditate or pray for long periods every day over the course of numerous years. Newberg's research has demonstrated impressive changes as a direct response to prayer in brain structures at the neuronal level. Furthermore, he has found that the longer and more frequently one is engaged in meditation or prayer, the more extensive the changes are in these brain structures.

Specifically, his brain-scan studies have shown that prayer powerfully stimulates the anterior cingulate in the brain, the center of the nervous system in which the balance between thought and feeling is sustained. Prayer seems to "exercise" the anterior cingulate by stimulating, strengthening, and enlarging it—while simultaneously decreasing neuronal activity in the limbic system, where emotions such as fear, shame, and anger are processed. Scientists have actually correlated this type of highly stimulated anterior cingulate with a unique kind of personality characterized by enhanced cognitive function and focus, along with increased stress resilience and a heightened ability to be able to withstand and handle physically, mentally, and emotionally difficult scenarios.

Thomas Merton, who I mentioned above, described in many of his writings moments of transcendence that he experienced during intense prayer, often characterized by feelings of selflessness and timelessness. Brain-scan studies have demonstrated at a structural level that this actually occurs because, during prayer, activity in the parietal lobe decreases, and one of the results of the decrease in activity in the parietal lobe is—you guessed it—an augmented perception of timelessness and spacelessness, very similar to what one might experience from the use of plant medicine or psychedelics.

These insights from neurotheological studies lend scientific credence and a physiological basis to what prophets, philosophers, and religious advocates have believed for millennia: Prayer seems to, nearly magically, change your life for the better. This appears to partially be because the brain becomes less prone to feeling anger, anxiety, aggression, and fear while simultaneously increasing tendencies towards empathy, compassion, and love. This reminds me a bit of the fascinating biological impact of a daily gratitude practice, which leads to the type of cardiovascular, mental, sleep and brain performance impacts I write more about in my book Fit Soul.

Perhaps this is why many notable religious figures of history who have all who have walked closely with God have also viewed prayer as an integral component in their lives. Many of these figures are described in Richard Foster's book *Prayer*, including:

- *Jesus: Jesus frequently slipped away to remote or quiet places to pray and meditate in solitude. In the gospel of Mark we are told, "And in the morning, a great while before day, he rose and went out to a lonely place, and there he prayed" (Mark 1:35).*

- *David: In Psalms 63:1, King David says, "Early will I seek Thee," highlighting the importance of morning prayer, in addition to his vast collection of written prayers throughout the book of Psalms."*

- *The apostles: Although I'm sure the apostles were tempted to invest their energy in many important and necessary tasks, they still gave themselves continually to prayer and the ministry of the word, "But we will give ourselves continually to prayer, and to the ministry of the word." (Acts 6:4).*

- *Martin Luther, German professor of theology, priest, author, composer, Augustinian monk, and seminal figure in the Reformation declared, "I have so much business I cannot get on without spending three hours in prayer." He held as a spiritual axiom that "He that has prayed well has studied well."*

- *English cleric, theologian, and evangelist John Wesley said, "God does nothing but in answer to prayer." He backed up this conviction by devoting two hours daily to a sacred exercise of prayer.*

- *One quite notable feature of David Brainerd, American missionary to the Native Americans was his praying. His personal journal is chock-full of accounts of prayer, fasting, and meditation, such as "I love to be alone in my cottage, where I can spend much time in prayer." and "I set apart this day for secret fasting and prayer to God."*

For these pioneers in the frontiers of faith, prayer was not just a small habit tacked onto the periphery of their lives—rather it was their lives. The following powerful anecdote from Christian evangelist George Muller's *Meditating on God's Word* is, in my opinion, a wonderful example of what can happen when we do not just read the Bible, but also meditate upon it and, most importantly, pray:

> *"While I was staying at Nailsworth, it pleased the Lord to teach me a truth, irrespective of human instrumentality, as far as I know, the benefit of which I have not lost, though now...more than forty years have since passed away. The point is this: I saw more clearly than*

ever, that the first great and primary business to which I ought to attend every day was, to have my soul happy in the Lord. The first thing to be concerned about was not, how much I might serve the Lord, how I might glorify the Lord; but how I might get my soul into a happy state, and how my inner man might be nourished. For I might seek to set the truth before the unconverted, I might seek to benefit believers, I might seek to relieve the distressed, I might in other ways seek to behave myself as it becomes a child of God in this world; and yet, not being happy in the Lord, and not being nourished and strengthened in my inner man day by day, all this might not be attended to in a right spirit. Before this time my practice had been, at least for ten years previously, as an habitual thing, to give myself to prayer, after having dressed in the morning.

Now I saw, that the most important thing I had to do was to give myself to the reading of the Word of God and to meditation on it, that thus my heart might be comforted, encouraged, warned, reproved, instructed; and that thus, whilst meditating, my heart might be brought into experiential communion with the Lord. I began, therefore, to meditate on the New Testament, from the beginning, early in the morning. The first thing I did, after having asked in a few words the Lord's blessing upon His precious Word, was to begin to meditate on the Word of God; searching, as it were, into every verse, to get blessing out of it; not for the sake of the public ministry of the Word; not for the sake or preaching on what I had meditated upon; but for the sake of obtaining food for my own soul. The result I have found to be almost invariably is this, that after a very few minutes my soul has been led to confession, or to thanksgiving, or to intercession, or to supplication; so that though I did not, as it were, give myself to prayer, but to meditation, yet it turned almost immediately more or less into prayer. When thus I have been for awhile making confession, or intercession, or supplication, or have given thanks, I go on to the next words or verse, turning all, as I go on, into prayer for myself or others, as the Word may lead to it; but still continually keeping before me, that food for my own soul is the object of my meditation.

The result of this is, that there is always a good deal of confession, thanksgiving, supplication, or intercession mingled with my meditation, and that my inner man almost invariably is even sensibly nourished and strengthened and that by breakfast time, with rare exceptions, I am in a peaceful, if not happy, state of heart. Thus also the Lord is pleased to communicate unto me that which, very soon after, I have found to become food for other believers, though it was not for the sake of the public ministry of the Word that I gave myself to meditation, but for the profit of my own inner man. The difference between my former practice and my present one is this. Formerly, when I rose, I began to pray as soon as possible, and generally spent all my time till breakfast in prayer, or almost all the time. At all events I almost invariably began with prayer... But what was the result? I often spent a quarter of an hour, or half an hour, or even an hour on my knees, before being conscious to myself of having derived comfort, encouragement, humbling of soul, etc.; and often after having suffered much from wandering of mind for the first ten minutes, or a quarter of an hour, or even half an hour, I only then began really to pray. I scarcely ever suffer now in this way.

For my heart being nourished by the truth, being brought into experiential fellowship with God, I speak to my Father, and to my Friend (vile though I am, and unworthy of it!) about the things that He has brought before me in His precious Word. It often now astonishes me that I did not sooner see this. In no book did I ever read about it. No public ministry ever brought the matter before me. No private intercourse with a brother stirred me up to this matter. And yet now, since God has taught me this point, it is as plain to me as anything, that the first thing the child of God has to do morning by morning is to obtain food for his inner man. As the outward man is not fit for work for any length of time, except we take food, and as this is one of the first things we do in the morning, so it should be with the inner man. We should take food for that, as every one must allow. Now what is the food for the inner man: not prayer, but the Word of God: and here again not the simple reading of the Word of God, so that it only passes through our minds, just as water runs through a pipe, but considering what we read, pondering over it, and applying it to our hearts... I dwell so particularly on this point because of the immense spiritual profit and refreshment I am conscious of having derived from it myself, and I affectionately and solemnly beseech all my fellow believers to ponder this matter.

By the blessing of God I ascribe to this mode the help and strength which I have had from God to pass in peace through deeper trials in various ways than I had ever had before; and after having now above forty years tried this way, I can most fully, in the fear of God, commend it. How different when the soul is refreshed and made happy early in the morning, from what is when, without spiritual preparation, the service, the trials and the temptations of the day come upon one!"

Christians are repeatedly encouraged by Jesus to pray. He tells us in the Gospel of Luke, "*How much more will the heavenly Father give the Holy Spirit to those who ask him (Luke 11:13)."* We are to pray so that God can help us to become more like Him in our own spiritual growth. We are to pray for the renewal and the growth of our soul. We are to pray to give thanks to God for all His blessings and provisions. We are to pray to seek forgiveness for our sins. We are to pray to seek help for others as well as ourselves.

Most importantly, we are to pray *without ceasing*. Here are several of the Scripture references to this concept of constant, incessant prayer:

- *1 Thessalonians 5:17: "Pray without ceasing."*

- *Ephesians 6:18: "Pray in the Spirit at all times and on every occasion."*

- *Matthew 6:5-7: "And when you pray, do not be like the hypocrites, for they love to pray standing in the synagogues and on the street corners to be seen by others. Truly I tell you, they have received their reward in full. But when you pray, go into your room, close the door and pray to your Father, who is unseen. Then your Father, who sees what is done in secret, will reward you. And when you pray, do not keep on babbling like pagans, for they think they will be heard because of their many words."*

- *Luke 11:9: "So I say to you: Ask and it will be given to you; seek and you will find; knock and the door will be opened to you."*

- *Luke 18:1: "Then Jesus told his disciples a parable to show them that they should always pray and not give up."*

- *Colossians 4:2: "Devote yourselves to prayer, being watchful and thankful."*

In other words, our life should ideally be one of constant prayer in which we are continually in union and relationship with God, drawing near to Him from morning to evening. Saint Isaac of Syria, a 7th-century Church of the East Syriac Christian bishop summed it up quite well when he said that *"...it is impossible to draw near to God by any means other than unceasing prayer."*

The Problem With Prayer

However, I don't know about you, but the prospect of praying all the time seems daunting.

After all, when I was growing up in a Christian church, prayer was usually positioned as a formal activity with a specific structure that required carving out time and forethought to wax poetic to the Creator. Not that there's anything wrong with that approach to prayer per se, but I think that when you consider prayer in that way only, it becomes something very much like the same type of formidable, intimidating activity that keeps many people from regular meditation: feeling as though they need to do it in some kind of perfectly systematized way, X number of times per day for Y minute sitting in Z position—which, as anyone who has taken a few simple and calming mindful breaths while stuck in traffic knows is not necessarily the case. Because of this conundrum, it can be easy to verbally attest to the importance of prayer as foundational to a Godly life, but based on our oft-faulty assumptions about how it should be conducted, prayer often gets crowded out as the calendar fills up with other duties or we simply become too mentally drained or fatigued during the day to conduct a "formal prayer session."

Sure, dedicated time to formal, traditional prayer (or meditation)—in which one goes off to a quiet place, kneels or adopts any other prayerful position, and speaks to God for a significant period of time—is certainly laudable and appropriate, but there can be other ways to pray that allow you to "pray without ceasing" without giving up your job, family time, hobbies, and other activities to move to a pristine Himalayan mountaintop so that you can be a constant and unceasing prayer warrior.

I suppose the best way to describe this problem with trying to pray without ceasing is that we tend to over-intellectualize prayer. As opposed to the simple prayer of early Christian hermits, ascetics, and monks such as the Desert Fathers and Mothers of the early church, intellectualized prayer is the common form of prayer encountered and encouraged in most mainstream churches, paired hand-in-hand with didactic and intellectual sermons, argumentative apologetics, and a focus on "prim-n-proper theology" that can stand in stark contrast to a more charismatic and aesthetic approach to speaking with and worshiping God.

For example, I was always taught that I, similar to the Lord's Prayer, should have a distinct prayer structure in which one opens with worship, thanksgiving and gratitude, then on to petitions, then on forgiveness and repentance, and finally, some kind of official prayer closure. The best way I can describe the feeling I sometimes have with this type of prayer is that it sometimes seems to keep me more in a mindset of praying "in the head" than praying "from the heart."

As I tell my children, it is one thing to know about God, but an entirely different thing to truly know God. The former is more mental, and the latter is more spiritual. Ideally, one has a grasp, understanding, and practice of *both*. Similarly, it is one thing to pray intellectually, and quite another to pray in a ripped-open, raw, and emotional manner.

Because of this mental, cognitive approach to prayer that is all-too-common for many people, prayer can often feel as though one is talking to God or talking at God in a lonely one-sided monologue rather than a dialogue...

"...thank you for this..."

"...please give me that..."

"...forgive me for this and that..."

"...whatever your will is in my life..."

"...amen."

In *The Way of the Heart: Connecting with God Through Prayer, Wisdom, and Silence* Henri J.M. Nouwen alludes to this over-intellectualization of prayer when he says:

> "For many of us, prayer means nothing more than speaking with God. And since it usually seems to be a quite one-sided affair, prayer

> *simply means talking to God. This idea is enough to create great frustrations. If I present a problem, I expect a solution; if I formulate a question, I expect an answer; if I ask for guidance, I expect a response. And when it seems, increasingly, that I am talking into the dark, it is not so strange that I soon begin to suspect that my dialogue with God is in fact a monologue. Then I may begin to ask myself: To whom am I really speaking, God or myself?"*

If you think of prayer as simply speaking at God or jumping through a set of structured prayer hoops, then it may not be long before you abandon prayer altogether, primarily because it can feel so intellectual and one-sided.

In contrast, the phrase *"pray without ceasing"* that the apostle Paul uses in his letter to the church in Thessalonians literally translates *"come to rest."* The Greek word for "rest" is *hesychia* and this kind of hesychastic prayer is associated with a style of prayer now called "contemplative prayer," which is very similar to the ancient form of Christian meditation practiced by the Desert Fathers and Mothers of the early church I alluded to above. Contemplative prayer is simply defined as a wordless, trusting opening of self to the divine presence—essentially moving from a "conversation" with God to "communion" with God.

This type of conversation with God abandons a formulaic approach to prayer. Instead, the main themes that characterize a contemplative prayer from the heart are that it tends to be short and sweet, unceasing, and an all-encompassing trusting and opening prayer that descends from the regions of the mind into the regions of the heart. Nouwen defines this descent like this:

> *"When we say to people, 'I will pray for you,' we make a very important commitment. The sad thing is that this remark often remains nothing but a well-meant expression of concern. But when we learn to descend with our mind into our heart, then all those who have become part of our lives are led into the healing presence of God and touched by Him in the center of our being. We are speaking here about a mystery for which words are inadequate. It is the mystery that the heart, which is the center of our being, is transformed by God into His own heart, a heart large enough to embrace the entire universe. Through prayer we can carry in our heart all human pain*

and sorrow, all conflicts and agonies, all torture and war, all hunger, loneliness, and misery, not because of some great psychological or emotional capacity, but because God's heart has become one with ours."

Contemplative prayer often focuses on one word or a simple phrase that is repeated throughout the prayer, or simply at various intervals throughout the day, in a form of near childlike repetition, such as:

"Jesus Christ, have mercy on me…"

or

"Oh God, thank you…"

or

"Lord, I'm so grateful…"

or

"I am here, God…"

I've personally found that a humble repetition of a single word or phrase helps "bring my mind into my heart" more significantly than a lengthy extemporaneous and theologically astute prayer and allows me to, throughout the day, pray without ceasing—without feeling intimidated or overwhelmed by the need to wax fancy or lengthy in my personal prayers. In addition, although I do have a prayer list that I keep for many people I have promised I'll pray for, or people God has placed upon my heart to pray for, I'll often simply draw an image of that person in my mind, or just say that person's name, and trust that God knows exactly what that person needs in the moment. This isn't done out of laziness or haste, but rather out of a desire to be able to simply feel God's presence and speak to God openly throughout the day.

Finally, this type of contemplative prayer lends itself well to meditation and breathwork as well, as one can simply sit still, breathe deeply, allow one's heart to fully open, then repeat a name of God, such as "Abba" or "Creator" over and over again, or an attribute of God, such as "love" or "mercy" over and over again.

Do you see what I'm saying here?

It's basically this: Don't feel as though every time you speak with God it must be a formal, intellectual, theological, and perfectly structured prayer. Don't get me wrong: this type of "complex" prayer is something that I think should be a part of one's prayer life, but doesn't need to be the sole means via which one prays. Instead, prayer can also be a simple acknowledgement of God's presence or a very basic mantra or series of mantras that you repeat at various points throughout the day. For me personally, this has allowed a consistent and achievable ability to be able to truly "pray without ceasing."

But there are other prayer tips and techniques I've discovered along my journey too, and so now I'll share the most helpful ones with you below.

How To Pray

Below are six ways that I've found effective for weaving prayer into my daily routine. As you read through these ways to pray, you may find that some particularly resonate with you, and I hope you find them helpful for enabling yourself to pray without ceasing, from the heart.

1. Memorize Certain Prayers That You Can Recite Throughout The Day

Having prayers that you have memorized or written down to recite throughout the day can be one effective way to pray without ceasing. For example, I recently visited my father Gary Greenfield and spent the weekend with him. He practices Orthodox Christianity and has multiple prayer books full of prayers that he has memorized and recites or reads at various points throughout the day.

One such prayer is known as "the Jesus Prayer," which is a short formulaic prayer esteemed and advocated especially within the Eastern Orthodox churches. It goes like this:

"Lord Jesus Christ, Son of God, have mercy on me, a sinner." This prayer is often repeated continually as a part of a personal ascetic practice and considered to be part of the hesychastic approach to prayer I mentioned earlier in this chapter. Often these types of short and simple memorized or ritualistic prayers are structured throughout the day. Below is an example of such an approach (and I'll link to more details on the history and reasoning behind this structure on the

resources webpage for this chapter):

- *Time: 6:30am and 11:00pm for 20 minutes each time*
- *Begin by lighting a candle, and making three prostrations and then stand quietly to collect yourself in your heart*
- *Trisagion Prayer*
- *One of six morning or evening Psalms*
- *Intercessions for the living and the dead*
- *Psalm 51 and confession of our sinfulness*
- *Doxology and the morning or evening prayer*
- *Personal dialogue with God*
- *Jesus prayer—repeat 100 times.*
- *Reflect quietly on the tasks of the day and prepare yourself for the difficulties you might face asking God to help you*
- *Dismissal prayer*
- *Stop mid-morning, noon, and mid-afternoon to say a simple prayer*
- *Repeat the Jesus Prayer in your mind whenever you can throughout the day*
- *Offer a prayer before and after each meal thanking God and asking for His blessing*

I fully realize that you may have raised an eyebrow at some of the elements above, such as repeating the Jesus Prayer 100 times, and while I fully agree that adherence to this type of rigid, repetitive, or timed prayer structure may not be attainable for many, there are other elements of this schedule that make sense, such as stopping mid-morning, noon, and mid-afternoon to say a simple prayer, or repeating the Jesus prayer in your mind whenever you can throughout the day.

Here's another example: I personally have a memorized prayer that I recite each morning when I jump into my cold pool and swim back and forth. Because the prayer is woven into something I'm already doing anyways each day as part of my routine, it's something that I very seldomly skip, and I've found this approach to actually allow me to systematize the process of speaking to God each morning:

> *"Our Father in heaven, I surrender all to you*
> *Turn me into the father and husband you would have for me to be*
> *Into a man who will fulfill your great commission*
> *And remove from me all judgment of others*
>
> *Grant me your heavenly wisdom*

> *Remove from me my worldly temptations*
> *Teach me to listen to your still, small voice in the silence*
> *And fill me with your peace, your love, and your joy. Amen."*

Of course, another example of a prayer that you can memorize and recite from your heart throughout the day is the Lord's Prayer, from Matthew 6:6-13 in the Bible:

> *"Our Father which art in heaven,*
> *Hallowed be Thy name.*
> *Thy kingdom come. Thy will be done in earth,*
> *as it is in heaven.*
> *Give us this day our daily bread.*
> *And forgive us our debts,*
> *as we forgive our debtors.*
> *And lead us not into temptation,*
> *but deliver us from evil:*
> *For Thine is the kingdom, and the power,*
> *and the glory, forever and ever.*
> *Amen."*

2. Keep A Prayer List

In Chapter 11 of *Fit Soul*, I told you plenty about how to read the Bible, and I filled you in on an app that my entire family uses called YouBible. In addition to offering the convenience of a host of done-for-you Bible reading plans, it also includes a handy prayer list that you can share with anyone else who is your friend or follower on the YouBible app (or you can just keep the prayer list to yourself if you'd like). Since I'm prone to forget people I've offered to pray for or specific things I want to pray about, I find it tremendously helpful to be able to simply open the prayer list on my phone, tablet or computer and have an at-a-glance list of anything or anyone that I want to bring before God. Each morning and evening, my family gathers together for our meditation and journaling practice, and as part of that, use the prayer list to remind us what to pray about. I know others who keep a prayer journal by their bedside or even on a scrap of paper tucked away into their Bible. As an added prayer incentive, motivation and reminder, my wife and I recently purchased a beautiful whiteboard that is now hung on the backside of our bedroom door. Each time I exit our bedroom, particularly when I wake in the morning, I can now see an at-a-glance list of all those we have offered to pray for, or particular needs we are praying for as a family. Keeping your prayer list top-of-mind like this is key for remembering to pray and remember who and what to pray for. In the same way that if you want to trim your waistline, you would hide all candy and sweets from daily visibility, or if you want to have better gut health, you would keep fresh ginger visible on the countertop and jar of sauerkraut prominently displayed in the fridge, if you want to pray more, you should keep your prayer list conveniently visible and accessible.

Some people find that an ever-expanding prayer list like this can be intimidating and lead to similar daunting or time-consuming issues with prayer that I've described earlier in this chapter, but here's the thing: you don't have to go through the *entire list* every time you pray. Often, I'll spend an entire day in multiple prayer sessions attending to just a few people or items who are on the list. What's most important is to actually have a written log *somewhere* of, for example, people who you've told you would pray for, along with the details of what you're praying about for them. Consider this to be built-in accountability for your prayer practice.

3. Pray Regularly With A Spouse Or Loved One

One of the best pieces of marriage advice that I ever received was to pray with my wife each night before bed. As a matter of fact, when I was recently reading the book *Gun Lap: Staying in the Race with Purpose*, which is a book written through the eyes of a faithful old man for old men to read in their later years, the author, Robert Wolgemuth commented that one of the things he wished he'd learned much earlier in life was the marital value of praying with your spouse every night before bed. Although I've slightly adapted that advice to now not only pray with my wife as our heads hit the pillow each night but to also pray with the entire family when we tuck my sons into bed, immediately after journaling and meditating, the concept remains the same as that outlined in Matthew 18:20: *"For where two or three gather in my name, there am I with them."* Not only does the power of prayer seem to become even more magnified when someone is there praying with you, muttering *"Amens"* and *"Yes, Lords"* and squeezing your shoulder or your hand as you pray, but, similar to a prayer list, having someone with which you regularly pray builds in accountability and encouragement to your practice of prayer - even if it's just a few, feeble, tired words uttered to God together as your faces hit the pillows and sleep sets in.

It's also important that there be an understanding between you and whoever it is you're praying with. It can't be a loosy-goosy, sometimes-remember/sometimes-don't morning or evening prayer routine. It needs to be as automatic as brushing your teeth, or pulling on your pajamas or flipping off the lights: whether it's a family affair or a spousal relationship, there must be a dedicated, identifiable time or times that you all pray together. For the Greenfield family, regular prayer times together as a family come at least three times per day: after morning meditation, before dinner, and before bed. I would encourage you to engage as many of your family members or loved ones as possible to join you in a practice of prayer, and to also, if possible, share the same prayer list.

4. Combine Fasting And Prayer

As I allude to in Chapter 1, Jesus experienced an extraordinary transformation following his forty-day stint of fasting in a rugged mountain wilderness location near the Jordan River.

It was only after this experience that Jesus returned to Galilee an entirely new man and commenced to perform a host of impressive miracles. It turns out that the combination of prayer and fasting has deep historical roots in Christianity. In the Old Testament, fasting combined with prayer was used when there was a deep need and dependence for God's work in one's life or in a particular set of often dire circumstances, such as abject helplessness in the face of actual or anticipated calamity. Prayer and fasting are historically combined for periods of mourning, repentance or deep spiritual need.

For example, Daniel 9:3 says, *"So I turned to the Lord God and pleaded with him in prayer and petition, in fasting, and in sackcloth and ashes."* King David prayed and fasted over his sick child in 2 Samuel 12:16, and wept before the Lord in his fasted state in earnest intercession in Verses 21 and 22 of that same chapter. In Esther 4:16, Esther urges Mordecai and the Jews to fast for her before she plans to appear before her husband the king. The first chapter of Nehemiah describes Nehemiah combining prayer and fasting because of his deep distress over the distressing news that Jerusalem had been desolated. We are told in Luke 2:37 that the prophetess Anna *"never left the temple but worshiped night and day, fasting and praying."*

The probable reason that fasting and prayer can be so powerful is that fasting dramatically sharpens the mind, reduces distractions or sluggishness brought on by calorie consumption, and denies the body in a manner that strengthens the resilience of soul and spirit, often causing prayers to become more deep, thoughtful and meaningful. In the book *Atomic Power With God* (which I recommend you read as an excellent, classic treatise on how to combine prayer and fasting), author

Franklin Hall describes prayer and fasting as follows:

> "PRAYER and FASTING move the hand that controls the Universe. When a person shuts out the world for a season of prayer, fasting, and consecration, it opens the heart of God and the windows of heaven and brings the forces of God into action on your behalf. When a person begins to fast and pray, they become a channel for the Holy Ghost to flow through as a yielded vessel. Fasting without much prayer is like having a car with no gas to operate the vehicle. Your set-aside season of fasting should be accompanied by much more prayer than just your normal daily prayer life of one hour a day. After about the third day of your fast, the flesh barrier has basically been broken through and these first few days of crucifying the flesh can feel like you are accomplishing nothing—because most of the time you FEEL nothing. Now, there are those special times when you are able to weep and cry under the power of God during these first few days of fasting, but my experience has been that it's very rare. Remember, fasting without prayer is only a diet. You MUST find a secret place and spend time with HIM alone while you fast. You need to find a place where you can speak things in private and take authority over personal circumstances you are addressing without feeling intimidated or feel like someone else is listening."

While I don't necessarily think that to be spiritually fit you must be in a state of constant fasting and prayer, I do encourage you, when there is a particularly problematic, distressing or meaningful thing that you need to pray about, that you consider a day of fasting, and that you take the twenty minutes to an hour that you'd normally spend eating a breakfast, lunch or dinner on that day to instead slip away for a deeper state of meditation and prayer than you would normally otherwise be able to experience.

5. Regularly Ask Others "How can I pray for you?"

I've been making it a habit, when I finish a dinner party, a social gathering, a phone conversation or any other meeting with a friend or friends, to ask around the table or to a specific person one simple question...

..."How can I pray for you?"

I'm constantly amazed at how open, transparent, honest and vulnerable the replies can be, even from those who would not classify themselves as spiritual or religious, but who nonetheless seem quite open to being prayed for. Often, someone will share a health condition, a personal struggle, a business or relationship difficulty, a need for clarity, insight, wisdom or discernment, or some other trouble, worry or setback that they hadn't brought up at any other point in the conversation. Sometimes, I'll pray with them right then and there, but other times I will, as an alternative to or in addition to that, jot that person and their specific need down in the prayer list I alluded to earlier so that their need stays top of mind in my prayer sessions for that week.

If you adopt this practice, I encourage you to text, call or speak with that same person one to two weeks afterwards to check in and see how they are doing with the particular issue you've been praying for them about. This can often lead to even more meaningful discussion and, for those who may not know or understand God, faith or salvation, the opportunity to open their eyes to the love and light of salvation and the hope that is within you.

6. Go On A Prayer Walk

The power of a prayer walk was something I hadn't fully realized until my friend Franklin visited my house one day and during a discussion about prayer, described to me his own personal prayer practice: namely, for thirty to sixty minutes each and every morning a dedicated conversation with God that included praying from verses of Scripture, praying songs, praying both aloud and silently, petitioning God, thanking God and steeping himself in a deep and meaningful daily conversation with God - most often at the beginning of the day, sometimes in the afternoon, but almost always in a dedicated prayer room of his house or on his prayer walk.

After Franklin described to me this practice, I asked him if he could take me on one of his prayer walks, and he agreed. So for an hour, we strolled through the quiet farm roads near my house, often with our hands in the air worshiping, often breaking into song, often injecting periods of silence and listening to God, and often reciting Scripture aloud (this is another very good reason to memorize verses from the Bible and place them on your heart or, as the Bible says in Proverbs 3, to "hang them around your neck"—you'll never run out of things to say to God or ways to worship God, even when you don't know exactly what to pray!).

The entire walk was so deeply transformative and impactful that I began to adopt this habit several times per week: simply heading out the door with nothing more than an intent to be with God for thirty to sixty minutes. There's just something about the energy of moving, being in nature, and seeing God reveal Himself to you through creation as you talk to Him and listen to Him that makes this a wonderful practice to include in your own prayer habits a few times a week, or even every day.

Summary

So there you have it: prayer is powerful, but it can be tricky sometimes to weave it into your day, especially if you "overthink" or excessively intellectualize it. But approaching prayer from a more pure and simple, near-childlike perspective of openly speaking to God throughout the day in a form of contemplative prayer—even with single words, phrases or mantras—you can indeed "pray without ceasing," without necessarily spending the entire day on your knees in your bedroom.

In addition, memorizing certain prayers, keeping a prayer list, praying regularly with a loved one, combining fasting and prayer, regularly asking others how you can pray for them, and going on prayer walks, can be incredibly helpful for building prayer into your life in a meaningful and profound way that, as you've just learned, can literally change your biology and neurology for the better while simultaneously bringing you closer to daily union with God.

Finally, I've found the following three books to be incredible resources for learning more about prayer, and well worth a read. I'll link to them all on the resources webpage for this chapter.

- *Spiritual Disciplines for the Christian Life* by Donald S. Whitney

- *The Celebration of Discipline* by Richard Foster

- *Prayer* by Richard Foster (particularly good for learning different prayers for different occasions, such as contemplation, healing, blessing, forgiveness, and rest).

How about you? Do you have favorite prayers that you rely upon on a regular basis? Do you find that certain forms of prayer bring you closer to union with God? Do you use or read resources, handbooks, journals, or have other literary tools or apps you use to support a prayer

practice? Do you ask others if you can pray for them, and do you keep a prayer list? If not, where do you plan to start?

For resources, references, links and additional reading and listening material for this chapter, visit GetEndure.com/Chapter15.

PART IV

LOVING OTHERS & LOVING GOD

Creatively weaving the Golden Rule into your life.

CHAPTER XVI
SHOES

You've no doubt heard it before...

...the Golden Rule of empathy...

...put yourself in someone else's shoes.

This allusion to seeing how it feels when you put yourself in someone's place has been credited by many as some kind of an ancient Native American aphorism. Others think that it has its origin in a poem published in 1895 by Mary T. Lathrap, entitled "Judge Softly" and later titled "Walk a Mile in His Moccasins."

The poem goes like this:

> "Pray, don't find fault with the man that limps,
> Or stumbles along the road
> Unless you have worn the moccasins he wears,
> Or stumbled beneath the same load.
> There may be tears in his soles that hurt
> Though hidden away from view.
> The burden he bears placed on your back
> May cause you to stumble and fall, too.
> Don't sneer at the man who is down today
> Unless you have felt the same blow
> That caused his fall or felt the shame
> That only the fallen know.
> You may be strong, but still the blows
> That were his, unknown to you in the same way,
> May cause you to stagger and fall, too.
> Don't be too harsh with the man that sins.
> Or pelt him with words, or stone, or disdain.
> Unless you are sure you have no sins of your own,

And it's only wisdom and love that your heart contains.
For you know if the tempter's voice
Should whisper as soft to you,
As it did to him when he went astray,
It might cause you to falter, too.
Just walk a mile in his moccasins
Before you abuse, criticize and accuse.
If just for one hour, you could find a way
To see through his eyes, instead of your own muse.
I believe you'd be surprised to see
That you've been blind and narrow-minded, even unkind.
There are people on reservations and in the ghettos
Who have so little hope, and too much worry on their minds.
Brother, there but for the grace of God go you and I.
Just for a moment, slip into his mind and traditions
And see the world through his spirit and eyes
Before you cast a stone or falsely judge his conditions.
Remember to walk a mile in his moccasins
And remember the lessons of humanity taught to you by your elders.
We will be known forever by the tracks we leave
In other people's lives, our kindnesses and generosity.
Take the time to walk a mile in his moccasins."

Now, that's a pretty darn good poem, but any student of ancient history or Scripture probably knows that the popularity of this rule also has its roots in the so-called "Golden Rule" found in the Bible, and elsewhere. In this chapter, I'll give you a bit more perspective on the Golden Rule, and share with you some deep insight I've had lately about how most of us are *aware* of the importance of the rule, but few of us actually implement it correctly—in a way that truly changes our own lives and the lives of others.

The Golden Rule

Like I briefly alluded to above, many of us Westerners are familiar with the Golden Rule because of its origins in Christianity and the Bible,

namely from the words of Jesus in the following passages:

Matthew 7:12: *"So in everything, do to others what you would have them do to you, for this sums up the Law and the Prophets."*

Luke 6:31: *"Do to others as you would have them do to you."*

A similar passage can be found in Matthew 22:36-40, in which the importance of the Golden Rule is heavily emphasized by Jesus again when he responds to the question *"Which is the greatest commandment of the law?"* Jesus says in reply:

> *"Thou shalt Love the Lord thy God with all thy heart and with all thy soul and with all thy mind. This is the first and great commandment. And the second is like unto it, Thou shalt love thy neighbor as thyself. On these two commandments hang all the law and the prophets."*

And also in Luke 10:25-28, which reads:

> *"Behold, a certain lawyer stood up and tested him, saying, 'Teacher, what shall I do to inherit eternal life?'*
>
> *He said to him, 'What is written in the law? How do you read it?'*
>
> *He answered, 'You shall love the Lord your God with all your heart, with all your soul, with all your strength, and with all your mind; and love your neighbor as yourself.'*
>
> *He said to him, 'You have answered correctly. Do this, and you will live.'"*

In another passage of the New Testament, Galatians 5:14, Paul the Apostle also refers to the Golden Rule: *"For all the law is fulfilled in one word, even in this; Thou shalt love thy neighbour as thyself."*

Now, that's not to say that the Golden Rule does not appear as a core element of most of the rest of the world's major religions and philosophies. Indeed, outside Christianity, the idea of the Golden Rule dates back at least to the early Confucian times (551–479 BC) and appears prominently in Buddhism, Islam, Hinduism, Judaism, Taoism, Zoroastrianism, and beyond.

As a matter of fact, 143 leaders of the world's major faiths endorsed the Golden

Rule as part of the 1993 "Declaration Toward a Global Ethic." Despite being an atheist and humanist, two philosophies with which I am not in agreement, Adam Lee sums up the importance of the Golden Rule as a worldwide moral axiom this way:

> "Do not do to others what you would not want them to do to you. This is the single greatest, simplest, and most important moral axiom humanity has ever invented, one which reappears in the writings of almost every culture and religion throughout history, the one we know as the Golden Rule. Moral directives do not need to be complex or obscure to be worthwhile, and in fact, it is precisely this rule's simplicity which makes it great. It is easy to come up with, easy to understand, and easy to apply, and these three things are the hallmarks of a strong and healthy moral system. The idea behind it is readily graspable: before performing an action which might harm another person, try to imagine yourself in their position, and consider whether you would want to be the recipient of that action. If you would not want to be in such a position, the other person probably would not either, and so you should not do it. It is the basic and fundamental human trait of empathy, the ability to vicariously experience how another is feeling, that makes this possible, and it is the principle of empathy by which we should live our lives."
> —Adam Lee, Ebon Musings, A Decalogue for The Modern World

Throughout history, this idea of reciprocity appears in a variety of proverbial forms, including:

> "Do to the doer to make him do." (Egyptian)

> "That which you hate to be done to you, do not do to another." (Egyptian)

> "One should never do something to others that one would regard as an injury to one's own self. In brief, this is dharma. Anything else is succumbing to desire." (Sanskrit)

> "Do not do to others what you know has hurt yourself." (Tamil)

> "Why does one hurt others knowing what it is to be hurt?" (Tamil)

> "Avoid doing what you would blame others for doing." (Greek)

"What you do not want to happen to you, do not do it yourself either." (Greek)

"Do not do to others that which angers you when they do it to you." (Greek)

"That nature alone is good which refrains from doing to another whatsoever is not good for itself." (Persia)

"Whatever is disagreeable to yourself do not do unto others." (Persia)

"Treat your inferior as you would wish your superior to treat you." (Rome)

"Seek for mankind that of which you are desirous for yourself, that you may be a believer." (Islam)

"None of you [truly] believes until he wishes for his brother what he wishes for himself." (Islam)

"Blessed is he who preferreth his brother before himself." (Bahá'í)

"Ascribe not to any soul that which thou wouldst not have ascribed to thee, and say not that which thou doest not." (Bahá'í)

"One should never do that to another which one regards as injurious to one's own self. This, in brief, is the rule of dharma. Other behavior is due to selfish desires." (Hindu)

"If the entire Dharma can be said in a few words, then it is—that which is unfavorable to us, do not do that to others." (Hindu)

"Hurt not others in ways that you yourself would find hurtful." (Buddhism)

"A man should wander about treating all creatures as he himself would be treated." (Jainism)

"Just as pain is not agreeable to you, it is so with others. Knowing this principle of equality treat other with respect and compassion." (Jainism)

"What you do not wish for yourself, do not do to others."

(Confucianism)

"Regard your neighbor's gain as your own gain, and your neighbor's loss as your own loss." (Taoism)

"Do not do unto others whatever is injurious to yourself." (Zoroastrianism)

And perhaps one of my all-time favorite versions, a Yoruba Proverb that goes like this:

"One who is going to take a pointed stick to pinch a baby bird should first try it on himself to feel how it hurts."

As I mentioned in the introduction to this chapter, this rule itself is not difficult to understand. Whether you're looking at it from the viewpoint of pinching a baby bird, not hurting other people, or loving your neighbor, psychologically, it means we empathize with others; philosophically, it means we perceive our fellow human beings also as "I" or "self"; sociologically, it means loving our neighbors, as both individuals and groups; and economically, it suggests that, as journalist Richard Swift, referring to ideas from anthropologist David Graeber puts it: *"without some kind of reciprocity society would no longer be able to exist."*

Through Their Eyes

But a few evenings ago, I was immersed in a conversation with my twin boys at the dinner table, and I experimented with a simple thought exercise that I've successfully repeated several times since with many other people—an exercise I came up with to truly be able to implement more empathy and a greater practical practice of the Golden Rule into my own life. Since trying this exercise, I've discovered that I wasn't really practicing the Golden Rule in its full power before, but I am now, and I must say, it's quite transformative, so I just had to share it with you.

It goes like this.

As my boys and I sat there talking, I thought *"I wonder how my sons perceive me,* as their father? How do they truly perceive me and how are they interpreting my very actions, words, and body language, even in this moment?"

So, I paused and closed my eyes. See, we allow each other to do weird things like this at the Greenfield family dinner table.

Using my imagination and visualization, I put myself in the same chair across the table from me as one of my sons, River Greenfield. Like seeing myself on a movie screen, I watched from his perspective exactly what I was doing: how I was carrying my head, which direction my torso was oriented in, whether both feet were flat on the floor, where my direct eye contact was settling upon, how I was breathing, the pitch and timbre of my voice, the seeming interest or disinterest in what he was saying, and the level of empathy and communication with which I was engaging him in dialogue.

Suddenly, I realized that I wasn't *really* facing his direction but was instead a bit more oriented towards my computer and smartphone located at the very end of the table. My feet were a bit restlessly shuffling on the floor, as though I was ready to be done with and disengaged with dinner and already thinking of moving on to the next task. My vocals were a bit flat and distant. My eye gaze was more focused upon my plate than upon his eyes.

Wow.

This is how people see me? *This* is how I'm making them potentially feel? *This* is what it feels like to *truly* put yourself in someone else's shoes: to literally translocate yourself using the powers of visualization and imagination into their very body, and look at yourself through their eyes?

Powerful.

I sat up, shifted my torso in his direction, placed both feet flat on the floor, looked into his eyes, and leaned forward.

And boom, just like that, I was engaged. Caring. Connected.

The next morning I found myself repeating the very same exercise, but this time at the grocery store. As the clerk tapped on her cash register and shoved each of my grocery items down the belt and to the grocery bagger, I briefly closed my eyes and imagined her seeing me through her eyes. I was wearing a baggy hoodie and a trucker cap, distantly eyeing the line of gum and magazines beyond her, fumbling for my credit card with one hand, lost in thought with headphones still attached to both ears and grunting a brief, curt reply to her salutation. *I realized I was coming across as a disinterested, distracted punk who really didn't care about her (as I write about in Chapter 4 of Fit Soul).*

I took out my headphones. I shifted my gaze to her. I tipped my cap up so she could really see my eyes. I looked at her and said, "How is *your* day going??

She smiled. She perked up. Her face lit. She stood taller.

"So good, thank you for asking, I'm a little tired but getting through the day."

I could tell that she was instantly happy that I even asked. That I showed I cared. That's *all* it took?

Gee. I've been living my whole life kind of disconnected from truly *feeling* the Golden Rule.

The next week, on a date night with my wife, I repeated the same exercise. As a result, I was more engaged and connected with her than any date I can think of in the past. I just had to truly place myself in her shoes and truly let myself see myself through her eyes. And this time, after practicing a bit the previous week, *I didn't have to close my eyes or anything weird like that to imaginatively see what she was seeing.* This time, it just took a mild upregulation of self-awareness and presence, and asking myself the question: how is *she seeing me*?

OK, your turn.

Try it.

How are your kids thinking of you? Can you see yourself through their eyes? What kind of parent are they perceiving you to be, and how much do they think you really care and are truly **interested** *in them based on your actions, words, and overall presence?*

The same for your spouse or lover. How do they see you? No, how do they **really** *see you, in the moment, right now?*

Your co-worker. Do they know you **care**? *Do you truly empathize with them about that issue they're having with their sick dog, or did your "gee that's too bad" and wandering down the hallway come across as mildly calloused?*

Can you imagine? Can you visualize? Can you empathize? Can you truly place yourself in the other person's shoes?

I know, I know: this may seem like a silly, simple exercise, but it actually works. Of course, it can be used "in reverse" too. As you sit at the coffee shop attempting to get deep work done are you inviting distractions from others by leaning back, looking people in the eye, smiling at passersby, and appearing to be fully ready for social engagement, or do you do your deep work like I do: headphones in (even if they're not playing anything, it's a universal language that says "I'm busy" or "I'm engaged elsewhere"), avoidance of eye contact, body language closed off to be oriented to the table you're working at, etc.? In other words, constant awareness of how others may be perceiving you can be used both to produce empathy or to discourage distractions, depending on how you use it.

THE SCIENCE OF THE GOLDEN RULE

So *how* does this visualization exercise work, exactly?

I suspect that it comes down to something called "mirror neurons." At least, that's my first hunch.

See, a mirror neuron is a neuron that fires both when one person acts and when the other person (the observer) observes the action performed by that person. They're the same neurons that make you cringe and feel pain when you see two athletes in the Super Bowl hit each other with bone-crushing speed or see a UFC fighter get mauled in the jaw by the giant paw of their opponent (especially if you've played football or fought before yourself and experienced anything similar, but even so if you've never been hit like that in your life!). These specific neurons "mirror" the behavior of the other, as though the observer were him or herself acting. These neurons have been directly studied and observed in humans, in primates, and in birds alike.

In humans, nervous system activity consistent in mirror neuron firing has been shown to be located in multiple areas of the brain, including the premotor cortex, the supplementary motor area, the primary somatosensory cortex, and the inferior parietal cortex. Researchers in cognitive neuroscience and psychology think that this system provides some kind of mechanism for the coupling of perception of other people and subsequent decisions and action taken on those perceptions. They hypothesize that mirror neurons may be important for understanding the actions of other people, and also for learning new skills by imitation. Neuroscientists such as Marco Lacoboni at UCLA have argued that mirror neuron systems in the human brain help us understand the actions and intentions of other people (*sound familiar?*). Heck, in one of his studies, Lacoboni reported that mirror neurons could discern whether another person who was picking up a cup of tea planned to drink from it or clear it from the table! In addition, he believes that mirror neurons are the neural basis of the human capacity for emotions such as empathy.

However, the subject of mirror neurons continues to generate intense debate, and many scientists express skepticism about the theories being advanced to explain the function of mirror neurons. In a 2013 article for Wired Magazine, author Christian Jarrett wrote that:

> *"...mirror neurons are an exciting, intriguing discovery—but when you see them mentioned in the media, remember that most of the research on these cells has been conducted in monkeys. Remember too that there are many different types of mirror neurons. And that we're still trying to establish for sure whether they exist in humans, and how they compare with the monkey versions. As for understanding the functional significance of these cells, don't be fooled: that journey has only just begun."*

So who knows...*maybe* it's not mirror neurons that make this Golden Rule visualization exercise so powerful.

Maybe it's a syncing and alignment of your own heart and brain electrical signals with that of the other person. This has never been studied, to my knowledge, though person-to-person and person-to-animal alignment of components such as the brain and heart's electrical field and the heart rate variability (HRV) rhythms has been studied and observed extensively by organizations such as the Heart Math Institute.

Maybe it's something a bit more quantum: the literal sharing of photonic energy via a process called "quantum entanglement," which has indeed been studied and observed in lovers. I'll link to that research, and the other studies I've cited above, on the resources webpage for this chapter.

Maybe it's simply an upregulation of pure, emotional empathy.

I'm not sure it really matters.

All I do know is that this visualization practice is like putting the Golden Rule on steroids. And you should try it.

Summary

So there you have it.

We all know the Golden Rule is immensely important for us to truly be able to empathize with others and love our neighbor in the way we have been called to do.

Many of us just fail to understand or fail to practice a full implementation of the rule.

But it's so simple to start: Just creatively and vividly see yourself through the other person's eyes. It takes practice. It takes time. And then it becomes automatic, and greater empathy becomes a subconscious, built-in part of your life. You become that person who really understands other people, can think what they're thinking, understand their actions, and most importantly, understand how what you are doing in the moment is affecting your fellow human.

Then, change your behavior accordingly if you find what you are doing makes you feel a bit disappointed in yourself, or at least less-than-elated to be in the other person's shoes. As that old Yoruba Proverb cited above goes, *quit using that pointed stick to pinch a baby bird*. It's a baby. It's a bird. Treat it softly, and the same way you'd want to be treated.

How about you? Have you tried a similar thought and visualization exercise like the one I've presented above?

For resources, references, links and additional reading and listening material for this chapter, visit GetEndure.com/Chapter16.

CHAPTER XVII

BABIES

Comedian, podcaster, and UFC commentator Joe Rogan has a fascinating thought about how parenting has changed the way that he interacts with people.

On multiple podcast interviews, Joe describes how having children of his own forced him to realize that we were all babies and children at one time, and that many adults are just kids walking around in a grown human shell, still thinking and acting with many of the same built-in belief patterns, habits, tendencies, temptations, and struggles as they experienced in childhood, often simply molded and shaped by a multitude of life experiences that have happened since the time they were a tiny, crying newborn baby, but not as far removed from who they were as a child as we might be led to believe.

Your doctor was once just a nerdy kid who was fascinated by the human body.

The greatest violin virtuoso used to be four feet tall, standing in their bedroom with a tiny bow, trying to squeak out a teeth-gritting, squeaky, nails-on-a-chalkboard version of *Twinkle, Twinkle, Little Star* for the first time.

Your favorite fantasy fiction author used to be a freckle-faced adolescent who would hunch over his or her keyboard sipping on a soda and scratching their head about how to describe a dragon.

The biggest Hollywood actors and actresses used to be tiny humans nervously huddled backstage at the school play, reciting their lines over and over again and hoping they didn't mess anything up.

Prolific modern-day inventors and business figures like Elon Musk, Richard Branson, and Bill Gates used to be teenagers tinkering in the garage with model airplanes, computer hard drives, and mail-order robot kits.

Your husband, your wife, your mother, your father, your brother, and your sister—

at a time really not too long ago—were pooping in their diapers, learning to awkwardly take their first step, throwing a tantrum, snatching away some other kid's precious toy, and checking under the bed and in the bedroom closet for scary monsters.

Joe Rogan describes in many of his podcasts in which he discusses parenting how, when someone says something to him that could be potentially upsetting, controversial, insulting, or just plain silly, now that he's a parent he really doesn't judge them quite as harshly nor allow his own feelings to get hurt because he's come to the realization that most people are just a grown-up baby or child trapped inside an adult-sized meat suit, still picking one shallow fight after another with each other, buying bigger and bigger toys, eating, drinking, pooping, laughing, masturbating, crying, talking and seeking entertainment and self-pleasure to deliver the surges of dopamine we are all hard-wired to crave, often abusing or misusing others to satisfy that craving.

Despite my belief that, by the grace of God, a man or woman can become more like Christ each day, and be renewed as a new creation in a "second birth" when they experience salvation, I'll admit that there are actually some shreds of truth to Joe's thoughts. After all, just because you're in possession of a full-grown body doesn't mean there's a responsible adult mind and soul inside, or that you've set aside childlike tendencies like selfishness, greed, anger, impatience or irresponsibility.

Just because you're a parent doesn't mean you're not still stricken with imposter syndrome and simply trying to stay "one step ahead" of your own kids in learning what it really means to be a parent, or even an adult for that matter. Just because you're supposed to "get a real job" to work to provide for and protect yourself and your family, that doesn't mean you don't still enjoy and find purpose in the same kind of activities and hobbies you enjoyed doing when you were a little kid.

Furthermore, there can be a great deal of value in not completely forsaking childhood. As childhood development physician Gabor Mate says, trauma doesn't have to necessarily involve some kind of intense, readily identifiable physical or spiritual event that noticeably scars you, but rather, as addiction, stress and other mildly distressing life events occur, can simply be a "disconnection" from the true self who we were quite intimately connected to a child. In addition, as I write about in Chapter 9, you should always retain in your life the joyful elements that came so easy to you when you were a child, such as dreaming, singing, and dancing, and that the fading away of our youthful, happy, and carefree dreaming, singing, and dancing can occur gradually over an extended period of time as we become more and more mindful of fulfilling the basic survival elements of [Maslow's hierarchy of needs](#) (find food, make money, start a family, get a home, etc.) and more and more obsessed with and satisfied with doing, accomplishing, and producing to the ultimate and sad sacrifice of being, savoring, and creating.

So what can we learn from this observation that we can tend to act like "grown human babies," each carrying many of the same tendencies and habits—both good and bad—that we did as children? I think there are three valuable lessons here: 1) empathizing with others in a different way; 2) coming to the self-awareness that certain elements from childhood that no longer serve us, serve others or serve God should be left behind; and 3) we should always retain in our lives some semblance of the magic and joy of childhood.

SEE OTHERS AS GROWN CHILDREN

In Chapter 16, I taught you a simple thought and visualization exercise that allows you to truly be able to implement more empathy and a greater practical practice of the Golden Rule into your life.

The basic idea was this: you can quite literally translocate yourself and, as though you were playing a movie in your mind, look at yourself through the actual eyes of anyone with whom you are interacting. Through the function of mirror neurons in your brain, this can allow you to really, truly feel what someone else is thinking, experiencing, and feeling as they interact with you, and allow you to adjust your own interactions with them to better sympathize, better empathize, and better communicate.

Very similarly, you can, based on this concept of everyone once being a child, see each adult human you interact with as someone who was once a baby.

Is your co-worker "throwing a tantrum?" Consider smiling at them, telling them everything is going to be OK, and perhaps fetching them a soothing coffee and a snack, just like that warm bottle of milk your mother delivered to you when you were a crying baby.

Is your husband or wife feeling down or depressed? Hold them, hug them, caress their hair, snuggle them, and pray with them. Remember how good it felt when you were sad and your parents or another adult who cared simply gave you a hug?

Are you frustrated with the actions of a politician or a leader or an employer? Write them a letter. Tell them how you're feeling. Vulnerably share your thoughts and emotions. Think back to when you were a kid and someone actually explained to you how they were feeling or why they were angry or impatient with you or why they made a certain decision. Don't assume these grown-up kids in some omniscient way know how their actions are affecting you. Maybe they never learned that in the days, weeks, months, and years since they were just getting a bath, taking a nap, and running around a playground somewhere. So tell them.

This practice can drastically change the way you interact with, view, and judge people. It can soften the way you treat them. It can transform your interactions with others into something more like the more gentle, loving, forgiving, and patient interaction you'd have with a baby, or with a child.

See, we're all just humans and we're all just basically grown-up baby humans.

So don't assume someone is "grown-up" in the sense that they are mentally and emotionally mindful and responsible in all aspects of life. We were all children once. Imagine all those influencers, all those gurus, all those teachers, all those employers, all those employees, all those lovers, all those adult bullies, all those in your life who you may be tempted to be fearful of, to disagree with, to argue against or to harshly judge as *children*. See them in your mind's eye as an awkward young boy or as a cute little girl who might be just a tad bit older now. Imagine them as a child, or even as a baby. Put yourself in their shoes.

Understanding and practicing this concept will give you more patience, more empathy, and more sympathy. Try it.

Leave Childish Things Behind

Next, now that you can hopefully see what it's like when many of those people around you act as though they haven't grown up as much as you'd expect, use that as inspiration to do a bit more growing up *yourself*, so that you're not personally acting as a giant, grown-up human baby in an adult shell. As Paul says in 1 Corinthians 13:11, *"When I was a child, I talked like a child, I thought like a child, I reasoned like a child. When I became a man, I put the ways of childhood behind me."* and later in Ephesians 4:14, *"…we should no longer be children, tossed to and fro and carried about with every wind of doctrine, by the trickery of men, in the cunning craftiness of deceitful plotting."*

If you get angry or stressed over small and pointless, meaningless or trite things (your spouse drinks all the morning coffee, your kids barge in on an important phone call, or someone is using "your machine" at the gym), tend to assume everything revolves around you (you narcissistically hog the bathroom, you're always first in line to get food at a party, or, as I discuss in Chapter 20 you're unwilling to sacrifice your precious yoga class or lunch hour to go help someone in need), and get upset when things don't go your way (waiting in line stresses you out, you get angry when you can't get a restaurant reservation, or you throw a tantrum when the Uber takes 20 minutes to arrive) and you generally treat others as though their sole purpose is to serve you, then you might indeed be living in an emotionally stunted childlike state, often described in modern psychology as Little Princess or Peter Pan syndrome.

One perfect example of the detrimental societal effects of this hanging on to irresponsible childish tendencies and living as a grown child in a sort of lifelong Peter Pan syndrome is the alarming and increased prevalence of fatherlessness, which has become what I would consider to be an epidemic, especially in America, but also beyond. If it were classified as a disease, fatherlessness would be an epidemic worthy of attention as a national emergency. More than 20 million children live in a home without the presence of a father. Millions more children have fathers who are physically present, yet emotionally absent. You can check out the resources webpage for this chapter to read plenty more statistics on the sad extent of fatherlessness.

A major contributor to this epidemic is the fact that many modern men are wandering through life as grown humans on the outside, but as mentally, emotionally, and spiritually immature boys on the inside. These men never experienced a formal recognition or ceremonial transition into adulthood, and consequently are often left scratching their head and trying to figure out when they became a man or if they're even a man yet, and, worse yet, these grown male adults subconsciously or consciously consider themselves to be and even *pride* themselves on being a happy-go-lucky boy on the inside, free to drive fast cars, listen to loud music, hit the clubs until 2 am, and knock up as many women as one's heart desires, with complete self-permission to walk away from any responsibility, because, well, *that's what little boys do.*

Male rites of passage—which I explore in detail on a podcast interview with Tim Corcoran available on my website, and which are also explained quite excellently in the book *Leaving Boyhood Behind*—begin with a separation from the tribe, followed by a transitional process of facing one's fears and dissolving one's ego through some kind of hardship or crucible, and finally, finish with a re-incorporation back into society accompanied by a ceremonial recognition that the new young man is now a responsible, contributory member of society. These types of rites have been woven into the fabric of culture and considered to be an integral part of a boy's transition into manhood for thousands of years, but are now noticeably absent in our modern, Westernized "cultured" tribes.

Mark my words: this absence of a male rite of passage is a time-honored tradition that we must reclaim. Masculine initiation in particular is a constant thread in ancient and classical literature and the upbringing of many well-recognized figures of history. Achilles, for example, was handed over by his father to Chiron, a centaur, to be initiated into manhood. "Jack and the Beanstalk" is the story of a boy being separated from his mother, experiencing a battle with a giant, and finally liberating his father so he could become a man like his father and reclaim his inheritance. Whether it's Telemachus in *The Odyssey* or Daniel in *The Karate Kid* or Jesus Christ wandering in the wilderness for forty days, mature, capable and enduring masculinity is forged by these types of harrowing but necessary experiences.

Fortunately, many organizations, often in the realm of wilderness survival and nature immersion, still exist to systematize the process of a rite of passage for a young man. For example, you can begin by Googling a term such as "wilderness rite of passage NAME OF YOUR CITY for boys." My own sons have experienced multiple solo, ego-dissolving days and nights in the wilderness between the ages of

7 and 13, with the most recent accompanied by a ceremonial coming of age and recognition of their passage into adolescence, all fostered by trained rite of passage guides at Twin Eagles Wilderness School. As a matter of fact, now that they are 13 and have completed their rite of passage, we don't even refer to them as "boys" anymore, but as sons, young men, fellows, or simply by their first name. They are equipped, not just physically, but also mentally, emotionally, and spiritually, to now become kings, leaders, fathers, and husbands for life. The rite of passage for your own boys doesn't need to be the same as mine, but hopefully, the examples above give you some idea of where to start. And yes, there's no reason that a full-grown adult male cannot also complete these same rites of passage. As the old Chinese proverb goes, *"The best time to plant a tree is twenty years ago, or today."*

While women naturally go through rites of passage to womanhood that are deeply rooted in their physical and psychological makeup (such as the onset of menstruation or giving birth to a first child) the same process for men is notoriously absent. For women, the problem is that even these experiences are often not recognized, honored, or celebrated, but instead hidden, pronounced shameful, or given a casual head-nod rather than a formal acknowledgment of their extreme importance and significance in signaling that a girl is prepared to become a woman, a caretaker, a minister to her family and eventually, a great and noble matriarch.

Ultimately, we must—as parents, as families, and as a society that desires responsible adults who have left childish things behind—reclaim these rites of passage and weave into our education and child-raising practices a ceremonial recognition of the passage of a man or woman into adulthood.

Yes, we all used to be babies. But that doesn't mean we need to be that way anymore.

Retain The Magic & Wonder Of Childhood

While it's a good idea to focus upon empathetically putting yourself in other's shoes by seeing them as grown adults still struggling with many

of the same temptations and tendencies from childhood, and simultaneously dedicate yourself to committing to set aside selfish and immature childish tendencies that don't serve you, you shouldn't necessarily *completely forsake* the magic of childhood.

As a matter of fact, when my twin sons recently set out upon their own wilderness rite of passage, I slipped them a letter full of observations, memories, and advice from me. One anecdote from that letter to one of my sons in particular went like this:

> *"...you have always loved good music, and always had a good voice, too, from singing muppet songs when you were a toddler, to belting out praise and worship songs at church, to playing all your epic music during school time, or workouts or tennis. I see how much you are connected to music and song. I was the same way growing up...*
>
> *...never, ever lose that love for music, and rhythm, and dancing, and singing. For some parts of my life, I lost my connection to the joys of singing and music but have since rediscovered it and the immense joy that instruments, singing, music, songs, bands, and even sound healing can bring to one's life. Keep on singing. Keep on playing your favorite music, as loudly as you'd like. Keep on learning and playing instruments. Both your Mom and I come from families that love music and it is woven into our DNA. I have a strong hunch it is woven into yours too...*
>
> *...oh also,* **don't ever give up on the other loves you've had since you were a baby, or think that they are so childish you need to leave them behind. Even as a man, they will bring joy to your heart.** *So don't give up your love for music. Or your love for dogs. Or your love for comics. Or your love for amazing works of fiction. Or your love for throwing snowballs. Or your love for playing tricks. Or your love for chasing puppies with laser pointers. Or your love for jumping on trampolines. Never stop dancing, singing and dreaming. Always keep just a little bit of fun-loving, youthful Peter Pan inside you. You can be a responsible and dangerous man, and a funny, light-hearted joyful man, too..."*

So yes, do avoid full-blown Little Princess or Peter Pan syndrome, but do also keep a bit of Little Princess or Peter Pan inside you.

Don't get so stuck in your mature, responsible adult hypnotic rhythms that you stop dancing, singing, and dreaming.

Go to the arcade.

Laugh more.

Sing in the shower.

Learn good jokes, and be the person that tells those jokes at dinner parties and social events.

Go on bike rides through the neighborhood at night to go get ice cream.

Play silly card games at dinner.

Build sandcastles at the beach.

Have dance parties.

Sing more.

Lay in your backyard staring at the sky, hands clasped behind your head, and daydream.

After all, even in the Bible, your transformation into a state of eternal happiness and salvation is described as a transformation dependent upon being like a little child. Matthew 18:3 says, *"Truly I tell you, unless you change and become like little children, you will never enter the kingdom of heaven."* and Mark 10:15 likewise says, *"Assuredly, I say to you, whoever does not receive the kingdom of God as a little child will by no means enter it."*

1 Peter 2:2 describes our love for the Word of God as follows, *"...as newborn babies, desire the pure milk of the word, that you may grow thereby..."*

And when it comes to retaining the love of our childhood, Psalm 71:5 says, *"For you, O Lord, are my hope, my trust, O Lord, from my youth."*

When I *interviewed anti-aging and longevity expert Marisa Peer on my podcast*, she described how surrounding ourselves with photos, memories, and activities from our younger years can inject youthfulness and vitality into our older years, describing studies in which older people were placed in a closed environment that resembled life 30 years prior, and the astounding results in their attitude, health, and longevity that resulted from that.

So yes, be responsible and mature and a contributory member of society who produces impactful work that loves God and loves others, but do so with a goofy smile on your face, a prank in your pocket, a voracious curiosity for God's creation, and perhaps the same kind of silly t-shirt with a witty slogan that you may have worn when you were ten. The world needs just a bit more responsible lightheartedness.

Summary

As I've written in this chapter, I believe that it is critically important to our societal stability that, like our ancestors, we learn how to weave into our culture a ceremonial recognition of passage into adulthood, and that we learn how to set aside the weaknesses of childhood that no longer serve us, God, or others. Sadly, many people simply can't say *when* they became a responsible adult, and *when* they set aside the silly, petty, irresponsible, or dependent elements of childhood.

If you fall into that category, I challenge you to set out upon your own rite of passage, whether that be a wilderness excursion, a meditation retreat, a hunting trip, a sabbatical, or any other immersive, preferably solo experience in which you face your own fears, dissolve your own ego, inspect any elements of your own inner child that still remain with you, and give yourself the time and focus to dwell upon how you are going to serve the world as a responsible, contributory, adult member of society.

Yet, it's also important that you maintain a sense of childlike wonder and joy as you savor each and every element of God's Creation. In the same way that, in Chapter 7, I told you that I consider myself to be a *temperate Christian hedonist*, I also consider myself to be a *grown, responsible adult still infused with childlike wonder...*

...still able to dance, sing, and dream...

...still plugged into enjoying, deriving satisfaction from—and even weaving into my own career in an act of self-actualization—those same productive and creative activities that I enjoyed and was good at as a child...

...yet also able to set aside the trite, silly, selfish habits and tendencies of that same child.

Allow me to finish with a thought-provoking poem by A. A. Milne, who you may recognize as the author of *Winnie the Pooh*, but who also penned the following poem, entitled: "Now We Are Six:"

> *"When I was One,*
> *I had just begun.*
> *When I was Two,*
> *I was nearly new.*
> *When I was Three*
> *I was hardly me.*
> *When I was Four,*
> *I was not much more.*
> *When I was Five,*
> *I was just alive.*
> *But now I am Six,*
> *I'm as clever as clever,*
> *So I think I'll be six now for ever and ever."*

How about you?

When did *you* become an adult?

Are you an adult yet, or are you still a child in an adult's body?

Are you able to look at others who may be upsetting you with their selfishness, silliness, or other childlike tendencies, and remind yourself to be patient, to have mercy, and to treat them kindly, because they were once a baby, they were once a child, and they are still learning how to—or perhaps don't know how to—forsake those rash, reckless, foolhardy, or irresponsible elements of childhood that they carried into adulthood?

Are you able to accept the fact that all the wisdom and insight and experience and depth of knowledge that you *think* you have now may be something you look back at two decades from now and laugh at, and can you therefore apply that same thought pattern towards your

interactions with those who may be years or even decades younger than you? Can you put yourself in *their* shoes when you were *their* age?

For resources, references, links and additional reading and listening material for this chapter, visit GetEndure.com/Chapter17.

PART V

END OF LIFE

Finding meaning in both life and death.

CHAPTER XVIII

DEATH

On a recent podcast, which included a Q&A from my listeners, someone asked me a specific question about my thoughts on "what happens after you die." While I certainly spitballed my gut response to the listener's question in that particular episode (which I'll link to on the resources webpage for this chapter), upon further reflection and study, I feel as though my reply wasn't entirely adequate…

…and for a matter as important as death and the afterlife, I think that such a topic—which I briefly visited in Fit Soul *when I wrote about what I think heaven itself will be like and what Jesus likely experienced during his three-day "harrowing in hell"—still requires a bit more of a thorough and considerate response.*

After all, death is a serious topic and not to be treated lightly or without deep thought. As author and theologian John Piper writes:

> *"Jesus kicked the teeth out of death, crushing its power over his people (Revelation 20:6) and promising one day to destroy it forever (Revelation 20:14). But because death has been conquered, it doesn't mean peace has been made with it. This isn't a tennis match. Death is no less terrible, and should be no less hated."*

Not a tennis match, indeed. Just think about it…

IMAGINE YOUR DEATH

No, really, really think about it. Your death, I mean. So seldom is it that we actually, apart from those who may have undergone an actual near-

death experience, truly imagine or experience death in vivid visualization.

Imagine, right now, as you are reading this very sentence, out of seemingly nowhere, a bullet rips through the wall of your room and buries itself with red hot fire into your upper right gut. You don't know where it came from. Perhaps it was a stray shot. Perhaps you're being assassinated. At this point, it doesn't matter. You've heard the tales of the temporary horror and debilitating pain of a sudden gallstone, or a heart attack, or a snapped femur, but this is far, far more horrific. As what feels like a live hornet's nest full of a million razor-sharp barbs is unleashed like a cluster bomb within your viscera and organs, your vision clouds over and your jaw drops open to scream in bone-chilling, blood-curdling terror.

You can't stop screaming. You keep trying to breathe through your screams, but as you struggle against the spasming in your gut to swallow precious air, blood instead bubbles up your throat and you choke violently on it, spitting thin flecks of bright crimson across the floor and walls in front of you. As the gore from your throat splatters against the wall, you double over and vomit dark green bile pooled with more blood, then you crumble to your side, your muscles failing as calcium floods into your cells and your entire musculoskeletal system begins to spasm.

You feel the cold, hard floor against your cheek. Desperately, you pull your knees to your chest in a fetal position, but this makes the pain even more unbearable, as though half a dozen daggers are plunging deep into your stomach and being twisted by a depraved demon again, and again, and again—each time causing bright bursts of lightning to flash across your eyes. Your head feels as though it is going to explode into a million fragments of brain and bones and more blood, but it doesn't explode. Instead, the unbearable pain stays inside your head, radiating more intensely with each second as the cluster of hornets travels into every corner of your skull, buzzing with a terrible fury, burrowing deeper and deeper, stinging, biting, and stinging again.

As the lightning bolts of pain continue to strike throughout your body, your head becomes heavy and feels nearly foreign. It seems as though there is a thick rope knotted around your neck in a noose, getting tighter and tighter. Your vision begins to cloud, and the puddle of thick blood in which your face lies slips in and out of visibility, flashing like a crimson strobe-light.

Somewhere in your bowels, something aggressively shifts, and you feel your own urine and fecal matter spill into your pants, along with pieces of your insides and more green, yellow, and red soupy fragments from within your intestines. You scream and squirm again and pain shoots through your body once more, but now your screams sound far away and muffled to your own ears as if your voice is echoing back at you from a distant cave.

Then, as endorphins, neurotransmitters, and photons of light pouring from your mitochondria and an enormous dump of DMT from your pineal gland all converge at once in a chemical thunderstorm in your bloodstream, pushed along with the final struggling beats of your heart, the pain begins to fade—and is replaced by an intense, black darkness that envelops your entire consciousness, accompanied by brief flashes of kaleidoscopes of color and, somewhere, still in the far distance, your own screams.

You cannot breathe. There is no oxygen. Everything becomes black. Dark, black, the velvetiest of black.

You glimpse a brief vision of your mangled body lying in a pool of blood and intestines.

Then that fades, too.

You realize you no longer have a body. You've never felt this before. No flesh. Just a faint awareness of existence. And somewhere, like a tiny speck in that blackness, a single photon of light between where your eyes used to be.

You are separated.

Your soul, your consciousness, is fully disconnected from your body.

Life as you know it has suddenly, drastically, even horribly and painfully...

...ended.

Are You Going To Be Reincarnated?

So what happens at that point, at the end, after your brain, your heart, and your entire lump of flesh have fully experienced physical death?

First, I'm not going to dive into reincarnation too heavily here, but in short, I believe it's an insult to God to believe that you are going to be reincarnated.

Why do I say that?

Perhaps you've read my writings in Chapter 9 of *Fit Soul* on the horrific, gory, shocking details of Jesus Christ's brutal beating, torture, and crucifixion. This was the murder of a deity, a sacrificial death that was so unimaginably painful and profound that it caused the very earth to shudder, the temple curtains to be torn in half, Satan to be overthrown, and the entire spiritual underworld to experience a vast and irreversible transformation. And God gifted that sacrifice of His dear son to us, as the well-recognized verse from John 3:16 in the Bible states: *"For God so loved the world that He gave His only begotten son…that whoever believes upon him shall not perish but have eternal life…"*

But the idea of reincarnation completely negates the necessity, meaning, and importance of that entire loving sacrifice.

See, both Judaism and Christianity believe in an important doctrine that directly challenges reincarnation: the resurrection of the dead. This resurrection means that our dead bodies will someday be revived and brought back to life on a New Earth. Reincarnation dictates that our immaterial souls will be inserted into a new human life and future human body, while resurrection dictates that our dead and decayed flesh will be brought back to a full and glorious, perfect life. In 1 Corinthians 15:13-14 and 17-18, the Apostle Paul is resolute in identifying this resurrection as the core of Christianity:

> *"If there is no resurrection of the dead, then not even Christ has been raised. And if Christ has not been raised, our preaching is useless and so is your faith… And if Christ has not been raised, your faith is futile; you are still in your sins. Then those also who have fallen asleep in Christ are lost."*

In short, reincarnation negates God's free gift of salvation that is described in the New Testament, a gift that was manifested in Christ's death, burial, and resurrection. If we are a disembodied self that isn't related to any particular time, then this means that our real self only has a sort of accidental connection to any specific body, because we'll go on to another body and another body and another body. But we are embodied beings, not separate from our souls, but with bodies so intimately intertwined to our souls that upon our resurrection, these same souls we possess now will be in the same bodies we possess now, but in a perfectly restored state of perfection.

Paul experienced quite a bit of resistance to this idea when he visited Athens, and preached Christ's resurrection to the Athenians. The Athenians derided Paul for teaching such an outlandish notion as resurrection. In Acts 17:32, we are told, *"When they heard about the resurrection of the dead, some of them sneered, but others said, 'We want to hear you again on this subject.'"*

See, Paul's reference to the resurrection of the dead ignited an interesting reaction among the Greeks, who repudiated the idea of a bodily resurrection. Though they embraced the concept of a soul living forever, they sneered at the idea of a bodily resurrection because they considered the body to be evil, and something to be discarded. This concept, known as dualism, was derived from the teachings of Socrates and Plato, who believed that everything physical is evil, everything spiritual is good, and that it really doesn't matter what one does with one's body so long as their spirit is good.

The Athenians' adherence to this philosophy blinded them to the truth of the gospel and the ability to be able to receive God's free gift of salvation for all humankind, in the very same way that an adherence to the philosophy of reincarnation blinds us from being able to accept God's free gift and Jesus's massive sacrifice. After all, if you (and you are both your body and your soul) are going to be resurrected, restored, and proceed to dwell in a blissful, eternal afterlife, then, if reincarnation is true, who's to say that "you" isn't a monk from a thousand years ago, you in your current state now, an astronaut living 2089, a butterfly, a bullfrog, or a brick?

It's as though reincarnation thrusts a giant middle finger up at God, shouting at him that we don't need salvation or resurrection because our souls are drifting along just fine down here, thank you very much, and we've already discovered eternal life—albeit a far less perfect eternal life than what God has promised us if we simply believe in Jesus, and go forth fully inspired to love God and love our neighbors.

What Happens After You Die

So if you're not reincarnated, what *does* happen after you die?

In summary, when the final breath empties like a wind-blown wisp from the lungs, the heart shudders in the death throes of its final contraction, and that last electrical wave fades from the brain, those who die in Christ will immediately find their souls in his presence, while awaiting the resurrection in their physical bodies that will occur at his return. As Psalms 16:11 says, we long to be near him and experience the fullness of joy and eternal pleasure that his presence offers. And as soon as we are out of this wrap of flesh for a temporary period of time, there is no reason that he will not welcome us into that presence upon our death, rather than making us wait in some kind of dark (or even blissful) state of floating consciousness.

Why do I believe this is what happens?

First, as I write about in Chapter 21 of *Fit Soul*, the Bible does not describe eternity in the afterlife as some kind of disembodied existence in the heavens, and such is not the language of the Scriptures. Rather, as Romans 8:23 says *"And not only they, but ourselves also, which have the firstfruits of the Spirit, even we ourselves groan within ourselves, waiting for the adoption, to wit, the redemption of our body."* This verse demonstrates the hope we can have in the eventual redemption of our physical bodies, which is ultimately what the resurrection will be.

That redemption and resurrection, however, does not happen upon our immediate death, but will rather occur upon the return of Christ at the end of the age, as 1 Corinthians 15:22-23 alludes to when Paul says, *"For as in Adam all die, so in Christ all will be made alive. But each in turn: Christ, the firstfruits; then, when he comes, those who belong to him."*

But in the meantime, what exactly occurs during that "waiting period" between death and resurrection?

Many people (including me when, upon reflection, I responded incorrectly to a listener question in the podcast I mentioned earlier, although I've subsequently studied up more on the matter) believe that we will experience something referred to as "soul sleep" during this time, which is a state of some kind of unconsciousness or soul floating or unattached, ethereal existence, after which we are to be awakened at the resurrection, whether that is a few years, a century or a millennia after our physical bodies have died. However, this seems to stand in stark contrast to what we can read in the Bible.

For example, in Luke 23:43, Jesus says to a thief who is dying on the cross beside him that today they would be together in paradise. Later, in Philippians 1:22-24, Paul expresses his hope to, upon his death, "depart and be with Christ." Even clearer is the testimony of 2 Corinthians 5:1-9:

> *"For we know that if the tent that is our earthly home is destroyed, we have a building from God, a house not made with hands, eternal in the heavens. For in this tent we groan, longing to put on our heavenly dwelling, if indeed by putting it on we may not be found naked. For while we are still in this tent, we groan, being burdened—not that we would be unclothed, but that we would be further clothed, so that what is mortal may be swallowed up by life. He who has prepared us for this very thing is God, who has given us the Spirit as a guarantee. So we are always of good courage. We know that while we are at home in the body we are away from the Lord, for we walk by faith, not by sight. Yes, we are of good courage, and we would rather be away from the body and at home with the Lord."*

If you read carefully here, Paul actually identifies three separate stages of existence for those who believe in Jesus: 1) life in this mortal, fleshly "tent," which is our earthly home—a home in which we, as Romans 8:23 alludes to, groan to await freedom from when our bodies are finally redeemed; 2) an unclothing into nakedness where we go to be at home with the Lord as our bodies rest in the dust of the earth, a home in a spiritual existence without a physical body and a home that is incomplete, but a home that is nonetheless far better than our existence away from the Lord in our present burdened body; and 3) finally, a complete clothing in a heavenly dwelling at the resurrection, and the ultimate, satisfied consummation of our longing to be with the Lord in which our bodies and souls are united once again and we are able to exist eternally on the New Earth, still in the presence of the Lord, as Revelations 21:1-7 tell us:

> *"Then I saw a New heaven and a New Earth, for the first heaven and the first earth had passed away, and the sea was no more. And I saw the holy city, new Jerusalem, coming down out of heaven from God, prepared as a bride adorned for her husband. And I heard a loud voice from the throne saying, 'Behold, the dwelling place of God is with man. He will dwell with them, and they will be his people, and God himself will be with them as their God. He will wipe away every tear from their eyes, and death shall be no more, neither shall there be mourning, nor crying, nor pain anymore, for the former things*

have passed away.' And he who was seated on the throne said, 'Behold, I am making all things new.' Also he said, 'Write this down, for these words are trustworthy and true.' And he said to me, 'It is done! I am the Alpha and the Omega, the beginning and the end. To the thirsty I will give from the spring of the water of life without payment. The one who conquers will have this heritage, and I will be his God and he will be my son.'"

So that is what happens after you die: Your soul is immediately whisked away from your body to be with the Lord in Heaven, you await Jesus' return, upon which you are finally resurrected in a state in which your soul and body are finally united, and that soul and body go on to live for all eternity, soaking up the full joy of a New Heaven and New Earth.

Summary

But wait a minute.

There's one glaring issue here: If accepting God's free gift, believing in Jesus, and laying all our burdens and sin at the foot of the cross gives us all the glory and the joy I've described above—a restoration of our new bodies in a New Earth for an exciting afterlife in eternity after our mortal bodies have breathed their last—then what happens if we **don't** *believe?*

In short, if we don't believe, then we, too, will go on to dwell in eternity.

But not with God.

Instead, we will be alone.

Forsaken.

Lost and wandering.

Isolated in complete and dark loneliness, staring up at the heavens, painfully gritting our teeth and licking our dry lips as we regret those short decades on this planet during which we decided that all this world's pleasures were far more attractive than a glorious existence with God for all time.

But that topic of what a horrible, hellish existence will be like is one that I'll address in Chapter 19. However, I can guarantee you now that when you die, and before you are potentially resurrected, there is no second chance. You do not, after your physical death, get another opportunity to be redeemed by believing in Jesus. The Bible is quite clear in Hebrews 9:27 that *"it is appointed for man to die once, and after that comes judgment."*

The powerful and convicting parable of the rich man and Lazarus from Luke 16 also backs this up:

> *"There was a rich man who was dressed in purple and fine linen and lived in luxury every day. At his gate was laid a beggar named Lazarus, covered with sores and longing to eat what fell from the rich man's table. Even the dogs came and licked his sores.*
>
> *The time came when the beggar died and the angels carried him to Abraham's side. The rich man also died and was buried. In Hades, where he was in torment, he looked up and saw Abraham far away, with Lazarus by his side. So he called to him, 'Father Abraham, have pity on me and send Lazarus to dip the tip of his finger in water and cool my tongue, because I am in agony in this fire.'*
>
> *But Abraham replied, 'Son, remember that in your lifetime you received your good things, while Lazarus received bad things, but now he is comforted here and you are in agony. And besides all this, between us and you a great chasm has been set in place, so that those who want to go from here to you cannot, nor can anyone cross over from there to us.'*
>
> *He answered, 'Then I beg you, father, send Lazarus to my family, for I have five brothers. Let him warn them, so that they will not also come to this place of torment.'*
>
> *Abraham replied, 'They have Moses and the Prophets; let them listen to them.'*
>
> *'No, father Abraham,' he said, 'but if someone from the dead goes to them, they will repent.'*
>
> *He said to him, 'If they do not listen to Moses and the Prophets, they will not be convinced even if someone rises from the dead.'"*

That parable should give you something to seriously think about as you consider your own death.

In the meantime, I challenge you to close your eyes and create your own "near-death experience." Imagine it. Visualize it in detail. Feel the discomfort. Feel the pain. Feel the separation from your physical body. Put yourself in your own shoes as you die, then, most importantly, dwell upon what will happen afterwards. It's a powerful exercise.

While you're thinking about the entire topic of death, you may also want to consider how you will be remembered, and whether your death will, as the Apostle Paul alluded to be "gain" and truly rock this planet. So how will you die, and how will you be remembered?

For resources, references, links and additional reading and listening material for this chapter, visit GetEndure.com/Chapter18.

CHAPTER XIX

HELL

In the previous chapter, I'm afraid I may have finished quite abruptly in a bit of a cliffhanger—if you will pardon the pun. If you recall, or if you go back and read that chapter, you will see that, while I described what passage into the eternal afterlife will be like after departing one's physical body, and how one's eventual resurrection to live forever in a New heaven and New Earth will manifest for those who believe in Jesus and have cast their burdens upon him...

...I didn't exactly get into too much detail about what happens when you die if you *don't* believe.

Ah, so am I about to answer the classic *"So you're saying I'm going to hell if I don't believe the way you do"* question?

Not exactly. Whether or not you are going to heaven or hell is between you and God. I'm not here to judge you or judge the answer to that question. It's not my role or responsibility.

But in this chapter, I would like to at least clear the air about how things will actually be, well, *down there*, which seems quite a logical next step since I've talked so much in my last book *Fit Soul* about Jesus's journey to hell as part of his Hero's Journey, what heaven will be like, and in the previous chapter of this book what death will be like.

Heck (sorry, I did it again), I'd be remiss not to address this topic. After all, if you were giving a friend directions to get to a restaurant, and you knew that one road led to the parking lot, but a second road ended at a broken bridge over a dark chasm, you probably wouldn't just tell them about the safe road. Instead, you would likely mention the existence of and warn them of the dangerous, wrong road.

What Will Hell Be Like?

One of the most well-known descriptions of hell comes from the Roman Catechism of the Council of Trent.

In it, hell is described as a *"most loathsome and dark prison in which the souls of the damned are tormented with the unclean spirits in eternal and inextinguishable fire. This place is called Gehenna, the bottomless pit, and is hell strictly so-called."*

This description is most likely derived from the words of Jesus in Mark 9:43, in which Jesus says, *"If your hand causes you to sin, cut it off. It is better for you to enter into life maimed than with two hands to go into Gehenna, into the unquenchable fire."* Gehenna was the Greek name for a valley southwest of Jerusalem, where pagan sacrifices occurred, including the burning sacrifice of children. In Jesus' time, Gehenna was a garbage dump where trash from the city was continually burned. Thus, hell is associated with a place of perpetual fire and pain.

But Jesus thought of hell as far more than just an evil trash-heap. Let's look at how Jesus viewed hell, since he spoke quite often about hell—more, in fact, than any other character in the Bible, and in quite bleak terms—and also, as a deity and the son of God, possessed a knowledge of hell that surpassed anything any mortal human might have.

In passages such as Matthew 10:28, Matthew 13:40-42 and Mark 9:43-48, Jesus not only referred to hell as a real place, but also described it in quite graphic terms, including as an eternal fire that burns but doesn't consume, a never-dying worm that slowly eats away at the damned, and a lonely, all-enveloping darkness with complete separation from God the Father.

Jesus also says in Matthew 8:12 that sinners *"will be thrown into the outer darkness. In that place there will be weeping and gnashing of teeth,"* and in his parable of Lazarus and Abraham refers to an uncrossable chasm that separates the wicked in hell from the righteous in Paradise. You can go back to Chapter 19 and read that passage from Luke 16:19-31 to see what I mean.

This passage implies that those in hell will not only suffer terribly, but will also remain entirely conscious and able to feel intense pain, able to retain their memories of life on earth, long incessantly for relief from their loneliness and pain, will never find comfort, cannot escape, and have lost any semblance of hope.

Again, it's important to understand that this fire and darkness is eternal, and not a temporary punishment or eventual "burning away" of one's sins, after which one is free to go. After all, in Matthew 25:46, Jesus says, *"And these will go away into eternal punishment, but the righteous into eternal life,"* Revelation 20:10 tells us of Satan being cast into a lake of fire and *"tormented day and night forever and ever,"* and Revelation 14:11 says, *"And the smoke of their torment goes up forever and ever."*

Compared to accepting God's free gift of salvation, and simply believing in the deity, death, burial, and resurrection of Jesus (something so simple that a child can do it) this picture of hell that Jesus painted is quite bleak indeed—but it really isn't even the worst of hell.

Will There Be Different "Levels" Of Hell?

Before telling you what the worst part about hell will be, there is one question that I need to address, because I think it's important: the question of whether or not there will be differing degrees of torment or intensity in hell.

For the answer to this question, we can once again turn to the Bible.

In Luke 12:47–48, we are told, *"That servant who knew his master's will but did not get ready or act according to his will, will receive a severe beating. But the one who did not know, and did what deserved a beating, will receive a light beating."*

Then there's Matthew 10:15, which says, *"Truly, I say to you, it will be more bearable on the day of judgment for the land of Sodom and Gomorrah than for that town."*

And in Matthew 11:21–22, it says, *"Woe to you, Chorazin! Woe to you, Bethsaida! For if the mighty works done in you had been done in Tyre and Sidon, they would have repented long ago in sackcloth and ashes. But I tell you, it will be more bearable on the day of judgment for Tyre and Sidon than for you."*

Finally, Romans 2:4–5 tells us, *"Do you presume on the riches of His kindness and forbearance and patience, not knowing that God's kindness is meant to lead you to repentance? But because of your hard and impenitent heart you are storing up wrath."*

Each of these passages implies that there will not only be greater and lesser amounts of suffering in hell, but in the same way that we can lay up treasures for ourselves in heaven here on earth (Matthew 6:20), we can also accumulate a greater intensity of wrath poured down upon us in hell, when, as Romans 2:5 says, *"God's righteous judgment will be revealed."* I can't say I know exactly what that will look like, but, rest assured, these sections of Scripture do indeed indicate that sinners will be punished according to the magnitude of their sinful deeds and unbelief.

The Worst Part About Hell

But the intensity of the levels of suffering, the consciousness, the ability to feel pain, the memories of life past, the longing for relief, the inability to ever escape, and souls burning alive for eternity are not the worst parts about hell.

There is indeed, in my opinion, one primary reason for which we should most greatly fear eternal damnation.

See, the chief punishment of hell is, as 2 Thessalonians 1:9 says, *"...eternal destruction, away from the presence of the Lord."* The Greek word for destruction used here is an interesting choice. It does not mean annihilation, which as nonexistence could technically not refer to an eternal disappearance, but rather refers to the loss of everything worthwhile. In 1 Corinthians, Paul used this same word to speak of the devastating temporal consequences of sin. Here, Paul uses the word to refer to the eternal consequences of sin: a penalty that is not annihilation, but rather eternal *separation* from the love of Christ.

This means eternal separation from the source of love itself, and a place of extreme loneliness the complete opposite of the glorious union with God that we will experience in heaven. Rather than the popular cartoonish portrayal of a Vegas-esque "party of sinners," hell—also in a manner completely opposite of the fellowship, reunion, laugher, relationships and happiness you can read about in books such as Randy Alcorn's *Heaven*—is actually a place where you are cut off from *everybody*, every friend, every family member, every loved one, every pet, every possession, and most importantly, God.

This amount of loneliness, combined with no hope, no good, no beauty, no pleasure, no satiation, no satisfaction, and complete, eternal separation from the source of all light and love should be terrifying to you. It means an eternity of solo darkness, separated from all humanity and from all that is true, good, and beautiful. Considering the [hidden killing epidemic called "loneliness" that we humans sometimes experience during our mortal life](#), that amount of complete darkness and separation should, well, scare the hell out of you.

As C.S. Lewis so succinctly says in his book *The Problem of Pain*, which is an excellent treatise of why God would allow his creation to suffer pain in the first place, *"To enter heaven is to become more human than you ever succeeded in being on earth; to enter hell is to be banished from humanity."*

Finally, as to why on earth God would have even invented such a concept as eternal damnation in the first place, which I'm sure you must be wondering or have wondered at some point, I'd like to acknowledge and quote one of my followers on [Instagram](#) who shared this excellent thought on the matter in a post I had made regarding death.

Here's what he had to say:

> *"...I struggled with the concept of eternal damnation for a LONG time (I think most people do). What has really helped me is to study and focus on the Holiness of God. When we can begin to see God for Who He really is, we start to see ourselves as we really are—sinful, utterly depraved. Part of God's holiness is that He is just; He HAS TO judge sin. It is His mercy and grace that He put that judgement upon Christ and then He gives each of us a choice: either see our sin for what it is (an affront to the Holy God), our need for a Savior, and choose to be IN Christ (accepting the forgiveness offered because of His sacrifice) OR be judged ourselves for our sin. That's what eternal damnation is—people who did not choose to have their sin judged in Christ but to be judged themselves. It's eternal separation from God*

because He's not going to force somebody to spend an eternity with Him if they don't WANT (i.e. choose) to..."

So I guess we really do get what we wish for, don't we? If it's independence from God, God's law, and the free gift of salvation that we crave, God serves all of that up on a silver platter to us at the very end, for eternity.

Summary

So there you have it.

Hell is loneliness.

Separation.

Eternal suffering.

And completely necessary as an integral part of God's perfect and holy character and our own utter depravity.

I'm afraid I can't paint it any differently than that.

Yes, it's quite sobering to think about. But there's hope. As Randy Alcorn, author of *Heaven* writes, *"For Christians, this present life is the closest they will come to Hell. For unbelievers, it is the closest they will come to Heaven."* In other words, for those who believe in Jesus, you're about as close now as you'll ever get to experiencing hell. But for those who do not believe, the loneliest moment you've ever experienced in your life comes nothing close to what you'll experience for an eternity in hell, completely separated from your Creator.

Sadly, many do not embark upon the narrow road to Heaven, but fortunately, the steps to begin down that road are not a hidden secret. Just believe in the message of simplicity that I'll tell you about in Chapter 21, and say a simple prayer.

What about you? What do you think hell will be like? Have you experienced a taste of union with God here on earth, and found it to offer just a tiny glimpse of what could happen if that intense feeling of joy, satisfaction, connection, and hope completely disappeared for all

eternity? What are some times you've experienced just a little bit of heaven here on earth, and what are some times you've experienced loneliness, lack of meaning, distance from God and a brief glimpse of what an eternity in hell will feel like?

For resources, references, links and additional reading and listening material for this chapter, visit GetEndure.com/Chapter19.

CHAPTER XX
FOREVER

Heaven. Hell. Death.

It seems you and I have covered quite a few afterlife-ish topics in the last several chapters.

But in this chapter, I'd like to present you with an important question and "thought exercise." Similar to the exercise of writing your own obituary as a potent practice to give you more insight into whether you are wasting your life or, instead, making maximum impact; or the exercise of sensually visualizing the experience of another to truly live out the Golden Rule, as I describe in Chapter 16 or even Warren Buffet's well-known "Ovarian Lottery" exercise (I'll definitely link to that one on the resources webpage for this chapter), this exercise will—if your experience anything like mine—give you valuable insight into what you should consider prioritizing during your relatively short physical existence here on earth.

Are you ready?

Let's begin.

WHAT IF YOU COULD LIVE FOREVER?

Imagine that you've suddenly discovered that you are going to live forever.

Yes, forever.

Now, forever is basically the equivalent of infinite. And infinity is a pretty darn massive idea. I mean, it's easy to understand the *concept* of infinity, but our frail human mind can't truly comprehend how "big" or "never-ending" infinity is, simply because our perception of time, from our very birth, has always had a beginning and an end, measured in seconds, minutes, days, years, and lifespans.

But just humor me for a moment and *try* to imagine what it would be like if you could truly exist *ad infinitum*—if you could actually live *forever*. That's right: the concept of limited time has suddenly vanished, and—even should you decide you still want to think about life in respect to time—your *affluence* of time is a never-ending bank account that will never diminish.

Furthermore, imagine that even though you are going to live forever, your current physical body will eventually fade and perish at the end of 70, 80, 90, or (if you're genetically blessed or some kind of biohacking-transhumanist-life-extension-obsessed-anti-aging-enthusiast) 100 years and perhaps slightly beyond. Yet imagine that even if your physical body fades, your soul will live on, and eventually, you will be given a perfectly new and restored body to enjoy and savor in a New heaven and New Earth for the rest of all time, a thrilling concept I write about in Chapter 18.

Next, imagine in that new and infinite existence, as I write about in Chapter 21 of my book *Fit Soul*, you're not limited to being dressed in a white fuzzy bathrobe and playing a harp while sitting on a fluffy cloud somewhere in the ether. Instead, all those things that you crave to do now, all those things you have a bit of FOMO (Fear Of Missing Out) built around, all those things you really want to do but just don't seem to have enough time of day to do are all things that will be fully available for you to engage in during your infinite existence.

That massive pile of books in your personal library that keep on piling up and driving you crazy or guilt-ridden because you simply don't have the opportunity to read them? No problem: you've got forever to read all those books and many, many more—should your heart desire.

All those sports you really want to learn but just don't have the time to deliberately practice? The New Earth will have all the golf courses, tennis courts, boats and wakeboards, snow covered-hills for skiing, mountains to summit, and ping pong tables you'll ever need for the rest of all time...

The language learning books and podcasts that have left you feeling like it should be so easy to learn a new language if you just had the time to implement those tips? Fear not, you'll have time to learn every language that has ever existed, for all time—with absolutely no rush...

All the new skills you wish you had the time or knowledge or connections to develop? There's also no good reason to think you won't also be able to devote as much time as you'd like to hobbies such as wood crafting, boat building, home construction, computer chip tinkering, car engine fixing, gardening, painting, discovering new recipes, and beyond...

That vast array of exotic locales you've always wanted to visit? The good news is that God made all his creation good (Genesis 1:31), and every last region, beach, mountain, valley, river, lake, and beautiful travel destination and hotspot isn't going to get suddenly wiped away and destroyed—instead each will be a perfect (both literally and figuratively) place for you to explore whenever and wherever your heart desires...

Ultimately, as the thought-provoking book *Not Home Yet* so clearly details, our final destiny is not some disembodied, heavenly existence but rather life with God on a renewed earth. Or as I write in my book *Fit Soul*:

> "What masterpieces could you form if you had millions or billions of years on your hands? This doesn't seem silly to me. God created the human constitution with a driven desire to create, experiment, design, manufacture, fashion, fabricate, and formulate. This isn't some modern evolutionarily acquired trait: archeology constantly reveals that from cave paintings to Stonehenge to the Pyramids, humankind has been created from our very beginnings. It's the way God made us and there's no reason to believe he won't continue to take joy and pleasure in our Creation when we are in eternal union with Him in Heaven (which the Bible clearly tells us is actually a 'New Heaven and New Earth').
>
> Being able to work on a watercolor art masterpiece for a thousand years, play a guitar until I have the skills of the greatest guitarist our current world has ever known, or design a new spacecraft that can carry me to the moon and beyond gets me pretty excited. Who knows? My passion for creating here on the 'Old Earth' is just a tiny slice of the creative cake I'll be blessed to consume on the 'new Earth.' Possessing an infinite and unchained power of Creation is a pretty exciting and stimulating thought, isn't it?"

I think you get it.

Vast, immeasurable time and opportunity at your fingertips, forever.

What Becomes The Most Important Thing?

So you are now equipped with the thrilling and exhilarating knowledge that you are going to live forever.

What, then, do you do *now*?

What becomes the most important thing that you can do with your short time here on this "Old Earth," for the span of those brief few decades that you have in your current physical body, before your *perfect and infinite existence* begins on a new perfect earth?

Would you continue to stress yourself out about that pile of books you don't have time to read?

Would you rush through your day in a frenzied attempt to squeeze in work, food, hobbies, family, friends, social life, learning, exploring, travel, and whatever else you desperately feel the urge to squeeze in before you die?

Would you experience FOMO every time you open a social media account and see your friends lounging on yet another beach in yet another exotic locale that you simply can't seem to fabricate the time to get to?

Would you grasp at every last second of life as though it might be your last?

Probably not.

Instead, here's what you might be thinking, and, if not, what you *should* be thinking, and saying to yourself and to others...

> ..."I've just found out I'm going to live forever! I have to go tell as many people as I can about how they can all go and live forever with me in a perfect existence and the fullest joy they could ever imagine for all time! I must rush out and share this good news with all my family, friends, neighbors, and shout this good news from the

rooftops! Hey, look everyone...I've discovered an opportunity to live forever and this means you can stop all your striving and rushing and worrying and stressing and squeezing and selfishness because you don't have to grasp at life anymore like it's a fading sunset! Your life can simply be a glorious beginning and a mere taste of what you're going to experience in the afterlife! C'mon everybody! Let's do this! Who wants to join me to savor God's creation forever, and ever, and ever?"

After all, how could you ever keep this "secret" to yourself?

Furthermore, who would ever want to live forever *all by themselves*? That's pretty much the definition of hell that you can read about in Chapter 19.

Instead, wouldn't it be nice to take a few of your fellow human beings, members of your own taxonomical species, those who you have a built-in ancestral drive to protect and to ensure long-term survival for, those with whom you have a deep hominid bond from the very dawn of time, along with you to live forever?

Isn't that the first most important thing to do if you know you're going to live forever? Isn't that a full manifestation of The Golden Rule?

Well, Jesus Christ certainly thought so. That is the whole point of his so-called Great Commission found in Matthew 28:19-20, in which he says, *"Therefore go and make disciples of all nations, baptizing them in the name of the Father and of the Son and of the Holy Spirit, and teaching them to obey everything I have commanded you. And surely I am with you always, to the very end of the age."*

How To Live Forever

See, the Great Commission that Jesus taught didn't simply involve a commandment to spend our lives finding random people, telling them they're sinful scumbags, sprinkling a bit of water on their heads, and then dragging them to a church.

Instead, the Great Commission was a message of good news. No: more like electrifying and exhilarating news.

It was a message that God so loved the world that He sent His only precious son Jesus—a great deity—down to our uncomfortable, sin-ridden, painful, hard Old Earth, to become human, to suffer, to be tortured, to die, to be buried, and to eventually conquer all of death and all of sin for all of time through an ultimate resurrection. That's the thrust of the entire greatest Hero's Journey tale described in Chapter 9 of *Fit Soul*.

It was a message that you and I *can indeed* live forever by simply believing that this epic event happened, and then laying all our burdens at the foot of the cross.

It was a message that, by simply saying a few words, we can unlock the door to eternal life and go on to live forever.

What are those simple words?

> *"Dear Lord Jesus, I know that I am a sinner, and I ask for Your forgiveness. I believe You died for my sins and rose from the dead. I turn from my sins and invite You to come into my heart and life. I want to trust and follow You as my Lord and Savior. In Your Name. Amen."*

And once those words are uttered, and spoken from the heart in an act of pure faithfulness, like taking the first step off a giant cliff and trusting that a staircase will materialize, or like being a child and showing up to the kitchen table and believing that somehow all the sustenance you need will be provided for you, your life becomes absolutely transformed. It becomes magical. You begin to live an existence filled with love, joy, peace, patience, kindness, goodness, faithfulness, gentleness, and self-control—not because you *have* to as some kind of litmus test to determine if you're actually good enough to be granted the gift of eternal life, but because you *want* to from the deepest corners of your heart because the love of Jesus washes over you with such an intense feeling of hope, joy, and salvation that you can't help but *crave* with the deepest of your heart's desires to not only *"obey everything I have commanded you"* with zero drudgery or obligation…

…but to shout that good news from the rooftops—that message of the secret of how to live forever—with every last person you can tell for the rest of your life, because you simply can't hold yourself back!

WHAT TO DO NOW

Wait, wait, wait.

Am I implying that, if you have discovered the secret to living forever, and if you have unlocked that secret to living forever by believing upon the message of Jesus's deity, death, burial, and resurrection, that you then must spend every last second of every day in an act of pure self-denial and an existence of utter poverty as you wander the planet in sandals and a toga as a selfless missionary?

Am I saying that since you're going to live forever, you should spend your short time here on Old Earth doing *nothing* but sharing the good news about living forever, and that ribeye steaks, a nice Bordeaux, a fine cigar, and all those books, hobbies, sports, travel locales, thrilling adventures, and wonderful joys of God's creation should be postponed until the afterlife, since they'll all be there waiting for you anyways, forever?

Not really.

See, as pastor John Piper often writes, *God is most glorified in us when we are most satisfied in Him.*

Furthermore, the two greatest commandments in all the Bible are to *"love God and love others"* (Matthew 22:37-40). We love God by glorifying him (e.g. being satisfied in Him) and we love others by not only sharing the good news with them, but also by, as I write about in Chapter 9, creating inspiring art, composing beautiful musical masterpieces, growing a garden that can feed you and perhaps your neighbors too, barbecuing mouthwatering chicken, crafting cabinets, writing thrilling tales, and sharing your unique creations with others in a spirit of love and altruism. This means that while our greatest purpose in life is to spread the good news of redemption, forgiveness, and eternal life, we can do so while *simultaneously* appreciating, enjoying, and relishing all of God's good creation in a manner that loves and shares that appreciation, enjoyment, and relishment with our fellow humans.

And here's the best part: by savoring God's creation, you are, in a very special way, fulfilling the Great Commission.

What do I mean by that?

It's simple, really...

...fellas, when you love your wife, dote on her, hug her, whisper sweet nothings into her ear, and hold her hand when you're walking through the parking lot into the grocery store, you're modeling for your family and for the world what true Christ-like love actually looks like, and you're also doing that when showing precision and honesty in all your business dealings and waking up to do the most excellent job you can with whatever tasks God has placed upon your plate for that day...

...ladies, when you are swaddling a child in a soft blanket to prepare them for refreshing sleep, caring for the family garden, yard, and home, driving an SUV full of excited neighborhood kids to the trampoline park, reading to a group of children at the local library, or revealing a mouth-watering pile of freshly grilled corn-on-the-cob and cheese-drenched burgers for a dinner party, you're displaying God's qualities of empathy, care, kindness, sacrifice, joy, ministry, and creation...

...when you or your family go on a hike and smile and wave at every last person on the trail, perhaps throwing in a "God bless you!" or "God is good!" to your fellow hikers as you bend down to pick up a stray littered beer can and stow it away into a plastic garbage bag, you're demonstrating a living, breathing example of holy gratefulness and savoring and caring for God's creation...

...just think about it: every last thing you do—from how you treat the waitstaff at your favorite restaurant, to who you invite to your home for a Sunday night dinner party, to how you care for your yard and home, to the songs you choose to blast in your car as you commute to work, to what you do when your neighbor needs help moving at the last minute—is all a special way for you to display what it truly means to be like Jesus, to the entire world, and a perfect way to demonstrate the secret to the forever life in your own daily dealings.

And it's actually quite joyful and satisfying to recognize that those six ribeye steaks smoking on the grill, that bottle of wine decanting on the kitchen counter, and that glorious salad of heirloom tomatoes from the garden are going to be enjoyed by your family and two neighborhood families, and those two neighborhood families may not really know the secret to living forever, but when they see the demonstration of God's love in your own lives, they're probably going to ask you questions about the hope and peace that they see vibrating within you as your family gathers, prays, sings, and begins to savor every last element of God's creation, and when they do ask, you can and should certainly share with them that secret to living forever that you have discovered in the form of a free gift God graced upon the world, as you simultaneously wipe steak juices from your chin and sip on a rich cabernet.

That, my friends, is basic "cultural evangelism," and that's the best thing you can do now if you have discovered the key to eternal life: live a satisfied, joyful life and share that satisfaction and joy with as many other people as you can. Demonstrate to others a tiny glimpse of heaven through the beauty and goodness that pours forth from you and your family.

But, I'll admit, in the whole process of being satisfied in God and savoring his creation, I have also, multiple times in the past, felt a bit guilty that I'm not "fulfilling the Great Commission" in a more boots-on-the-ground sort of way, such as via "inconvenient" and laborious mission trips, helping build schools, churches or hospitals in needy, foreign countries, or supporting missionaries in a very direct manner via financial giving or hospitality outreach vs. spending that money on groceries for a neighborhood party.

In other words, I often ask myself whether I should be at home entertaining and caring for my friends and family with beer and roasted chicken, or whether that time would better be spent under a bridge serving soup, or wearing sandals, or holding a hammer, or climbing a ladder, all while getting eaten alive by mosquitos somewhere in a disadvantaged village in Africa. After all, the world needs missionaries—people sent into an area to declare their faith and perform ministries of service, such as education, literacy, social justice, health care, and economic development—just as much as it needs neighborhood parties, barbecue bashes, and church potlucks, doesn't it?

Frankly, why not have both?

As I write in Chapter 6:

> *"Ultimately, most people could do a better job striking a balance between enjoying and savoring the beauty of God's creation and self-denial or delayed gratification specifically for the purpose of helping and blessing others, and not necessarily for the purpose of self-improvement or self-growth.*
>
> *...When was the last time you fasted not as an exercise of righteous self-denial or some kind of selfish anti-aging tactic, but as an exercise to delay gratification, bless others with a bit of extra food, money, or*

time, and pass up a marshmallow now for a reward in heaven later?

When was the last time you skipped dinner to free up an extra hour to go serve the homeless, and perhaps drop dinner off at the soup kitchen on your way?

When was the last time you pulled a big ol' ribeye steak from your freezer and a nice bottle of wine from the pantry, walked past your dinner table, put it into a padded cooler, and sauntered it down to your neighbor's mailbox instead?

When was the last time you took the same mental resilience, fortitude, and ability to engage in delayed gratification that you've used for so many years to 'eat the frog,' do the hardest task of the day first, squeeze in a morning workout or meditation session prior to jumping into e-mails, etc., and applied that same ability to simply forego a few pleasures to free up money, time, or resources to help others?"

What I mean by that is that you simply need balance.

In the same way that living an extraordinary life and savoring God's creation while simultaneously sharing the message of eternal life are not at odds with one another, neither are evangelism and missions at odds with one another. That's the beauty of Christianity. While hedonistic Epicureanism that involves lounging in bed all day sucking on greasy roasted turkey bones while being fanned with grape leaves is certainly incongruous with a Stoic, puritanical self-denial approach of sipping plain soup, eating crackers, and plowing a field for sixteen hours a day, hosting glorious dinner parties at your home on a Sunday night while simultaneously serving soup at a homeless shelter on a Monday night are hardly paradoxical.

So yes, you can certainly be both an evangelist for the forever life that you have discovered *and* a missionary who gets your hands dirty and serves others in the streets, and you can strike a beautiful balance between the two.

Summary

You have been given the glorious opportunity to live *forever*, and that's a mind-blowing thought. As a result, you don't need to mightily hustle to selfishly and stressfully squeeze every last drop out of life because you only have a few decades to enjoy your short existence.

Access to that eternal life is as simple as *saying a prayer of pure faith and simplicity*: acknowledging Jesus's deity, death, burial, and resurrection, then casting all your burdens at the foot of the cross.

Knowing that you will live forever, you can now fully *enjoy* the life God has blessed you with on this planet, while not necessarily *grasping* desperately at that life.

Furthermore, your very best purpose and calling, upon knowing the secret of eternal life and being blessed with the secret to being able to live forever, is to *share that message with as many of your fellow human beings as possible*, particularly by demonstrating an extraordinary life as a sort of "divine image bearer," then, when people ask you, sharing with them the secret to eternal life and the reason for the hope and peace that is within you.

Finally, the knowledge that you are going to live forever *doesn't* mean that you must spend your relatively short time here on this Old Earth living a life of stoic drudgery, self-denial, and perpetual service, but it *does* mean that you should constantly be asking yourself whether you are excessively "chasing" pleasures that, frankly, you'll have an entire infinite existence to enjoy, or whether you're spending your time in wise balance by caring for others, serving others and ministering to others while simultaneously demonstrating to others what pure and powerful gratefulness and enjoyment of God's creation actually looks like.

Finally, you may enjoy this little gem I recently discovered, written by Eric Berne, an author and psychiatrist (who also happened to create the theory of transactional relationships I discuss in Chapter 4 of *Fit Soul*). It goes something like this:

> "...the way to walk the earth like a prince is to cast golden apples wherever you walk, and then finish your own apple upon your deathbed."

What about you?

What would you do if you knew you were going to live forever?

More importantly, *are* you going to live forever?

Do you see how simple it is to accept the free gift of eternal life by, like a little child, simply taking one giant step of faith and saying a simple prayer—then proceeding to live an extraordinary life that inspires as many other people as possible to join you in that eternal life?

For resources, references, links and additional reading and listening material for this chapter, visit GetEndure.com/Chapter20.

PART VI

LIVING FULLY

*Being most glorified in God
by being most satisfied in Him.*

CHAPTER XXI
SIMPLICITY

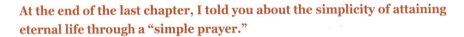

At the end of the last chapter, I told you about the simplicity of attaining eternal life through a "simple prayer."

I want to visit the topic of simplicity in this chapter, because I think that—especially when it comes to "spiritual enlightenment" (which is difficult to describe, but often portrayed as some kind of higher consciousness and deeper mental awareness)—people tend to make things pretty complex these days.

For example...

...want to meditate? Sitting cross-legged on the floor next to your bed, perhaps seated on a bath towel, simply won't do. No, no, no. You must instead have an app (preferably one with paid upgrades to unlock the *cooler* meditations) and also, if possible, some kind of actual *course* or *certification* you've taken to ensure that you're meditating properly. To keep you motivated, you'd better have signed up for a 10-day silent Vipassana meditation retreat, and in the meantime, to ensure all your self-quantification of neural metrics is in order during your meditation, use a self-quantified headband or wearable to track those metrics, and possibly a few additional wearables that drive you deeper into the meditative state. Oh, and if you run out of any plant medicine or microdosing pills, your meditation is useless, and also non-existent unless accompanied by an Instagram selfie...

...do you desire to pray more? As I write about in Chapter 16, when I was growing up in a Christian church, prayer was usually positioned (often paired hand-in-hand with didactic and intellectual sermons, argumentative apologetics, and a focus on "prim-n-proper theology") as a formal, oft-overintellectualized activity with a specific structure that required carving out time and forethought to wax poetic to the Creator. As a result, prayer often becomes something very much like the same type of formidable, intimidating activity that keeps many people from regular meditation: feeling as though they need to do it in some kind of perfectly systematized way, X number of times per day for Y minute sitting in Z position—

which, as anyone who has taken a few simple and calming mindful breaths while stuck in traffic knows, is not necessarily the case. Because of this conundrum, it can be easy to verbally attest to the importance of prayer as foundational to a Godly life, but based on our oft-faulty assumptions about how it should be conducted, prayer often gets crowded out as the calendar fills up with other duties or we simply become too mentally drained or fatigued during the day to conduct a "formal prayer session," as opposed to the simple prayer and prayer constancy of early Christian hermits, ascetics, and monks such as the Desert Fathers and Mothers of the early church (by the way, the wonderful book *Where Prayer Becomes Real* could be a great read for you if you struggle with this same complexity of prayer issue)...

...Bible reading can also be quite complex, can't it? You've no doubt heard of stout theologians taking deep 4 am forays into Scripture, following complex Bible study reading plans, accompanied by spendy pieces of Bible exploration software and study apps, oodles of highlighting and margin writing, and deep dives into word origins, Biblical dictionaries and encyclopedias, exegetical text analysis, and hermeneutics. The act of simply opening the pages of a basic, inexpensive Bible to the book of Psalms and reading for the precious few minutes that you have each morning perhaps leaves you a bit guilty that you aren't driving downtown to meet up with a Bible study group or keeping up with the theologically superior Joneses down the street with their fancy leatherbound Scriptures, Bible study meetings on all days that end in Y, and thick tomes of Bible commentary adorning their bookshelves...

...fasting and breathwork, which are, a bit like Bible reading and prayer, the veritable "turkey and cranberries" of the spiritual disciplines kingdom, can also be fraught with complications. These days, fasting cannot simply involve a focused abstinence from eating. Instead, you must choose from a dizzying array of options, including a bone broth fast, a juice fast, a fasting-mimicking diet (FMD), an alternate-day fasting (ADF) diet, a one meal a day (OMAD) fast, a 5:2 fast, a time-restricted fast, a one-, three-, or five-day water fast, an eat-stop-eat fast, or a pre-packaged, done-for-you fasting kit that can be sent to your house, chock full of all the teas, tinctures, potions, powders, and pills to keep you from getting hungry during your fast, although that's kind of one of the whole *points* of fasting as a spiritual discipline in the first place. You must then track your fast with an equally dizzying variety of fasting apps out there, and do heaps of research on the ideal meal to break your fast, what kind of things you can eat that allow you to fast but not *really* be fasting, and join a special fasting club or online social media group for

support and accountability because, let's face it, unlike Jesus, *nobody* can fast alone. Neither can you simply stop eating, deny the body, and put up with the hunger and embrace the pain and discomfort of fasting, because you could have *sworn* you heard on a health podcast somewhere that it might inhibit your metabolism or do some kind of hormonal damage if your body feels too uncomfortable without eating…

…should you want to include breathwork as one of the additional physical elements of your spiritual discipline habits, things get just as complicated as fasting. Breathe in, preferably through your nose, hold briefly, then breathe out slowly. There you have it. That's breathwork. But get a good app too, so you can have bells, whistles, and chimes that tell you when to breathe in, how long to hold, and when to breathe out. Be sure also to consume blood flow precursor agents like beet root, citrulline, arginine, cordyceps, and oxygenated water so that you can maximize that breath-hold time. Purchase a hyberbaric oxygen chamber, or at least some kind of fancy breath restriction wearable or facial and/or waist-worn device to enhance the effects of said breathwork. Like fasting, be sure to join an online membership or club so that you don't forget to breathe, and so that others can hold you accountable to breathe. Do not, under any circumstances, do your breathwork near hard surfaces, water, hot stoves, irritated dogs, or in public places, so as not to injure yourself or disrupt the peace, and attempt to only practice in a sauna or a room lined with plush pillows that can protect you should you forget to breathe and subsequently pass out. And finally, ensure that any breathwork practice you choose—similar to any fasts you embark upon—has an appropriate name, such as "Wim Hof" or "Buteyko" or "Carbon Dioxide Tolerance Training" or "Holotropic" or "Reduced Frequency." Otherwise, it's just "breathing," and that's far too plain-jane and cardboard to work for anyone…

…next, gratitude. Gratitude is something else that can pour forth positive fruits and health improvements into your life, but, let's face it: it can be difficult to be grateful without a bit of fancy assistance, such as a study guide, a journal, an accountability group, and some kind of online gratefulness immersion course that you take to learn how to properly time your gratefulness practice and the exact number of items that are ideal to be grateful for…

…you get the idea. Really, "spiritual enlightenment" in general seems like it increasingly requires not only many of the complexities above, but also, should one want to truly connect with God, experience a connection to Jesus Christ, or become, as Paul says in 2 Corinthians 5:17 in the Bible, a "new creation," but also

necessitates some kind of a trip to an Ayahuasca center in the Amazon, a stint of properly timed microdosing with plant medicines and perhaps a hefty DMT experience *(though neither of those are hardly an ecologically friendly, much less permanent and reliable methods, for equipping everyone on the planet to "find God")*, along with a chakra balancing session, sound healing tools, body protection jewelry, a decently fashionable toga...

...and, for you fellas out there, some kind of man bun.

It's So Simple To "Be Spiritual"

Obviously, I'm being sarcastic.

In reality, what most people are truly seeking when they seek so-called "spiritual enlightenment" is some kind of fulfillment of the God-shaped abyss in their soul that only God can fill.

As I write in Chapter 20 of *Fit Soul*:

> *"See, we each feel a pull of heaven and yearn for an eternal bliss that goes on far after our bodies have exhaled their last breath. This is what C.S. Lewis described as a 'God-shaped' hole in our hearts—an endless abyss that we can dump more money and fancy cars and bigger homes and exercise and diet and even noble pursuits such as family and charity into—but an abyss that will never feel complete, satisfying or fulfilling unless we have discovered the deep satisfaction and joy that comes from peaceful union with God.*
>
> *Augustine also highlighted a similar idea when he famously wrote, 'Thou hast made us for Thyself, and our hearts are restless until they rest in Thee,' and Indian Christian missionary Sadhu Sundar Singh writes in his book With and Without Christ: 'In comparison with this big world, the human heart is only a small thing. Though the world is so large, it is utterly unable to satisfy this tiny heart. Man's ever-groaning soul and its capacities can only be satisfied in the infinite God. As water is restless until it reaches its level, so the soul has not peace until it rests in God.'"*

Perhaps the best summation of this God-shaped hole and the original concept of it can be found in Blaise Pascal's writings Pensées, which are a series of defenses of the Christian religion. In Pensées, Pascal says:

> *"What else does this craving, and this helplessness, proclaim but that there was once in man a true happiness, of which all that now remains is the empty print and trace? This he tries in vain to fill with everything around him, seeking in things that are not there the help he cannot find in those that are, though none can help, since this infinite abyss can be filled only with an infinite and immutable object; in other words by God himself."*

When that endless pursuit for true spiritual fulfillment, meaning, and happiness is discovered through union with God and salvation through Jesus, that is when you can ultimately become a new creation.

As 2 Corinthians 5:17 says: *"Therefore, if anyone is in Christ, he is a new creation; old things have passed away; behold, all things have become new."*

And the beautiful fact is that it is so, so simple to become that very new creation—a new creation who will go on to live for all of eternity in pure bliss and joy.

How simple?

Romans 10:9 puts it this way: *"... if you confess with your mouth the Lord Jesus and believe in your heart that God has raised Him from the dead, you will be saved. For with the heart one believes unto righteousness, and with the mouth confession is made to salvation."*

This confession itself is also beautifully described in the book *Pilgrim's Progress* by John Bunyan. The book was originally published in 1678, so the anecdote below may seem a bit clunky to get through, but I think you'll do just fine. A character called "Hopeful" in the book puts it like this:

> *"Then I asked him what I must do when I came; and he told me I must entreat upon my knees, (Ps 95:6) (Dan 6:10) with all my heart and soul, [Jer 29:12,13] the Father to reveal him to me. Then I asked him further, how I must make my supplications to him; and he said, Go, and thou shalt find him upon a mercy-seat, where he sits all the year long to give pardon and forgiveness to them that come. I told*

him, that I knew not what to say when I came; and he bid say to this effect: God be merciful to me a sinner, and make me to know and believe in Jesus Christ; for I see, that if his righteousness had not been, or I have not faith in that righteousness, I am utterly cast away. Lord, I have heard that thou art a merciful God, and hast ordained that thy Son Jesus Christ should be the Savior of the world; and moreover, that thou art willing to bestow him upon such a poor sinner as I am—and I am a sinner indeed. Lord, take therefore this opportunity, and magnify thy grace in the salvation of my soul, through thy Son Jesus Christ. Amen."

William Franklin Graham Jr.—AKA "Billy Franklin"—born November 7, 1918 and died February 21, 2018—was a prominent and influential American evangelist who took that same confession, and crafted it into an even simpler "Sinner's Prayer." That prayer goes like this:

"Dear Lord Jesus, I know that I am a sinner, and I ask for Your forgiveness. I believe You died for my sins and rose from the dead. I turn from my sins and invite You to come into my heart and life. I want to trust and follow You as my Lord and Savior. In Your Name. Amen."

That's it.

You can simply recognize that you do not have the mental or emotional capacity within your own being—no matter how many books, journals, apps, clubs, supplements, teas, tinctures, powders, lotions, oils, meditation cushions, and pure grit you apply to become "spiritually enlightened"—to truly change yourself for the better, and then you utter those simple words, that simple acknowledgment that you are a sinner in need of salvation, and an entirely new life begins for you as you become anointed with the elixir of the Holy Spirit, and a sudden satisfaction fills your entire being as you become, in a quite magical sense, full of a lasting peace, hope, and fulfillment, unlike anything you've ever experienced before.

Upon receiving God's free gift of eternal salvation through His Son Jesus Christ and his sacrificial death on the cross, and accepting the grace, mercy, love, and goodness that saves you from yourself and your sinful state, you truly become a brand new creation. Just imagine—by uttering those simple words written above, you will have been gifted with a brand new life and a brand new start, along with a brand new heart and a brand new spirit.

You will have now become a brand new creation ("Therefore, if anyone is in Christ, he is a new creation; old things have passed away; behold, all things have become new." (2 Corinthians 5:17)).

You will have now been made fully alive ("And you He made alive, who were dead in trespasses and sins, in which you once walked according to the course of this world..." (Ephesians 2:1)).

You will have been delivered from darkness ("He has delivered us from the power of darkness and translated us into the kingdom of the Son of His love, in whom we have redemption through His blood, the forgiveness of sins." (Colossians 1:13)).

You will have been fully cleansed ("Then I will sprinkle clean water on you, and you shall be clean; I will cleanse you from all your filthiness and from all your idols. I will give you a new heart and put a new spirit within you; I will take the heart of stone out of your flesh and give you a heart of flesh. I will put my Spirit within you and cause you to walk in My statutes, and you will keep My judgments and do them." (Ezekiel 36:25)).

You will have been given the gift of the Holy Spirit (Then Peter said to them, "Repent, and let everyone of you be baptized in the name of Jesus Christ for the remission of sins; and you shall receive the gift of the Holy Spirit. For the promise is to you and to your children, and to all who are far off, as many as the Lord our God will call." (Acts 2:38)).

Your salvation will have been sealed and guaranteed ("In Him you also trusted, after you heard the word of truth, the gospel of your salvation; in whom also, having believed, you were sealed with the Holy Spirit of promise, who is the guarantee of our inheritance until the redemption of the purchased possession, to the praise of His glory." (Ephesians 1:13) and "And do not grieve the Holy Spirit of God, by whom you were sealed for the day of redemption." (Ephesians 4:30) and "Now He who establishes us with you in Christ and has anointed us is God, who also sealed us and given us the Spirit in our hearts as a deposit." (2 Corinthians 1:21) and "Now He who has prepared us for this very thing is God, who also has given us the Spirit as a guarantee." (2 Corinthians 5:5)).

All old things will have now passed away and all things will have now been made brand new! How glorious a thought is that? It is so glorious that it goes far above and beyond a mere "spiritual enlightenment" and instead involves a complete transformation by the work of God's supernatural power within you that is so profound and so intense that the feeling of pure joy, hope, and peace is absolutely indescribable. It is my deepest wish that, if you are reading this chapter, you can experience that for yourself by saying the simple words I will repeat once more here:

> *"Dear Lord Jesus, I know that I am a sinner, and I ask for Your forgiveness. I believe You died for my sins and rose from the dead. I turn from my sins and invite You to come into my heart and life. I want to trust and follow You as my Lord and Savior. In Your Name. Amen."*

And if perhaps you have already uttered those words, or some semblance of them, at some point in your life, and have already accepted the free gift of salvation, but subsequently become overwhelmed with the "complexity" of the dizzying variety of "strategies" for spiritual growth, then I challenge you to consider stepping back and simplifying. In the same way that a complex workout comprised of calisthenics, kettlebells, mobility moves, interval timing, and breathwork can be daunting, defeating, and intimidating, so can a spiritual life that is gummed up with too many to-dos and toys. So perhaps it's time for your spiritual workout to instead involve a simple peaceful walk in a beautiful forest instead of a foray to a spiritual gym littered with oft-distracting tools.

Take a deep breath, read a Psalms, say the Lord's Prayer, *write down something you're grateful for, close your eyes and meditate for a few moments, then rinse, wash and repeat the next day. Just try that for a few days. See how it feels.*

SUMMARY

Look, I—a self-professed "biohacker" who on the daily uses a wide variety of technology, apps, wearables, and devices; who has launched on social media fasting challenges (including all those fasts with the weird acronyms), meditation challenges, and cold water challenges; and who uses Bible apps, prayer bracelets, fringe supplements, and plant medicines—won't deny that there is a time, a place and a benefit to enhancing one's life with what may seem like complex, yet often valuable variables.

But let's face it.

You don't *need* journals, apps, wearables, and retreats to meditate. You can simply close your eyes, relax and go into the void, so long as you give yourself permission to do so.

You don't *need* fancy phone apps and flowery phrases to connect with God daily in constancy of prayer. You can simply start by getting on your knees each morning and reciting the Lord's Prayer.

You don't *need* to join a Bible study group or get an online seminary degree to feast upon and attain deep nutrition from God's word. You can simply open the Bible and begin to read (I recommend beginning with Psalms, Proverbs, or 1 John particularly).

You don't *need* a thick book, accountability club, appetite satiating compounds from the Orient, and a nutrition certification to wrap your head around fasting, nor a hyperbaric chamber, nighttime mouth tape, and infrared sauna to engage in meaningful breathwork. You can simply not eat for a while, breathe through your nose, and exhale longer than you inhale.

You don't *need* a journal or a checklist or a daily habit reminder to be grateful. You can simply close your eyes, give thanks, and let that feeling of gratefulness wash over your body.

And you don't *need* a giant tent revival, a plant medicine immersion, an Ayahuasca retreat, or a lick on a Sonoran desert toad to "see God" or "find Jesus." You can simply say a simple sinner's prayer, then begin to allow God to grace you with the spiritual fruits of love, joy, peace, patience, kindness, goodness, faithfulness, gentleness, and self-control that will subsequently pour forth into your life.

Make sense?

Good. Now go commit (perhaps with a cheap pencil and a common Post-It note) to daily Bible reading, prayer, meditation, fasting, breathwork, and gratitude. I guarantee your life will be better for it. Eventually, if complex tools prove to be of some benefit, then that's fine too. Just don't fool yourself into thinking they're necessary, despite their trendiness and perceived criticality.

Want more of my thoughts on simplicity?

You may want to check out an article I wrote about the simplicity of sleeping better, an article I wrote about the "death of heart rate training zones," and also (this one is written more from an exercise standpoint, but interesting nonetheless) the book *Unplugged*. I'll link to them all on the resources webpage for this chapter.

How about you? Have you been caught up in the modern, trendy complexities of being spiritual? Have you, like me, become a bit distracted and subsequently disillusioned with feeling as though a practice of the spiritual disciplines has become too complex or commercialized? Do you want to embrace simplicity and choose to seek with wisdom only those elements that *truly* enhance your spiritual life, without distracting you? Do you see how simple eternal spiritual enlightenment through the acceptance of the free gift of salvation from God in the form of the sacrifice of His son Jesus can be?

For resources, references, links and additional reading and listening material for this chapter, visit GetEndure.com/Chapter21.

CHAPTER XXII

LAUGH

In Chapter 9, I explained how you know you've gotten stuck in a ho-hum hypnotic rhythm of life when you've found that you're no longer regularly dancing, singing, and dreaming.

However, I was recently re-reading my friend Randy Alcorn's excellent book Happiness (you may have already noticed I highly recommend this book and his Heaven book as must-reads), and in Chapter 16 came across the odd and compelling story of a man named Norman Cousins. It really got me thinking that to live a joyful, adventurous, and fulfilling life, in addition to ensuring you don't forsake dancing, singing, and dreaming, you should also...

...laugh more.

Allow me to explain.

ANATOMY OF AN ILLNESS

Let's begin with the story of Norman Cousins, which is detailed in his fascinating book *Anatomy of an Illness as Perceived by the Patient: Reflections on Healing and Regeneration*.

As a political journalist and activist, Cousins was also a professor of medical humanities at UCLA, where he studied the biochemistry of human emotions and their relationship to healing. So this guy did indeed understood basic human medicine, and wasn't just some happy-go-lucky alternative health hippie.

In 1964, Cousins was hospitalized with a crippling disease of his collagen, along with a debilitating and painful condition called ankylosing spondylitis. Told by his physicians that he had a 1 in 500 chance of recovery, he opted to take his health into his own hands. He and one of his doctors, Dr. William Hitzig, combated the disease together by creating a regimen of laughter (interestingly, along with hefty doses of vitamin C), and were not only able to reverse the damage but allow Cousins to live to the ripe ol' age of 75, decades after his collagen illness first occurred.

In the book, Cousins describes how he educated himself with research and books that described the link between negative emotions and illness. One of the more notable resources he mentions is Hans Selye's *The Stress of Life*, although I've also found other similar titles to be *The Biology Of Belief*, *The Body Keeps The Score* and *The Emotion Code*, all of which I mention—along with the science behind emotions and healing—in Chapter 15 of *Fit Soul*.

Cousins learned that negative emotions, such as frustration or suppressed rage, are linked to the type of conditions he was experiencing, and he of course assumed the opposite to be true: that positive emotions such as love, hope, faith, confidence, and—you guessed it—laughter, would yield similar results. Now you must understand that in addition to his debilitating condition, the pain medications he was being administered—the equivalent of roughly 38 pills of aspirin and phenylbutazone per day—were causing even more tissue damage and internal bleeding. So, to repair his immune system, Dr. Hitzig utilized high doses of intravenous Vitamin C to combat inflammation and nurture Cousin's deteriorating adrenal glands. Then, to combat the unbearable pain, Cousins leaped into a daily digest of comedy and laughter, most notably Marx Brothers films, Candid Camera, and selections from E.B. White's *A Subtreasury of American Humor*. He quickly discovered that just ten minutes of strategically induced hearty laughter seemed to produce significant hours of painless sleep.

The continued results were quite impressive. After several years of regularly scheduled "laughter therapy," Cousins began to experience little to no pain in his day-to-day living, noting that:

"I made the joyous discovery that ten minutes of genuine belly laughter had an anesthetic effect and would give me at least two hours of pain-free sleep."

and also...

"When the pain-killing effect of the laughter wore off, we would switch on the motion picture projector again and not infrequently, it would lead to another

pain-free interval."

...and finally, my favorite:

"Hearty laughter is a good way to jog internally without having to go outdoors."

Impressive, huh? When paired with wise words from the Bible such as ***"A joyful heart is good medicine."*** **(Proverbs 17:22);** ***"A glad heart makes a cheerful face, but by sorrow of heart the spirit is crushed."*** **(Proverbs 15:13); and** ***"Be glad in the Lord, and rejoice, O righteous, and shout for joy, all you upright in heart!"*** **(Psalm 32:11), along with many examples of our Creator laughing, smiling and displaying the emotion of joy, this story of Norman Cousins backs up the fact that we humans were designed to laugh, smile, and be happy as a core part of our existence.**

THE POWER OF LAUGHTER

Of course, it's one thing to say that an emotion—say, gratitude or humor—is important to overall health and can cause positive biological healing effects, and quite another to demonstrably prove it in research.

But, it's been done.

For example, one of the most cited studies on laughter therapy is Dr. Michael Miller's research at the University of Maryland. Dr. Miller measured the blood flow of twenty healthy volunteers before they watched 15 minutes of two different movies: either the dramatic, violent opening to the war film *Saving Private Ryan* or a segment from the Woody Harrelson comedy, *Kingpin*. The goal of the study was to measure the expansion or contraction of the endothelium, which is the inner lining of blood vessels (a test I personally had performed and reported upon at BenGreenfieldFitness.com/hearthealth, albeit without being equipped with a scary or a funny movie). A flow-mediated vasodilation test was also used for the evaluation. This measures blood flow in the brachial artery in an arm that is restricted by a blood pressure cuff and then released. An ultrasound device then measures how well the blood vessel responds to the sudden increase in flow. A total of eight of these tests were given to each of the participants.

After watching the stressful intro to *Saving Private Ryan*, Dr. Miller found that 14 of 20 participants' brachial blood flow was reduced by a constricted endothelium, while 19 of 20 participants' endothelial lining seemed to do the opposite and significantly relax after the Kingpin comedy segments. The results were quite dramatically opposite: Blood flow decreased by an average of 35% during the war movie and increased by an average of 22% during the comedy. This led Dr. Miller to conclude that laughter may be almost as healthy as exercise.

In a similar study, also led by Dr. Miller, researchers asked several questions about humor experienced in everyday activities to volunteers, half of which had experienced a heart attack or undergone coronary artery bypass surgery, and half of which had not. The results correlated with his previous study, displaying that people with heart disease responded less humorously to everyday life situations.

But there's more. For 15 years, spanning a timeline from 1984 to 1999, researchers at Loma Linda University in California studied the effects of laughter on the immune system. In one of these studies, participants watched Laurel and Hardy comedy shows with IVs in their arms, while researchers drew continuous blood samples. Their results were astounding. Natural killer cells that attack virus and tumor cells significantly increased in number and activity. The immune system's T cells, along with signaling components such as antibody Immunoglobulin A, Immunoglobulin G, and gamma interferon (which helps antibodies attack dysfunctional or infected cells) all also increased both during laughter and well into the following day.

Researchers at the University of Tsukuba in Ibaraki, Japan have also found surprising results related to blood sugar levels and laughter. They collected blood-sugar measurements from participants with type 2 diabetes, both before and two hours after a meal. After dinner on the first day, the patients attended a "boring" 40-minute lecture. Then, on the second day, the identical dinner was consumed, but this time it was followed by a 40-minute comedy show. The post-prandial (after meal) rise in blood sugar was significantly lower following the comedy show compared to the lecture, and the same results seemed to occur even in healthy subjects without type 2 diabetes. The researchers stated that: *"In conclusion, the present study elucidates the inhibitory effect of laughter on the increase in post-prandial blood glucose and suggests the importance of daily opportunities for laughter in patients with diabetes."*

Finally, from a research standpoint, and not necessarily related to "laughter" per se, as I was researching happiness, humor, and health, I came across an interesting study titled *Hand Grip Strength and Self-Perceptions of Physical Attractiveness and Psychological Well-Being*. This study investigated the link between handgrip strength and self-rated physical attractiveness, sexual history, and social characteristics in 145 male university students. Handgrip strength correlated, not surprisingly, with both height and weight, but also with levels of self-perceived happiness, social confidence, and even overall physical attractiveness. So one might hypothesize that healthy doses of good humor not only make you healthier but could make you stronger too!

Based on this research into the field of laughter therapy, multiple organizations have now been created, including *Patient TV*, which is audiovisual communication service that offers comical programming on patient television stations; *SMILE (Subjective Multidimensional Interactive Laughter Evaluation)*, a service that allows participants to answer questions about how they're feeling and what types of humor they enjoy, followed by "prescription" list of suggested reading materials, videos, and audios that person might enjoy; and even a "Laughter First Aid Kit" designed by humor therapist *Peggy Stabholz*, which is basically a done-for-you container filled with jokes, videos, and comics targeted to combat depression.

Then, all hardcore science aside, there's the frequency and energy effects of laughter that, from the energy, body frequency and quantum physics standpoint I discuss in Chapter 15 of *Fit Soul*, also seem to be quite profound. As Brian Scott notes in the humor section of his excellent book *The Reality Revolution*:

> *"...a level of energy that is really powerful and accessible is that of humor and laughter. We can diffuse dark, depressing situations with a little humor to lighten the energy in the room. Books about ghosts will tell you that you can protect yourself from ghosts by laughing. It literally raises the vibrations of energy in a room and can instantaneously change your own energy. For that reason, I believe humor is the most powerful energy that we can focus on and become part of."*

So whether it's raising your vibrations, scaring away all the ghosts in your closet, decreasing your blood sugar, lowering your blood pressure, or increasing your healthspan and lifespan in general, laughter is a demonstrably powerful addition to your life toolbox.

How To Have More Laughter In Your Life

So I hope that by now you are convinced of the significant relationship between positive emotions, humor, laughter, and overall health. I'll link to all the research from the last section of this chapter on the resources webpage should you want to read more.

But, it's one thing to know you should be laughing more, and quite another to know how to practically implement more laughter, comedy, and humor into your own life. Admittedly, this is still something I'm working on myself, as I'm one of those guys who can crush a 16-hour workday totally straight-faced and completely forget to smile, laugh, joke, or introduce any other humor or comedy into my life because—let's face it—I'm busy.

However, I have found a few tactics that have seemed to work well for me lately that I'd like to share with you now.

1. **Family Dinners.** For our nightly family dinners, which are one of the most cherished and magical parts of my day, we all prepare a mouth-watering meal together, then gather around the table over our food and, for nearly an hour, play hilarious games such as Exploding Kittens, Unstable Unicorns, Bears Vs. Babies, Moustache, Gubs, Scattergories, Telestrations, Idiomaddict, and all manner of other funny card and board games that are inevitably covered in food crumbs and grease by the time dinner is done (a gradual game destruction that is well worth the laughter that ensues during our entire family feast). Often, we'll precede these dinners by putting on a silly song and having a bit of a dance-off, or slipping away after dinner upstairs into the boys' bedroom to read a humorous story by authors such as P.G. Wodehouse, Mark Twain, or even Jack Handey.

2. **Stand-Up Comedy.** While I eschewed stand-up comedy for many years because I considered it to be either A) a waste of time; or B) usually chock full of offensive material, I've recently refreshed my love for a good, family-friendly comedian, and now, when driving in the car and wanting some light-hearted audio, or looking for the occasional fun show to watch with the family, I'm now enjoying stand-up once again, particularly from the likes of funny folks like *Jim Gaffigan, Brian Regan, Jerry Seinfield,* and *Jim Breuer.*

3. **Jokes.** Recently I have begun, leading up to holidays such as Thanksgiving, Christmas, the New Year, etc., hunting down holiday-topic-oriented joke websites and telling my children and wife themed jokes leading up to or on the holiday. You know, silly quips such as *"What goes "Oh, Oh, Oh?" "Santa walking backwards!"* or *"What did the turkey say to the turkey hunter on Thanksgiving Day? Quack, quack!"* For some reason, jokes and holidays seem to go together like, well, turkey and cranberry.

4. **Songs**. Songs don't have to be funny, per se, to elicit feelings of joy and happiness. Heck, just the other night, as I was listening to a relatively "stale" science podcast, I pushed the wrong button on my iPhone and accidentally switched it into full-blast Kanye West's song "Stronger" (yeah I have a lot of old songs on my phone!). I immediately felt a surge of energy, which isn't surprising, especially relative to the podcast I was listening to before the song came on, but I also felt an uptick in overall positivity of mood and even broke out into a smile as I began to sing along. So, occasionally taking a break from audiobooks, podcasts, or pure silence to pipe upbeat tunes into your eardrums, bedroom, living room, or office can be a sort of "gateway drug" into laughing and smiling more as the beats pick up your spirit.

5. **Pranks.** Every day doesn't necessarily have to be April Fool's Day at your home, but lighthearted, relatively harmless pranks, such as a bit of extra hot sauce mixed into a family member's ketchup, drawing a mustache on a sleeping friend, putting a fake plastic spider into a briefcase, topping off a toilet with dry ice, or filling someone's closet with blown-up balloons can all be ways to keep spontaneity, dopamine, smiles, and laughter high in your household. On the resources webpage for this chapter, I'll link to more ideas for harmless, funny pranks you can play, without necessarily needing to buy Walmart out of toilet paper to go TP an entire house.

6. **Outfits/Clothing**. Let's face it: Dressing up in silly outfits can instantly spread infectious laughter and giggles amongst any crowd. So get some funny t-shirts with witty slogans and actually wear them to places you normally wouldn't: like a fancy restaurant or a kid's piano recital. Host an ugly sweater party. Make your own hoodies, sweaters, and other clothing with witty phrases or cartoons (I like to use the website Zazzle for this). I have one friend who takes his family out to dinner once a month with everyone dressed up in their favorite pair of footie pajamas or craziest hat. You get the idea: Use your wardrobe to spice things up a bit too, even if it's not Halloween day.

7. **Just Smile.** Finally, as one of my favorite recent songs by the Black Eyed Peas reminds us: just smile. The mere act of turning up the corners of one's mouth and forcing a smile has been shown in research to create a sort of positive feedback loop cycle that can pick up your mood, even if you're not really, truly happy at the time. So, whether you're by yourself, or with others, try smiling more. Yep, research has shown that turning up the corners of your mouth actually works to trick your brain into happiness. The name of that song, by the way, is "Be Nice," and the infectiously catchy chorus goes like this:

Hey, be different
Be nice
Just smile, I promise it'll change your life
Hey, be different
Be nice
Just smile, I promise it'll change your life

Summary

Ultimately, as Randy Alcorn details over the course of 479 pages in his book *Happiness* (which I cannot recommend more highly to you as a companion read or audiobook listen for a deeper dive into the topic of joy, laughter, and humor from a spiritual and physical healing standpoint, along with the book *Anatomy of an Illness*)...

...God is a happy, joyful God, and He wants us to be happy too.

The entire gospel is called "the good news of great joy" for good reason, and the fact that God has gone through extraordinary lengths like the great sacrifice of Jesus to ensure our eternal happiness speaks volumes to the unimaginable happiness you can experience in eternal life in Heaven.

But in the meantime, here on the Old Earth, joy and happiness are within our reach, especially if we understand their immense importance in our lives and take practical measures such as those I've given you in this chapter to ensure we are surrounded by happy moments of laughter throughout each day. So grab your ugly sweater, smile, break into song, tell a joke, play a prank, watch some comedy, and stop being so serious, already. Like I said, this is still something I'm working on, but with each passing day, I find myself more and more capable of being funny, feeling joyful, laughing, smiling, and enjoying the positive physical vibrations that seem to manifest from doing so.

What tactics have you found to be helpful to stay smiling and joyful on an "average day?" How often do you laugh during the day? Do you have ways you plan to inject more humor and smiles into your life? How do you feel your emotions and energy change if you simply smile to yourself right now? Try plastering on a big, goofy one to see what I mean.

For resources, references, links and additional reading and listening material for this chapter, visit GetEndure.com/Chapter22.

CONCLUSION

Congratulations.

You've come a long way. Throughout the pages of this book, you've passed many, many mile markers on your training course for spiritual stamina.

You've discovered common temptations, obstacles, pitfalls and struggles you and I both face, and have learned how to deal with them.

You're now familiar with the concept of temperance, the mastery of passions and desires, and how to strike a balance between savoring God's creation and self-discipline.

You've familiarized yourself with how to enhance your purpose and productivity, while working deep, creating meaningful beauty, and simultaneously experiencing rest and refreshment.

You've learned how to love others and love God more fully, while creatively weaving the Golden Rule into your life, using a mindful and people-connected approach that will change your personal interactions for the rest of your life.

You're now aware of what exactly happens at the end of your existence, and how to find more meaning in both life and death.

You've grown to embrace laughter, simplicity, joy, relationships and the magical feeling of being most glorified in God by being most satisfied in Him.

Ultimately, you have discovered and learned how to implement a wide variety of potent tools, tactics and habits for enhancing your spiritual stamina and endurance.

So what's next?

How can you *not* be that person who finishes a book like this, nods their head in agreement, feels inspired to experience a life saturated with persistence, perseverance and patience, then gets completely derailed as all the distractions, busy-ness and old routines and habits seem to set right back in once the book has found its final resting place in a dusty spot on your bookshelf or disappeared into the archived section of your e-reader?

Perhaps it would be helpful to briefly review a few key habits that you can implement now so that doesn't happen to you. So I'll give you a simple seven-count list of my own personal tips to make this all do-able—without you feeling as though you need to drop everything now to go read the entire Bible, sign up for five different volunteer organizations in your community, go on a ten-day silent meditation retreat, and sell all that you own to live a life of puritanical, sanctimonious Stoicism.

1. *For the next week, commit to reading the Bible, every day. Any habit like this that you want to "stick" needs a very low barrier-to-entry, so just keep it by your bedside and do it first thing, before you even get out of bed. You may eventually branch out and find a special place and time to read in another fashion, but for now, trust me: start in bed, first thing. Download the YouBible app if you need a plan to follow. If you're new to the Bible, I recommend the First Steps Reading Plan by Wayne Cordeiro.*

2. *For the next week, do the exact morning and evening spiritual disciplines journaling, meditation and prayer protocol outlined in Chapter 14. As a reminder, this will take you 5-10 minutes in the morning and 3-6 minutes in the evening. Finish with the Lord's Prayer. You'll have that prayer memorized within a week, I guarantee.*

3. *For the next week, pray before breakfast, lunch and dinner. Just thank God for the food and ask Him to bless it to your body. That's it. Again, start simple.*

4. *Today, purchase an inexpensive bracelet from a website like Amazon (mine, a simple wooden bead bracelet, cost five bucks), and as soon as it arrives, begin to pray every time you look at it. What exactly should you pray? Simply utter a gratitude prayer for whatever it is you're experiencing in that moment (quite literally: "thank you, God"), pray for someone or something you know needs a prayer at that time (such as the person you named in your journal that day), or or simply tell God "I am here," then take 30-60 seconds of quietness to listen to His still, small voice in the silence.*

5. For the next week, if you suspect you are addicted to, excessively reliant upon, or emotionally, psychologically or biologically attached to anything, then look at it and say, as Anthony DeMello recommends in his book *Awareness*:

> *"I really do not need you to be happy. I'm only deluding myself in the belief that without you I will not be happy. But I really don't need you for my happiness; I can be happy without you. You are not my happiness, you are not my joy."*

I challenge you this week to say that statement to anything and everything you're attached to: verbally, aloud and enthusiastically. Memorize this statement if you must. I did, then I spent a month practicing saying this phrase—even to my morning cup of coffee—and it was quite powerful and eye-opening.

As you begin this practice, also consider the following: in the same way that it is not within your human power to resist every last temptation that this world throws at you, it is also not within your human power to fully detach from anything in life. To experience both resistance to temptation and release from attachments, you must rely upon the power that God bestows upon you. Read Chapter 1 of *Fit Soul*, and also pay attention to my concluding statements below, to learn plenty more about this strategy of detachment.

6. For the next week, listen to one (preferably spiritual) song per day that charges you up, inspires you, gives you goosebumps or makes you want to move your body. You can even play it immediately after you've read your Bible—meaning, for this first week, right when you get out of bed in the morning. I've personally found this is a wonderful and inspiring way to begin the day (I literally dance my way down to the living room to make coffee or tea as my song plays). Sing, dance, move, and smile as the music plays. Don't worry: life won't pass you by as you spend three to six minutes enjoying the emotional, psychological, biological and spiritual benefits of interacting with a good tune. During a work break, a commute, or directly before dinner is another excellent time for a practice like this, and I recommend you check out songs by groups from Bethel, Hillsong or Elevation Worship for Christian inspiration and motivation.

7. For the next week, do one nice thing for someone, every day. Make your loved one coffee and bring it to them. Give cash to a homeless person. Help somebody carry their groceries to their car. Leave the server or waiter or

waitress a surprisingly larger-than-normal tip. Buy the person behind you in line at a coffee shop or grocery store their coffee or tea or groceries. Drop some packaged food off at the soup kitchen or homeless shelter. Send your Mom or Dad or Grandma or Grandpa a nice card with a handwritten note. Walk over to your neighbor's house and ask them if they need help with anything. You get the idea. I think you'll find this practice to be less of a teeth-gritting, begrudgingly time-consuming activity than you may think.

That's it. That's just seven habits that you implement over the next seven days. Do you think you can do it? I know you can and I guarantee if you implement nothing else or take nothing else away from this book, these seven habits alone will change your life and make you far more impactful for loving God, loving others, and increasing your spiritual stamina and endurance.

Finally, as I've mentioned multiple times throughout this book, resistance to temptation accompanied by the ability to be able to run this spiritual marathon that you and I are in is not something we can do on our own, no matter how many fancy journals, single-minded resoluteness, tools, tactics, programming, scheduling, or even Bible reading and prayer that we weave into our daily lives.

No matter how hard you and I try to be a good person, our passions and desires run so contrary to our natural inclinations that it eventually becomes utterly impossible to run the race relying upon our own strength and willpower.

This is because, as Galatians 5:16-17 says, we wage a constant war against the carnal, sinful desires of our flesh:

> *"But I say, walk by the Spirit, and do not gratify the desires of the flesh. For the desires of the flesh are against the Spirit, and the desires of the Spirit are against the flesh; for these are opposed to each other, to prevent you from doing what you would."*

But in the passage above, Paul also reveals a secret to eventually winning this battle between the flesh and the Spirit, namely to "walk by the Spirit." In other words, if living a life fully immersed in loving God and loving others seems too difficult, we must remember that we are not called to pull this off by *ourselves*. We can only endure when we walk by the Spirit of God: otherwise, resistance to temptation becomes hopelessly hard and ultimately impossible.

So what does it mean to walk by the Spirit?

First, it means living each day in perpetual prayer, immersion in Scripture, and union with God.

Second, it means to love God and love others. As Paul also says in that same chapter, in Galatians 5:13, *"For you were called to freedom, brothers. Only do not use your freedom as an opportunity for the flesh, but through love serve one another."* and in Verse 22, *"The fruit of the Spirit is love, joy, peace…"*. So to walk in the Spirit means to bear the fruit of the Spirit, especially, and greatest of all, expressing and experiencing love for God and love for others throughout each day. Backing this up, in Colossians 3:12-14, Paul says, *"Therefore, as God's chosen people, holy and dearly loved, clothe yourselves with compassion, kindness, humility, gentleness and patience. Bear with each other and forgive one another if any of you has a grievance against someone. Forgive as the Lord forgave you. And over all these virtues put on love, which binds them all together in perfect unity."*

Third, denying and "crucifying" the flesh requires us to be saved by the blood of Jesus Christ (read Chapter 20 for more on how exactly that is done). Galatians 5:24 says, *"Those who belong to Christ Jesus have crucified the flesh with its passions and desires."* and Galatians 2:20, *"I have been crucified with Christ, it is no longer I who live, but Christ who lives in me; and the life I now live in the flesh I live by faith in the Son of God who loved me and gave himself for me."*

Related to that third point, does that mean that if you struggle with temptation, you aren't a Christian? Not really. A Christian is not necessarily a person who experiences no temptations or bad desires. Rather, a Christian is a person who is aware that they are at *war* with those desires, and someone who understands that they are indeed engaged in a sort of competition—a daily battle against the flesh. So you should actually take heart if your spirit feels like a battlefield sometimes, because that's a sign that you haven't actually set up shop to live in daily comfort with your fleshly desires, but rather that you are at war with them because you care so much about loving God and loving others!

And when you walk by the Spirit, that broken flesh will ultimately be conquered. You can mount up with wings like an eagle, you can run and not be weary, you can walk and not faint.

You can walk with confidence, knowing that you will never be tempted beyond what you are able, because with any temptation, God has promised that He will make a way of escape, that you may be able to bear it.

You can run with endurance the race that is set before you, looking to Jesus, the author and finisher of your faith, who for the joy that was set before him also endured, even to the cross.

You can rejoice in hope and be patient in tribulation.

You can be strengthened with all might, according to God's glorious power, for all patience and long suffering with joy.

You can receive the crown of life which the Lord has promised to those who love Him.

*You can, by God's grace, **endure**.*

BEN GREENFIELD

For resources, references, links and additional reading and listening material for this chapter, visit GetEndure.com/Conclusion.

ADDITIONAL RESOURCES

Though I consider the Bible to be my go-to resource for tackling temptations and building spiritual stamina (I highly recommend investing in a good study Bible that you keep on hand at all times, and I'll link to a few of my favorites on the resources webpage for this concluding section), and I also hope that you have found *Endure* to also be helpful, there are several additional resources—listed below—that I've found to be quite beneficial for setting aside or establishing new habits or routines, learning how to "reprogram" thought patterns that aren't serving God, you or others, and reframing the way that you approach aspects of life you've identified you need to change or adjust.

- *Atomic Habits* by James Clear
- *Boundless* by Ben Greenfield
- *Boundless Cookbook* by Ben Greenfield
- *Power Of Your Subconscious Mind* by Joseph Murphy
- *Spiritual Disciplines Journal* by Ben Greenfield
- *Stillness Is The Key* by Ryan Holiday
- *Willpower Doesn't Work* by Benjamin Hardy
- *Loving What Is* book and *The Work* smartphone app by Byron Katie
- The Ben Greenfield Podcast
- The Michael Singer Podcast
- *The Power Of Habit* by Charles Duhigg
- Dr. Don Wood's The Inspired Performance Program (TIPP™)

For links to these resources, visit GetEndure.com/AdditionalResources.

NOTES